DATE DUE

FEB 0 4 2010			
MAY 1 0 2010			
AUG 0 3 2010			
AUG 3 0 2010			
OCT 0 6 2010			

Demco, Inc. 38-293

The Next Front

Southeast Asia and the Road to Global Peace with Islam

Senator Christopher S. Bond
and Lewis M. Simons

WILEY

John Wiley & Sons, Inc.

Published by John Wiley & Sons, Inc., Hoboken, New Jersey
Published simultaneously in Canada

For general information about our other products and services, please contact our Customer Care Department within the United States at (800) 762-2974, outside the United States at (317) 572-3993 or fax (317) 572-4002.

Wiley also publishes its books in a variety of electronic formats. Some content that appears in print may not be available in electronic books. For more information about Wiley products, visit our web site at www.wiley.com.

ISBN 978-0470-503904

Printed in the United States of America
10 9 8 7 6 5 4 3 2

To my wife, Linda, for encouraging me to put my ideas in a book, and for her constant encouragement and support without which this book would never have happened
and
To my son, Sam, whom I regard as my hero for his service in Iraq, and whose reports from the field as a Marine ground intelligence officer convinced me that we needed a smart power strategy.

—CSB

To Carol
and
to Eleanor, Jonah, Nathaniel, Noah, and Sophie, in the hope that your world will be smarter.

— LMS

A great nation is one which is capable of looking beyond its own view of the world, or recognizing that, however convinced it may be of the beneficence of its own role and aims, other nations may be equally persuaded of their benevolence and good intent.

—J. WILLIAM FULBRIGHT, on the U.S. Senate floor,
June 1965, at the height of the bitter and
protracted Vietnam debate

We have a great opportunity to extend a just peace, by replacing poverty, repression, and resentment around the world with hope of a better day.

—PRESIDENT GEORGE W. BUSH,
to the West Point graduating class, May 2002

The supposed "clash of cultures" is in reality nothing more than a manifestation of mutual ignorance.

—THE AGA KHAN, leader of the world's
15 million Ismaili Muslims, July 2007

Contents

Acknowledgments

This book is much more the product of firsthand discussions with scores of people in their own backyards than of library-based research. Many conversations resulted from prior arrangements, while others just happened. We are indebted not only to those individuals whose interviews we have included in the text, but also to many others who helped us along the way. Some guided us through their nation's religious and political mazes, others down teeming streets and muddy pathways. Some sat with us for hours in offices or at restaurant tables, sharing their insights and expertise, while others provided cool drinks, shelter, and personal experiences.

Among those to whom we offer particular thanks and gratitude is Chan Heng Chee, the ambassador of Singapore to the United States. Throughout our project, Ambassador Chan has been extraordinarily helpful, gracious, and generous with her time and knowledge.

We are grateful to the U.S. Institute of Peace and its president, Richard H. Solomon, for helping fund our reporting travel. And special thanks to former USIP executive director G. Eugene Martin, who took great interest in our project. Others in and around Washington whose assistance has made a difference are Ambassador Alphonse F. La Porta, former president of USINDO, the United States–Indonesia Society; W. Keith Luse, senior member of Senator Richard Lugar's staff; Kate Clemans, director, C & M International Ltd.; former deputy undersecretary of commerce Dr. Paul London; Albert Santoli, president, Asia America Initiative; Ambassador John S. Wolf, president, Eisenhower Fellowships; Australian ambassador Dennis Richardson; Ken Ballen, president, Terror Free Tomorrow; Allen Cissell of the East-West Community College Partnership; and Astari M. Daeuwy, Johns Hopkins University.

U.S. ambassadors Ralph L. "Skip" Boyce and Lynn Pascoe couldn't have been more helpful in providing their own exceptional insights and making members of their embassy staffs available to us.

To Bond Senate staff members Brent Franzel, Jack Bartling, Mike Dubois, and Louis Tucker, minority staff director of the Senate Select Committee on Intelligence, our thanks for giving of your own time and for help in preparing research and providing background for the genesis of this book.

Colonel James Linder, an officer and a gentleman, head of the joint task force in Mindanao, gave freely of his time to help us observe and understand what smart power looks like at work on the ground.

In Indonesia, Islamic communications specialist Mohammed Iqbal of Gadjah Mada University guided us across the archipelago and through the gray zones of religious fundamentalism. We are also grateful to Ambassdor Sudjadnan Parnohadiningrat; former U.S. Public Affairs counselor Charles N. Silver; Sidney Jones of the International Crisis Group; Dr. Alwi Shihab, presidential envoy to the Middle East; Rev. Lidya K. Tandirerung; Faqihudin Abdul Kadir, secretary-general, Fahmina, Cirebon; and presidential spokesperson Dr. Dino Patti Djalal. Particular thanks to Dharmawan Ronodipuro, who unfailingly kept us up to date.

In the Philippines, we owe much to a dear old friend, Abby Tan, and to another journalist, Greg Hutchinson, who made marvelous arrangements for us in Manila and Mindanao. Also, Maria A. Ressa, ABS-CBN Broadcasting Corp., and Benjamin Philip G. Romualdez, president, Benguet Corp. From the University of the Philippines: Aileen S. P. Baviera, dean, Asian Center; Asiri J. Abubakar, professor of Asian Studies; and Dr. Carmen A. Abubakar, dean, Institute of Islamic Studies. Ellen H. Palanca, director of Chinese Studies, Atteneo de Manila University. In addition, General Benjamin Defensor, chief, APEC Counterterrorism Task Force; Major General Dato Pahlawan Soheimi bin Abbas of the Malaysian Army, head, International Monitoring Team, Mindanao. Ray D. Roderos, chief superintendent, Philippines National Police, Directorate for

Intelligence. And our special appreciation to attorney Ishak Mastura for his river of information from Bangsamoro.

In Thailand, Busaba Sivasomboon bravely accompanied us through dangerous territory in the South. We are thankful to her and apologize to her husband, who worried about her safety. Monsour Salleh, a journalist who lives in the South and covers his homeland courageously, is due our appreciation for leading us to particularly informative sources. Thanks, too, to author and scholar Jeffrey Race; Colonel Denny Lane of Saint Anthony's College, Oxford University; Lin Hang Hing of the embassy of Singapore in Bangkok; Abdul Rahman Abdul Samad, chairman of the al-Iman Foundation; Anthony Davis, Asia correspondent, *Jane's Intelligence Review*; and Denis Gray of the Associated Press.

In Malaysia, veteran journalist Kuah Guan Oo organized our way throughout the country. Juhaidi Yean Abdullah led us along the northern border. We are also most thankful to Philip Mathews, an old friend and assistant director-general of the Institute of Strategic and International Studies in Kuala Lumpur.

In Singapore, for sharing their insights into their own country and the surrounding region, our thanks to Benny Lim, the crackerjack permanent secretary of the Ministry of Home Affairs; Amitav Acharya, head of research at the Institute of Defense and Strategic Studies, Nanyang Technological University; Chua Siew San, deputy secretary of the Ministry of Defense; and Stanley Loh, director, Middle East, North Africa, and Central Asia Directorate, Ministry of Foreign Affairs.

And in Hong Kong, we owe particular thanks to Harvey Stockwin and Isabel Escoda, two Old Asia Hands who have forgotten more than we will ever know.

Finally, we offer our sincere appreciation to our editor, Hana Lane, who *got it*, right off the bat.

Introduction

The last time Americans took a sober look at Southeast Asia, military helicopters were snatching U.S. diplomats and terrified South Vietnamese off Saigon rooftops. It was noon, Tuesday, April 29, 1975. A few hours later, Communist North Vietnamese troops marched into Saigon. They had won.

More than three decades later, Americans are no longer very concerned about Southeast Asia. This is a serious mistake. The region is home to one of the greatest concentrations of Muslims on Earth. They are spread among Vietnam's neighbors—Indonesia and Malaysia, the southern Philippines and southern Thailand, and Singapore. At 250 million, they outnumber the entire Muslim Middle East. The world's most populous Muslim-majority nation is Indonesia, 220 million, three times the largest Arab country, Egypt. But the Muslims of Southeast Asia do not register in our mind's eye. We turned our backs on them and their homelands when we abandoned the quagmire of Vietnam. We can no longer afford this complacency and the ignorance it breeds.

While Southeast Asia's Muslims have for centuries stood apart from their Arab coreligionists, the differences are beginning to shrink. And that is cause for concern and action, from Southeast Asians as well as Americans. Thirty years ago, while we were fully engaged fighting Vietnam's Communists, the Muslims of Southeast Asia were almost universally what we would have termed "moderate," had we been paying attention. But because they were God-fearing Muslims, and therefore anti-Communist, we paid them little heed. We took them for granted. They might have prayed the required five times a day or they might not have prayed at all. Many felt comfortable dining in restaurants with non-Muslim friends, as long

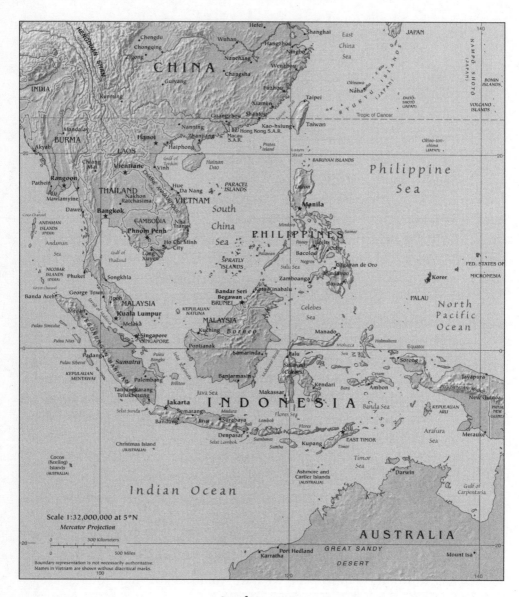

Southeast Asia

as pork wasn't served. Men seldom grew beards, even those sufficiently hirsute to do so. Some women covered their hair; almost none masked their faces. People greeted each other in the vernacular *salamat pagi*, never the Arabic *salaam aleikum*. They thought of themselves first as ethnic Malays and only then as Muslims.

All of that, and much more, is shifting dramatically as the Muslims of Southeast Asia turn increasingly to the Middle East to reaffirm their identity. Moderation is losing the moral high ground, looked down upon as a tool of Western manipulation. And still we are paying scant attention.

The flame of puritanical religious practice, which more and more Muslims perceive as the Islam that Mohammed transmitted from God, was reignited by two events in the Middle East during the latter decades of the twentieth century. Only in retrospect have they been recognized as Earth-shattering. First, the mullahs' revolution of 1979 in Iran demonstrated to Muslims everywhere that Islam was not merely a litany of rites to be performed in the mosque, but a way of life meant to control their every move as well as the legal system and governance of the state. The second was Saudi Arabia's pouring of vast amounts from its staggering oil earnings into building and running ultraconservative Wahhabi mosques and religious schools throughout Southeast Asia. Saudi-trained imams and teachers spread the word that their intense practice alone was the true Islam of Mohammed and that the watered-dawn versions of the region were *haram* (forbidden).

At about the same time, Osama bin Laden began agitating for stricter implementation of the faith within the Saudi kingdom. He preached that the influence of Christian-Jewish "Crusaders" was eroding the purity of Islam and that the presence of U.S. troops was sullying the very land of its birth. This culminated in the 9/11 attacks. In direct reprisal, on October 7, 2001, the United States attacked Afghanistan in what the Pentagon called Operation Enduring Freedom. Seventeen months afterward, beginning on March 20, 2003, U.S. forces unleashed the Shock and Awe bombing campaign of Baghdad, laying the groundwork for a swift, cross-country armored assault. The basis of the argument President George W. Bush and Britain's prime minister, Tony Blair, employed was "to disarm Iraq of weapons of mass destruction

[WMD], to end Saddam Hussein's support for terrorism, and to free the Iraqi people." It quickly became evident that Saddam did not possess any weapons of mass destruction, and U.S. credibility suffered its greatest blow since we abandoned our friends in the Indochinese states of Vietnam, Cambodia, and Laos. Throughout the Muslim world and beyond, America became not a defender of freedom, but an aggressor.

Many of the Muslims with whom we spoke during our research travels through Southeast Asia said they had been horrified by 9/11. Many others admitted readily that they were pleased. They acknowledged exhaling a collective, long-held sigh of relief and vindication for a score settled. Still, they bit their tongues and swallowed their instinctive resentment when the Bush administration ordered the invasion of Afghanistan. They had little empathy for the Taliban and they understood, even if they did not condone, Americans' need to settle their own score with bin Laden and his hosts.

But the invasion of Iraq, the overthrow of Saddam Hussein, and the protracted and violent occupation appalled them. They condemned the war, not because they admired Saddam but because they viewed it as unprovoked and a clear demonstration of Americans' universal disregard for Muslims. They found in the killing, the Abu Ghraib torturing, and what they perceived as the blatant hypocrisy of the Guantánamo Bay imprisonments all the proof they needed that Americans cared little, if at all, about the human rights of Muslims and about bringing the blessings of democracy to Iraqis.

In their reality, the United States wanted Iraq's oil, its strategic location as a permanent base for U.S. military forces, and a springboard from which to better defend Israel—the quintessential symbol of Islam's humiliation. After years of theoretical teachings, Iraq provided them with incontrovertible evidence of America's anti-Islamic bias.

Resentment of Western influence, never very far beneath the surface after centuries of colonial domination in Southeast Asia, percolated up to ground level. Muslims we had considered moderate— or "mainstream"—began to take on the fundamentalist trappings of Arabs, though not necessarily their intellectual comprehension. Small percentages of Southeast Asian Muslims, mainly undereducated, unemployable young men, heard the siren call of terrorism and bought into it as the best weapon available to them to fight against their own disadvantaged status and what they believed was the evil of the West. In Indonesia, officials estimate that 2 percent of Muslims fit within the "radical" rubric. While initially that seems reassuring, in a nation of 238 million, 90 percent of them Muslim, 2 percent works out to well over 4 million.

After some of these young men traveled to Afghanistan and Pakistan to undergo martial training with bin Laden's al-Qaeda organization, they returned home and began launching suicide-bombing attacks on Westerners and their supporters in their midst. Yet most Southeast Asian Muslims continue to fit Western standards of moderation. Most value democracy and want to live in democratic societies. Most admire much of what Americans believe in and want the United States to remain an active participant in their region's economic and diplomatic lives. But they will no longer accept the big brother–small brother relationship that we have long demanded of them and that their own governments have accepted as unavoidable.

Because we lacked insight the last time we bumbled into the jungles of Southeast Asia, we left with 58,000 of our own and perhaps 6 million Vietnamese, Cambodians, and Laotians dead. Our greatest failure in the 1960s and 1970s was in not realizing that Ho Chi Minh could be, indeed was, both a Communist and a Vietnamese nationalist. Instead, we convinced ourselves that if Ho came to power over the South, a reunited Communist Vietnam would align with China, its millennial enemy, and the Soviet Union. This melded giant would then overrun the rest of Southeast Asia—the "dominoes"—and stain the East indelibly red.

Today, by continuing to lump religious fundamentalists together with radical extremists and assuming that they all hate Americans, we are compounding the same kind of simplistic mistakes. First among these is the widespread and insulting tendency to think of all Muslims as Arabs and as terrorists. In fact, numerous variables exist within Islam, and they readily can be traced geographically. The Muslims of Southeast Asia are at the far end of a religious feeding chain that originates in the Arabian desert. There, the Arab

Muslims of the Middle East, with Saudi Arabia at their core, comprise the beating heart, the wellspring of Islamic orthodoxy. The religion teaches that it was there that God, Allah, speaking through the Archangel Gabriel, dictated the Koran to an illiterate trader in a desert cave fifteen hundred years ago. And it is there today that many feel most powerfully the renewed summons of that man, anointed the Prophet Mohammed, the Messenger of God, to once again eliminate the governments and laws of men and reestablish the pure form of Islam that he delivered.

To the east of the Arabian heartland, in South Asia, are the Muslims of Afghanistan, Pakistan, India, and Bangladesh. With notable exceptions (the Taliban, for one), they are less intense in their practice than the direct descendants of the Arab legions that forced them at scimitarpoint to convert more than a thousand years ago. Former adherents of Hinduism and Buddhism, both faiths much older than Islam, they retain measures of their previous cultural identities, which leaven fundamentalist tendencies.

Finally, the Muslims of Southeast Asia, from southern Thailand to peninsular Malaysia and the far-flung archipelagoes of Indonesia and the southern Philippines, accepted Islam of their own free will. The faith was brought to them peacefully, beginning in the thirteenth century, first by Sufi mystics who wandered down from India, and later, to a much greater extent, by Arab traders, whose objective was accumulating spices and other Oriental riches rather than souls. Many of those Arabs remained behind in what must have seemed a tropical paradise, seduced by soft ocean breezes, the joys of the monsoon rains, the succulent fruits, and the women in graceful sarongs. They enjoyed other benefits as well. The darker-skinned ethnic Malays of the islands treated the fairer Arabs with deference. To this day, indigenous people honor the descendants of the early Arabs as being closer to the progenitors of the faith than they, latter-day converts.

Thus, the Islam that evolved among Southeast Asians is an amalgam, adapted, distilled and modulated first by distance and then by blending over time with their own cultural and religious precursors. The result is not only less doctrinaire but also in some ways almost unrecognizable to modern Arab travelers. They angrily dismiss indigenous medicine men and mystics who commune with spirits of volcanoes as haram. Traditional female court dancers from the island of Java, the heartland of Indonesian culture, performing with arms bared in elaborate, jeweled costumes, are an affront to Arab sensibilities.

Superficially, Indonesian Muslims have more in common with the relaxed attitudes of Thai Buddhists and South Indian Hindus than with the austerity of Middle Easterners. The application of Islamic law, Sharia, is comparatively limited. Most women cover their hair with scarves and many, though not nearly all, wear some type of loose, form-concealing overgarment. Still, far fewer women on the streets of Jakarta and Kuala Lumpur shroud themselves in the black abaya or mask their faces behind a niqab than do in London and Paris, leave aside Jiddah and Tehran, though the practice is spreading. In Indonesia and Malaysia, it is common for Muslims to live, work, and study alongside Christians and Buddhists (mostly ethnic Chinese), Hindus, and animists—though not without periodic bloody outbursts. (There is reason that the only Malay/Indonesian word used commonly in English is "amok.") Also common in Southeast Asia is elected, secular government. Although the degree of liberal democracy and the brightness of the line between religion and state differ, the basic precepts are common to the people of the region and of the United States.

We focus our attention in this book on five Southeast Asian states: Indonesia and Malaysia, which have Muslim majorities; the Philippines and Thailand, with violent Islamic minorities in their southern districts; and Singapore, overwhelmingly ethnic Chinese but bracketed by Islamic neighbors and newly uncertain of the loyalty of its own Muslim minority. As we will make clear, the stability of these governments, their levels of corruption, and their commitment to the well-being of their citizens vary widely, as do the challenges and opportunities they offer Americans.

Indonesia is unarguably the centerpiece. Astonishingly, after breaking free in 1998 from half a century of "guided democracy" under President Sukarno and the authoritarian "new order" of Suharto, it has become the most genuinely democratic country in the region.

At the opposite end of the scale is Singapore. Tiny, bourgeois, essentially a one-party town, it enforces rigid strictures on democracy. It has the most secular government in the region and is, along with Japan and Australia, America's most supportive friend in Asia.

It would be tempting—understandable, even—for Americans to quickly size up these and most of the other Muslims of Southeast Asia as "our kind." We could assure ourselves that they are, for the most part, as President George W. Bush famously put it at the outset of the war on terror, "with us." But that would be presumptuous and mistaken. We could assuage our consciences with the belief, doubtless held by many Americans, that the United States already has done more than enough to help Muslims, to no avail. The real issue, however, is that what we have done until now has been simply wrong. Not only do we need to continue helping, our help must be effective. Although the Muslims of Southeast Asia begin from a very different theological place than the Arabs, they increasingly are heading toward a religious junction with them. "Compared with the Middle East, Islam in Southeast Asia is still tolerant and respectful of other faiths," Tommy Koh, Singapore's former longtime ambassador to the United Nations and one of Asia's most astute world affairs analysts, told us. "But there's a movement afoot for 'pure' Islam; not backward-looking like the Taliban but, nevertheless, far more conservative than has traditionally been the case. There is no denying it: there is a 'green tide' and it is rising."

Members of Singapore's ethnic Chinese majority, like Koh, nervously glancing over their shoulders at Indonesia and Malaysia, are fixated on the tide analogy. Unspoken is the alarming prospect that should it rise much higher, it could surge across the entire region, leaving behind devastation. The tide—green being the symbolic color of Islam because the Prophet is believed to have dressed in a green cloak and turban—has risen to such a level of anger and frustration over the past seven or eight years that secular political leaders are increasingly fearful of attempting to resist it.

The tendency toward Islamic fundamentalism and its potential degeneration into terrorism could become a huge and dangerous reversal for Southeast Asia as well as for the United States. For sixty years, beginning with the stunning post–World War II independence upheaval that shut down European colonialism in Asia, American-style democracy was the model many in the region dreamed of.

When Malaysia's first prime minister, the courtly Tunku Abdul Rahman, first saw the new and evocative Iwo Jima Memorial in Washington, he immediately commissioned artist Felix de Weldon to craft a similar heroic bronze monument in Kuala Lumpur, honoring Malaysia's independence fighters. The red, white, gold, and blue flag of Malaysia bears a remarkable likeness to the Stars and Stripes. At one time or another, all ten countries of Southeast Asia, Muslim and non-Muslim—Brunei, Burma, Cambodia, Indonesia, Laos, Malaysia, the Philippines, Singapore, Thailand, and Vietnam—shared the great hope that they would incorporate some pieces of the American way in their nationhood.

For those who have gained at least a tenuous footing on the economic ladder, part of the dream has come true. But for millions of Muslims, it was shattered, first and still foremost, by the realization in 1948 that the United States would stand aligned with Israelis against Palestinians. This bitter pill has lodged ever deeper in their throats as successive U.S. presidents have embraced Israel, enshrining it as America's closest ally in the Middle East and the largest recipient of its military aid. America's quiet acquiescence to Israel's unacknowledged nuclear weapons program, contrasted with its volatile rejection of Iran's presumed effort to develop its own, has further infuriated most Muslims, the Iranian Shia themselves as well as the majority Sunni. Likewise, they interpreted America's rejection of the Hamas election victory in the Palestinian territories in January 2006 and its dragged-out inaction before demanding a halt to Israel's invasion of Lebanon the following July as further affirmation of an American double standard. The hesitant U.S. response to Israel's invasion of Gaza in January 2009 refueled the fires of resentment. Now the eyes of the world's Muslims are focused intently on President Barack Hussein Obama, watching and waiting for change.

Although Israel-Palestine remains the baseline, the invasion and occupation of Iraq elevated anti-American bitterness to unprecedented heights. We are now commonly seen as bullies. As we press Southeast Asian governments for assistance in routing out the terrorists in their midst—and they are providing that help— what is on their minds is: the only time the Americans show up is when they're in trouble; and then they don't ask, they demand. Certainly, there are some marked exceptions to the pattern. The enormous, life-saving U.S. military relief effort following the 2004 Indian Ocean tsunami was hugely appreciated and went a long way toward offsetting the underlying animus, though just temporarily. Otherwise, from Southeast Asia's viewpoint, it's all terrorism (formerly all communism) all the time. While they consider fighting terrorists important, they're far more worried about reducing the poverty that cripples them.

If we are to begin reversing our relationships, we'll need to accept that with our awesome position at the pinnacle of power must come a new sense of responsible behavior. The United States, at least for the moment, is something the world has never known, not simply a greater power among lesser ones but a behemoth utterly without peer. Yet, such isolated splendor means we are more dependent, not less, on others. No longer can we continually put our self-interest first.

In a 2007 PBS television special titled "The Case for War," Richard Perle, a neoconservative Reagan administration official and a chief architect of the Iraq war, complained, "There's got to be *some* advantage to being a superpower." We suggest that the advantage is, we get to try to convince developing countries that democracy may hold the answer to their problems and we have the wherewithal to help them become democratic—if that is what they want. No longer can we toss the raw bone of "with us or against us" at other nations and expect them to snatch it up with gratitude. We have seen how such self-centered policies redound to hurt us.

So long is the shadow we cast and so deep the footprint we leave that no other country seriously challenges us, at least not in the sense that the Axis challenged us in World War II or the Soviets in the Cold War. But, in warfare so absurdly asymmetric as that we're fighting today, seemingly petty foes such as Iraqi and Afghan insurgents and other nongovernmental groups, such as al-Qaeda, which previously we might have expected to swat aside as mere annoyances, can cause us extreme pain.

While the George W. Bush administration viewed itself as democracy's singular champion, Muslims (and many non-Muslims) in Southeast Asia considered it no less evil and brutal than we do al-Qaeda. In facing this judgment we need to set aside our own self-indulgence, our instinctive defensiveness. For hundreds of millions of people, America as Satan is an obvious truth. To comprehend why, we must walk in Vietnamese or Iraqi or Palestinian shoes: How would we respond if foreigners invaded the United States? How did we respond when they flew airplanes into our buildings? How would we react if that foreign army occupied the United States year after year; its armored vehicles rumbling day and night through the streets of our cities; its soldiers demanding that we identify ourselves to them, entering our homes at will at any hour, shooting us because we look suspicious to them, and those soldiers didn't understand our language or know the first thing about our way of life?

People are enraged, not pacified, when they perceive that power, certainly foreign power, is being used unjustly against them. They don't roll over; they lash out. If anyone doubts that, think again about Vietnam, where ninety-pound, malnourished soldiers, who humped artillery pieces over mountain trails on bicycles, outlasted first France and then the United States. Consider Afghanistan, where illiterate, untrained peasants on foot and horseback drove out the British Empire a century ago and their great-grandchildren crushed the Soviet Union eighty years later. Today, that generation's children are fighting U.S. and NATO troops. And think again of Iraq, where the most powerful and sophisticated armed force the world has ever known could not halt furious young men who planted crude explosives in the roads. That grisly chapter began to wind down only after Americans on the ground finally learned to *listen* to Iraqis, specifically to local leaders, and then empower them to provide their own security and meet their own pressing human needs.

If one lesson is to be drawn from this bloody history it is this: people will do almost anything, for as long as necessary, to defend their country and their way of life against foreigners. Invaders simply cannot match their passion. This is a painful admission for Americans, whatever our politics and biases. As a nation we think of ourselves as good. We are sure that the rest of the world hungers

for our way of life and understands our helpful intentions, our optimism and spontaneity. And we believe that we can change anything
we set out to do. There are times when the people of other nations
do admire these upbeat qualities. But there are other times when
they regard our soaring self-confidence as arrogance. In Southeast
Asia, we are teetering between those times right now.

Yet it is in Southeast Asia where we have the best opportunity
to regain our balance and begin moving toward global peace with
Islam. The first step requires that we simply *listen*. The two of us
have spent careers doing that, listening to the people of this part
of the world, among them presidents and prime ministers, radical
clerics and terrorists, businessmen, students, peasant farmers, legislators, soldiers, police officers, and intellectuals. In the following
pages we give some of them the opportunity to speak for themselves
and their societies. Some speak in favor of the United States; others are hostile. Rising anti-Americanism and terrorism are on all of
their minds.

A common thread running through our conversations was
that poverty and inadequate education lead to the recruitment of
religious foot soldiers, the so-called *jihadi* warriors, to plant home-
made bombs along roads and to drive explosives-laden vehicles into
targets selected by their better-educated and wealthier superiors.
Whether in Iraq or Indonesia, these young men (and occasionally
women) step forward—knowing almost certainly that they will die,
either by suicide or in combat—with one ambition: to kill Americans
before they are killed.

It is a straightforward matter to trace the path of violence eastward, from Iraq to Afghanistan, through the sievelike frontier into
Pakistan, and—since the November 2008 assault on Mumbai—
onward into India. To the east, Bangladesh has long been fragile
and dangerous. Then come the vulnerable states of Southeast Asia.
This is a much more realistic and worrisome queue of dominoes
than existed during the Vietnam War. With Islamic resentment
and pride swelling, it is predictable that more will volunteer and
continue waging what they rationalize as jihad.

Yet, Americans can find encouragement in this bleak picture, not
in the poisonous Middle East but among the Muslims of Southeast

Asia. To them, Barack Hussein Obama is a heroic figure. Like them, he is a person of color. Though a Christian, he has a recognizably Muslim name. Indeed, his father was a Kenyan Muslim. He is an American who as a child lived for a time among them with his mother and Indonesian stepfather. And now he is president of the United States.

As far as the people of the region are concerned, the new administration began work with a clean slate. They want to open a mutually beneficial level of exchange, one that would help provide them with sorely needed help, especially in education, small-scale business, manufacturing, and job training. In return, they offer Americans much-improved relations with a vast number of the world's Muslims. Surely such an outcome, at a small fraction of the cost of a war, would be a win-win. If the Obama administration wants to reduce the threat of radical Islam in Southeast Asia, it will do so by creating and fine-tuning proactive policies that previous administrations failed to develop.

The fact that Islam in Southeast Asia, although under rising fundamentalist pressure, is not yet in crisis, should be all the encouragement the United States needs to step up to the challenge by putting what foreign-policy experts know as "smart power" to work in the region. The very prospect of avoiding open-ended warfare such as we face in the Middle East and parts of South Asia gives us all the cause needed for considered, positive proactivity. If we wait for extremism to reach tsunami level in Southeast Asia, the region could indeed fulfill the prophecy of becoming the second bloody front in the war against radical Islamists.

Southeast Asia is and long has been home to a number of deadly terrorist organizations, such as Jemaah Islamiya, the Abu Sayyaf Group, and the Moro Islamic Liberation Front. Recently declassified U.S. intelligence revealed that a post-9/11 follow-up attack on Los Angeles was being led by a prominent terrorist known by the nom de guerre Hambali and his Jemaah Islamiya followers in coordination with al-Qaeda. It was about the time that the Los Angeles plans were discovered that intelligence analysts began speaking of Southeast Asia as "the second front" in the "war on terror." As we delved into the security situation in Southeast Asia, however, we came to understand that the problem was more one of rising Islamic fundamentalism and less a massive terrorist threat. Most importantly, we recognized that Southeast Asia presented a rare opportunity for us to learn how to deal with Islamic countries that were not torn by war. By helping them establish successful governments that would discourage the development of violent extremists, we would be helping them, and the rest of the Muslims in other countries, including the United States. We chose *The Next Front* as the title for this book because we believe it is there where we can and must develop and test an entirely new approach applicable to Muslims everywhere.

These are the key questions for Americans to consider at the outset:

- Should we make the effort to win the understanding, if not necessarily the hearts and minds, of a vast number of the world's Muslims?
- Are we willing to change long-held policy models based on demand for quick results and invest, financially and otherwise, for the long term?
- Are we to write off the people of Southeast Asia to China's careering economic locomotive, or do we attempt seriously to compete for their appreciation?
- Should we go on twisting their arms for cooperation—currently, it's exclusively about their home-grown terrorists—when it suits our needs, otherwise ignoring them, as we have since the ignominious outcome of the war in Vietnam?
- Do we step up our propaganda, which they see through as though it were made of plate glass, simply wiping on a bright new sheen?
- Do we replace image with action?

We will address each of these questions fully. In sum, though, we believe that Americans cannot afford any longer to ignore the Muslims of Southeast Asia. There is simply too much at stake, and not just the economic and strategic basics, which, to the small community of U.S. specialists who study the region, are historically all that have mattered. More important is the need to penetrate the thinking of the region's people.

Respect for the United States as a force for good has plummeted dramatically, not only in Southeast Asia but among all people of the worldwide Islamic community, the *umma*. According to a November 2006 poll by the University of Maryland, Arab dislike of President George W. Bush surpassed that of Israeli prime minister Ehud Olmert by nearly two to one. But with the change of U.S. administrations, the extent of anti-Americanism in Southeast Asia certainly is becoming less deeply rooted and less often expressed in acts of violence. Obama has been given an important opportunity. Southeast Asia's governments are anxious for the United States to step up trade, investment, security, and public diplomacy to cool the extremist rhetoric that threatens them and offset the dexterously managed, low-key, high-speed rise of China throughout the region.

The steps Americans take, if we take them, could have an effect as profound and long-lasting as the missteps we took in the past. Forty years ago, we misread the hopes and intentions of the Vietnamese. Two generations later, we misread Iraqis, presuming that because they had suffered under a dictator, they wanted to become us. As Iraq has proven, there is no way to crush the jihad in the way we crushed Germany and Japan; no thirty-eighth parallel, as there was in Korea, behind which to drive them. Those enemies were governments with armies; defeat the army and the entire structure collapses. Today's enemies have no government to defend. More often—and this applies to South and Southeast Asia as well as the Middle East—they despise their governments. They're fighting not for a country but for an ideal.

The ideal is all they have. But it does us no good to tell ourselves that because they have bought into the most extreme interpretation of religion, they are simply evil zealots who despise us. Those who best understand the terrorist movements of Southeast Asia say that most sign on simply because everything else in life has failed them, not because they hate our freedoms. In truth—and they themselves say so—they envy us for our privileges. That is very different, though, from wanting to *be* us. Most of all, what they want is hope. Having and working toward realistic hope is the essence of what it means to be American, and it is the best of what we can offer. To interpret this sense of the possible for people who have so few

possibilities, we must help them break the cycle of poverty, ignorance, and injustice in which they are caught.

To begin, we will need nonmilitary armies of energetic
Americans to deliver the information and skills that Americans
know and do well. We will have to give this help freely and with
no presumption that those who receive it will become our friends
or even thank us. Some may end up disliking us more than they
do now. It happens. But most will benefit, and so will we. The
task will be costly, though far cheaper than war. This likely is
the only way for us to help a huge bloc of Muslims draw back
from the brink of extremism and build a mutually advantageous
relationship with a United States that exercises the responsibility, as well as the prerogatives, of world leader.

As George W. Bush observed more presciently than he could
have known, during his first presidential campaign, "If we're an
arrogant nation, they'll resent us; if we're a humble nation, but
strong, they'll welcome us."

PART ONE

Brown Brothers: The Philippines

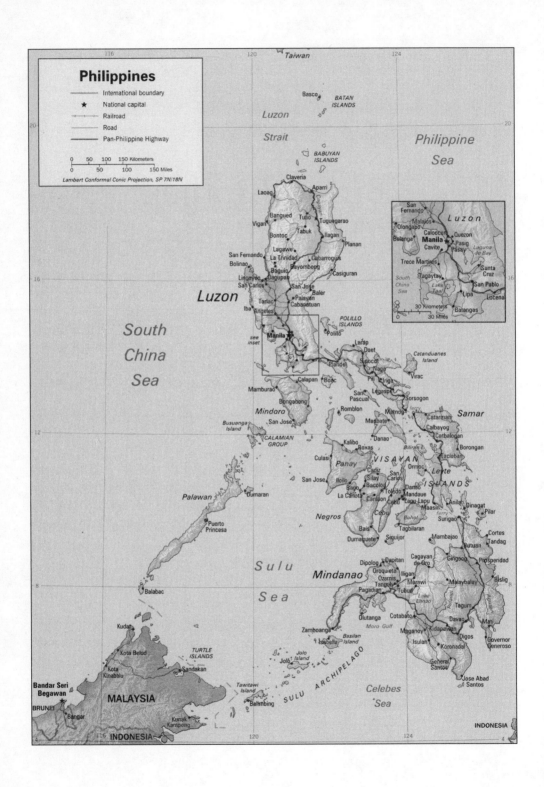

1

The Doctor

The morning after the aerial attacks on the World Trade Center and the Pentagon, September 12, 2001, Americans awoke to the realization that al-Qaeda was a worldwide organization. In addition to its core Arab fighters and funders in the Middle East, Afghanistan, and Pakistan, other operatives lived, worked, and were winning favor among the Muslims of Southeast Asia. Al-Qaeda's contacts and contractors in the Philippines, Malaysia, Thailand, Indonesia, and Singapore, it developed, were numerous.

There was the Pakistani Khalid Sheikh Mohammed, whom the 9/11 Commission called "the principal architect" of the 2001 attacks. He had operated out of Manila in 1994, planning other attacks and recruiting for al-Qaeda.

Then there was Khalid's nephew Ramzi Yousef. After successfully blasting a six-story-deep crater in the foundation of the World Trade Center on February 26, 1993, he shifted his base of operations to Manila and began concocting a bizarre and ultimately failed plot known as Operation Bojinka, to simultaneously blow six American airliners out of the sky while assassinating Pope John Paul II and President Bill Clinton.

Riduan Isamuddin, an Indonesian better known as Hambali and a protégé of Kalid, recruited seventeen members of the Indonesian terrorist group Jemaah Islamiya to participate in a 9/11-style "second wave" aerial attack on the U.S. Bank Tower in Los Angeles.

Saudis Khalid al-Mihdhar and Nawaf al-Hazmi, both connected to the 1998 bombings of U.S. embassies in East Africa and both aboard American Airlines Flight 77 when it plowed into the Pentagon, attended a critical al-Qaeda planning session in January 2000 at a golf resort condominium outside Kuala Lumpur. Their host was Yazid Sufaat, a Malaysian biochemist and a graduate of California State University.

These men and numerous others were linked to al-Qaeda either directly or through its Southeast Asian franchises. Their goals and tactics varied extensively at the time and they still do. Likewise, the degree of violence they employ, their impact on local populations, and the effectiveness of governments in containing them differ significantly from country to country in the region. Consequently, the countries in which they operate require individually tailored attention from the United States. Many of the people with whom we spoke, whose daily existences were intimately affected by the radical Islamist threat, are hoping that the Obama administration will begin paying them that level of attention. Based on what we heard, a new template of educational and economic assistance would help relieve the extremist pressure. If we can help them in ways they need and want, we will help ourselves.

The first stop on our journey through Southeast Asia was Mindanao, at the southern end of the thousand-mile-long Philippines archipelago, the ancestral home of the country's four-million-member Muslim minority. Decades of continuing war in Mindanao between Muslims and the Christian-dominated central government have followed America's botched and only attempt at colonial rule. In much the same way, today's bloody messes in Iraq and Kashmir resulted from Britain's inept efforts to extricate itself from the responsibility of ruling no-longer-profitable imperial outposts.

U.S. colonial rule began in 1898, when Washington annexed the islands during the brief Spanish-American War and paid Spain $20 million. The Philippine-American war of resistance, which began six weeks later, lasted for three years. Little taught in U.S. schools today, it was a particularly brutal conflict, resulting in tens of thousands of Filipinos and thousands of Americans being killed. Forty-eight years later, in 1946, the United States got out of the colonial business and granted independence to the Philippines. To this day, the relationship remains erratic, and numerous Filipinos believe that an amorphous "Washington" somehow controls their homeland. Still, the great majority hold deep affection for all things American.

Dr. Nilo Barandino and his wife, Cristina, who live on the Mindanao island of Basilan, put the Islamist threat in blunt, personal terms. On November 28, 1992, a group of Muslim men armed with automatic weapons kidnapped the couple and nine of their children as they were driving from their home, in the small city of Isabela, to their farm in the countryside. The assailants were members of the Abu Sayyaf Group, a particularly vicious Islamic separatist organization that operates throughout the southern Philippines. Basilan, a tiny, deceptively lovely island some 575 miles south of Manila in the deep-emerald Celebes Sea, was an Abu Sayyaf stronghold.

After thirteen days of captivity at a jungle hideout, where some of the men raped Cristina in front of him, Barandino was released and instructed to come up with ransom money. Two weeks later he bought the family's freedom with $45,000 raised by mortgaging the farm.

Barandino, a physician, garrulous and given to a touch of self-aggrandizement, is also a deep brooder, a man who doesn't easily forgive or forget. At age seventy, when we met, he was compactly built and looked as fit as a well-conditioned man twenty years his junior. He claimed to have challenged Abu Sayyaf to put up five of its gunmen in an automatic-weapons duel with him. "They've never responded," he told us.

Barandino wanted revenge. In May 1993, he talked his way into accompanying a team of fifty-three government troops in an amphibious raid on Abu Sayyaf's Camp al-Madina. "I was old enough to be the father of most of them and still I was the best shot," he said. In the course of a running, nine-day gun battle, Barandino and the soldiers killed thirty-four terrorists and suffered no casualties of their own. "I settled the score," he said. For that he would pay a price much stiffer than the $45,000 ransom money. Two years after the raid, one of his sons was gunned down at a fish market. The shooter allegedly was a young Abu Sayyaf initiate making his bones. Whether Barandino's son had been singled out or was just a random target was never officially determined.

A Roman Catholic, Barandino was born in Isabela, a city of seventy-four thousand, and has lived there his entire life. He has numerous Muslim friends. "I went to school with Abdurajak Janjalani [who founded Abu Sayyaf in 1991 and was killed by police in 1998] and I know many of their people. . . . They're protected by the police and many are family members of police officers and government people. The military doesn't know who's who because the soldiers are not from this area. The only way they can arrest someone is if a friend or a family member volunteers to identify them."

In December 2004, representatives of the U.S. embassy in Manila presented the State Department's $1 million "Rewards for Justice" program payment, in bricks of Philippine pesos packed in three suitcases, to three unnamed Filipinos at a public cere-mony. The three, who fingered the brutal Abu Sayyaf commander Hamsiraji Sali, considered it prudent to disguise themselves with masks, sunglasses, oversized white sweatshirts, blue trousers, blue baseball caps, and even gloves at the reward ceremony.

Since their release, the Barandinos have taken costly steps to protect themselves. They completely rebuilt their house. The new structure, which stands on a hilly roadside above Isabela's bustling ferry dock, has sloped, 18-inch concrete walls, small barred win-dows, and a heavy black steel door. It looks more like a bunker than a dwelling. Belowground is a gloomy, claustrophobic, one-room clinic where Dr. Barandino sees patients when he's not on hospital duty. With no sunlight, the floor is constantly damp. When we were there, the room smelled of disinfectant. "Last January—the eigh-teenth, actually—someone tossed a grenade at us," said Cristina, with about the same level of emotion as a housewife elsewhere might complain of a clogged garbage disposal. "It just bounced off and exploded on the street."

After passing around cups of sweet, milky instant coffee, Cristina pulled three fat red photo albums from a cramped bookshelf and handed them to her husband. One by one, Nilo opened the books across his knees. He turned the plasticized pages slowly, as though to maximize dramatic effect, and recited the names of the figures in the three-by-five snapshots, the dates and circumstances of each killing.

He knew them all by heart. "This is from April 8, 2004," he said with clinical remove. "It's Commander Hamsiraji Sali, also known as José Ramirez. You will see that the side of the head has been blown away." Until troops ambushed and killed him, Hamsiraji was one of the top five leaders of Abu Sayyaf and was considered its most successful assassin.

The photos amounted to a gruesome history of Basilan. Some, like that of Hamsiraji, were of alleged terrorists government forces killed; others were of their victims. All were gut-churning—corpses torn by gaping wounds, blackened in the sodden heat of the equatorial southern Philippines, many with limbs or heads missing. One was no more than a torso. "It was found in the mangroves," Nilo said. "The arms and legs were chopped off and it was decapitated. We couldn't locate the head, so it was never identified."

The grisly collection showed twelve decapitations, a trademark of the Abu Sayyaf Group. "Actually," the doctor said as he unfolded a white sheet of figures his wife had begun typing fourteen years ago, "there have been more than 56 beheadings. Sorry, our records are not up to date, but this gives a general idea; also, more than 452 killings and 183 kidnappings."

Abu Sayyaf–related violence is just a small piece of the complex jigsaw puzzle of Islamic separatist-related bloodshed in the southern Philippines. Since the early 1970s, an estimated 120,000 people have been killed and property damage has been put at $3 billion. Well over 240,000 people remain displaced from their homes. Horror is so tightly woven into the fabric of Basilan's daily life that it is barely discernible to those who live there as anything other than ordinary, a subject for a family scrapbook. A small but particularly violent terror organization, Abu Sayyaf operates on

Basilan and other heavily Muslim islands of Mindanao and the Sulu Archipelago. Its members, never more than seven hundred and now down to perhaps half that, use kidnapping, extortion, bombing, and assassination to pursue their goal of breaking away from the predominantly Catholic Philippines government and reestablishing what historically had been an independent Islamic sultanate.

Abu Sayyaf, Arabic for "Bearer of the Sword," is only one link in a loose chain of extremist Islamic groups strung across Southeast Asia from the southern end of Thailand through the arc of Malaysia, Singapore, Indonesia, and the Philippines. Newer links have begun appearing of late in such unlikely places as Vietnam and Cambodia. Some of these groups are narrowly focused independent operators, seeking greater autonomy for Muslim minorities within countries dominated by Christians or Buddhists or where ethnic Chinese minorities run the economies. Others are tied to each other and to al-Qaeda, sharing Osama bin Laden's grand vision of rescuing Islamic states from perceived American and other Western neocolonialism.

Like Osama, those who study jihad at his feet nourish the vision of restoring the caliphate, the theocratic leadership that governed the world's Muslims and dominated much of North Africa, Europe, and Asia for more than three hundred years after the death of the Prophet Mohammed in A.D. 634. The caliphate is the only form of governance that has ever been fully approved by Muslims. Toward the end of the ninth century, the caliphate began slipping into a long, drawn-out decline. In 1924, Mustafa Kemal Ataturk, the secular dictator of modern Turkey, abolished it altogether, along with the veil for women and the fez for men, which he considered unacceptable symbols of Islamic backwardness.

Ever since, some Muslims throughout the world have stewed in bitter frustration over what they consider the vicious emasculation by the West and its acolytes of Islam as a global power. They believe that only by reestablishing a borderless, ultraconservative caliphate will Muslims reclaim greatness.

Like Abu Sayyaf in the Philippines, some of Southeast Asia's other Islamist groups use terror as their principal weapon in the struggle; others rely more on political manipulation, peer pressure, propagandizing, and fundamentalist indoctrination of school-children. It is by no means clear yet which tactic will yield the most effective, long-term results. For obvious though not necessarily the wisest reasons, the United States has focused its attention almost entirely on the terrorists.

Yet fundamentalist social pressure, with minimal violence, may well prove more powerful over time than bombings and murder in shifting Southeast Asia's Muslims toward ultraconservatism. At this stage, with social progress and regression pitted against each other in a protracted struggle, it's too soon to tell.

As grim as daily life can be in places such as Basilan, faint glimmers of better times do on occasion break through the clouds. Across the Isabela town square from the Barandinos' house, a Jollibee restaurant, an outpost of the Philippines' leading homegrown fast-food chain, sparkled a brilliant, mock-McDonald's red and yellow, its trademark smiling bumblebee buzzing with corporate confidence in Basilan's future. Hopeful residents see the arrival of a new Jollibee in any hard-pressed Philippines town as a sign that they are joining the world. The Isabela branch opened in 2005, shortly after a U.S. military Joint Special Operations task force wrapped up a three-year campaign of training Philippine soldiers and marines in counterterrorism and civic action techniques.

Judged by the sharp reduction in kidnappings and beheadings along with the elimination of many Abu Sayyaf fighters, the task force achieved great success. The Americans then transferred the "Basilan model" to Jolo, the next troubled island down the archipelago. But while Nilo Barandino acknowledged that Basilan had become much more peaceful, he was reserving final judgment. "It's simply too soon to tell," he said.

To help us gain better insight as to what remained undone and what ought to be done, the doctor offered to take us to meet his friend the judge. As always, before leaving home, he packed a green, zippered gym bag with three high-powered automatic handguns, all fully loaded, and spare magazines. He slung it over his shoulder, where it settled with a clank. "A precaution," Nilo explained, heading out the door with his guests.

2

The Judge

Parked snug to the door of the Barandinos' house was a pearl-gray van, an armed driver, and a pistol-packing security man up front. We piled in the back.

Within minutes after speeding out of town, the van was skirting tiny farms and villages of green, blue, pink, and yellow bungalows set among matching tropical flowers. We sped past billboards alternately appealing to islanders to "Support Cease-fire" and to "Practice Family Planning." After half an hour's drive, we pulled up to a modest, brown wooden bungalow draped in lavender bougainvillea.

It was late Sunday morning, after Mass, and the judge was dressed for comfort: green flip-flops, brown plaid shorts, and a white singlet. He was seated in a small dirt front yard, at a square card table covered with faded yellow oilcloth. Arrayed before him were a drained coffee mug, a pack of Marlboros, a plastic throwaway lighter, and a loosely holstered .45 pistol, its butt glistening with oil in the brilliant sunshine. A few steps away, a thin young man in cutoff jeans and running shoes perched quietly and seemingly without curiosity on a stool alongside the fence. A black Uzi bridged his thighs.

As the judge rose to shake our hands, a large and exquisitely worked gold crucifix swayed on a thick gold chain around his neck. A small man with a bar code of dyed black hair slicked across his pate, he casually waved us to the table with a Marlboro clamped in a white faux ivory holder. "This place is something like your Wild

West," he said while discreetly slipping the .45 out of sight somewhere beneath the table. "But things are much better now, since
the Americans were here and helped build roads and development
projects. That shows that you can't defeat these people just by military
operations. You have to alleviate poverty at the same time."

Considering the source, this sympathetic assessment was
surprising. The judge was Danilo M. Bucoy, known across Basilan
and throughout Mindanao for handing down harsh sentences against
young Muslim men. In the American West of the nineteenth century
Bucoy would have been spoken of with the trepidation accorded
Isaac Parker, the "hanging judge" of Indian Territory. Bucoy's record
of severity from the bench included sentencing all seventeen Abu
Sayyaf members he had recently tried to three death penalties
apiece. Now he was about to begin the trials of ten more. Yet here
he was, urging American visitors to further help the Philippines
government ease the terrorists' economic plight.

How did he rationalize this seeming contradiction? "When they
come before me in court I never hear them say that they believe
in this or that cause or that they want to die a martyr's death,"
Bucoy answered. "No, they deny their involvement and beg me
to save their lives." This made it obvious to him that they were
not committed ideologues but poor, uneducated young men with
no prospects. A few leaders of Abu Sayyaf and other Philippine
Islamist terror groups may be knowledgeable religious fundamentalists, educated and middle class, but their foot soldiers are for the
most part ignorant, both secularly and religiously, unemployed, and
motivated to violence by desperation. "Very few are indoctrinated
with an ideology and it's rare that they know anything about Islam,"
said the judge. So, while he was prepared to sentence the guilty
to the full extent the law allowed, he believed that many could be
directed away from extremism by economic opportunity.

Bucoy's experience suggests that poverty-bound ignorance of religious doctrine, rather than educated understanding of it, accounts
for the rise of Islamic fundamentalism and outbursts of brutal violence in a region of the world where Muslims traditionally have
been known for moderation. Ignorance combined with frustration
over their inability to sway events governing their lives have opened

growing numbers to the appeals of radical clergymen. And they are increasingly focusing their fury on the United States, a country they once honored and sought to emulate.

If the United States is to avert an unending war of cultures, spinning out of the Middle East to distant Islamic centers, it is critical that Americans determine to their own satisfaction whether Muslim bitterness is in fact based on poverty and lack of educational and economic opportunity or is a result of religious psychosis. While there is no shortage of lunacy among those who plot and conduct suicide attacks on innocent civilians, most of their followers are themselves victims, and the acts of terror they carry out are more symptom than cause.

Tinted glass towers and glittering department stores are the face of globalization Southeast Asia's financial and political elites like to show the world. But the outsider who walks the big cities' fetid back streets and the dirt lanes of Muslim villages is certain to take away a stark and discouraging picture. The lasting image is of young men squatting in doorways and on corners, with nothing more to occupy themselves than sharing cigarettes and staring into the shabby middle distance. If these aimless men and teenagers are not wide open to a wild-eyed imam's pitch or a terrorist's wad of cash, then the world has nothing to fear from Islamic radicalism.

Many national leaders in Southeast Asia believe that the United States could best cool anti-American fever by shifting its priorities from killing terrorists to providing low-key, essentially open-ended investment in preparing young Muslims to earn a living. And not in Southeast Asia alone, but also in the broader Middle East tied ever closer by fundamentalist practice and religious law. Some American terrorism analysts challenge this seemingly straightforward thesis, arguing that it is naïve; that economic hardship is not the underlying cause of terrorism and that Islamic terrorists act on an irrational hatred of the United States and its allies. They point out that none of the nineteen suicide hijackers on 9/11 was a product of poverty.

But those whose expertise is gained on the ground—military and police officials, government leaders, and numerous less consequential people who live among the terrorists of the Philippines and elsewhere in Southeast Asia—contend that the Americans are missing the point. To them, it is evident that terrorist leaders, who take their lead from al-Qaeda and other radical Arab organizations, are distinct from the masses who follow orders and carry out the suicide bombings.

This is an argument that came up repeatedly as we traveled through the region. The simplest answer to the debate is that there is no simple, and certainly no single, answer. The most likely truth is that poverty underlies other hard-to-swallow factors, among them protracted Muslim humiliation over being left behind as the rest of the world presses into the twenty-first century; their inability to speak out against the betrayal of corrupt and despotic political leaders; and their anger at the United States in general and the George W. Bush administration in particular for what they consider its judgment of Islam by a different standard than it applied to perpetrators of violence in non-Muslim societies.

The election of Barack Obama in November 2008 came as a great relief to many Muslims, especially in Indonesia, where he lived as a child, raising hopes and expectations of warmer relations with the United States as well as greater understanding from the American people. Still, under Bush, there was positive movement toward resolving the nagging dilemma of coexistence between Islam and the West. The Defense Department devised for the Mindanao region, which includes Basilan, a military and civic-action blueprint to meet the conflicting needs of the Muslim minority and the Christian majority, which regard each other as threats. It was called Operation Balikatan, meaning "shoulder-to-shoulder." If successful, the Balikatan plan could be applied throughout the southern Philippines, across Southeast and South Asia, and perhaps into the Middle East itself. In the broadest sense, some of General David Petraeus's key tactics for the "surge" in 2007, when U.S. troops started helping rebuild Iraq, were based on the plan.

The first step of Balikatan was to dig beneath the layer of terrorism on Basilan and accept that it was an extreme expression of Muslim discontentment and not necessarily an irrational one. Next was to examine the perceived wrongs that prompted the violence, and then, finally, to set some of these wrongs right.

The lush jungles of Basilan offered an ideal setting in which to start digging. It is one of the poorest of the 7,107 islands of the Philippines. In a nation as impoverished as the Philippines, one must look long and hard to find a place so badly off that it makes the rest of the country appear prosperous by comparison. Basilan is that place. While 35 percent of the nation's population lives below the government poverty line of a monthly income of $131 for a family of five, 63 percent of Basilan's 340,000 people do. Sixty-three of every 1,000 newborns on Basilan die in infancy, compared with 49 for the general population. Only 39 percent of children on the island are enrolled in school, as compared with 72 percent throughout the country.

Christian control of the area—80 percent of the population is Roman Catholic—began under the Spaniards, who encouraged migrants from the northern islands to migrate to help develop the virgin forests. The American colonial authorities continued the migration process, further contributing to marginalizing Muslims in their homeland and raising tensions and armed struggle between the two religious groups. Between 1972 and 1981, under martial law, President Ferdinand E. Marcos downgraded suffrage require- ments and granted voting rights to eighteen-year-olds and illiterates, swinging the balance of political power in Mindanao permanently to the Christian side. Marcos's move was just one example of how Roman Catholics have long outmuscled the indigenous Muslims. The central government in Manila, on the main island of Luzon far to the north and even more distant in empathy, encouraged the newcomers to seize ancestral Muslim land. The result was a volatile mix, an explosive formula that has fired extended periods of Muslim insurgency over the past three decades.

Since the days of the Spanish, economics has always been a criti- cal part of the Mindanao struggle. The province is a grocery basket of agricultural products and a trove of natural resources. Late in 2006, ExxonMobil bought a 50 percent interest in a two-million- acre offshore site in the Sulu Sea. The plot's potential one billion barrels have added to the friction between the revolutionary Moro Islamic Liberation Front and the government. Another area under contention is the Ligawasan Marsh, an immense wetlands known to be rich in oil and natural gas. The MILF and its precursor, the Moro National Liberation Front, have grappled for decades with the central government over ownership.

The current unrest may be traced in a fairly straight line to the early 1970s, when a young University of the Philippines political science lecturer named Nurallaji Misuari helped establish the MNLF, to struggle for Muslim independence, and became its chairman. Misuari, known to Filipinos simply as Nur, recognized that his fellow Muslims had become a distinct minority in their homeland. Under his leadership, the MNLF eventually numbered thirty thousand armed men, and its battles with the government from 1972 to 1976 accounted for as many as two hundred thousand people killed on both sides.

In fact, though, the Muslims of the southern Philippines have been at war with outside rulers in varying degrees of intensity since soon after the Spanish explorer Ferdinand Magellan came upon the islands in 1521. Twenty-one years later, Spain laid claim and named the islands in honor of Prince Phillip, who later became King Phillip II. In full-blown imperial mode, the conquistadors, who didn't know what to make of the dark-skinned Muslim natives they encountered, misnamed them Moros, Spanish for Moors. As with Christopher Columbus splashing ashore in the Bahamas, thinking he was in Bengal and identifying the natives as "Indians," the name stuck. In one of their history's ironies, the Moros adopted the once-hated pejorative as a label of nationalist pride, even as they ferociously resisted four hundred years of harsh attempts by Spanish friars to convert them to Catholicism. Today they call the homeland of their dreams Bangsamoro (Moro Nation).

The outlines of that glimmering homeland were defined in 1976 under an agreement worked out in Tripoli. President Ferdinand E. Marcos, believing that Libyan dictator Muammar Qadaffi was financially supporting the MNLF, dispatched his wife Imelda, a onetime beauty queen, to charm the eccentric colonel. It worked, at least to the extent that an agreement was reached to establish an autonomous Muslim homeland in Mindanao.

Indicating the lack of priority with which successive Manila governments customarily treat Mindanao affairs, it was only in August

1989 that the government and the MNLF, under Misuari, set up the Autonomous Region in Muslim Mindanao (ARMM) to implement the Tripoli accord signed thirteen years earlier. It comprises nearly 12 percent of Mindanao's population and its four poorest provinces. Misuari was appointed governor of the ARMM. Because the ARMM was so small and poor, most Moros were further embittered, and fighting with government forces continued unabated.

Then, in 1996, the two sides signed a peace agreement. Like the Tripoli agreement and the ARMM, it has been honored far more in the breach than in practice, with each side accusing the other of bad faith and dirty tricks. In the three decades since Misuari founded the MNLF, his and its fortunes have waned. After years of him protesting the nonimplementation of the Tripoli agreement, President Gloria Macapagal Arroyo had him arrested in 2001 and imprisoned for five years on charges of rebellion. Since 2007 he has been held under house arrest in a suburb of Manila.

In 1981, the MNLF organization split and a more violent faction, calling itself the Moro Islamic Liberation Front, launched a full-throated war against the central government as well as against Misuari's forces. The MILF accused Misuari of selling out for peace.

Dr. Barandino's old schoolmate Abdurajak Abubakar Janjalani, far more extreme than Misuari or any of his successors in the MNLF and MILF, founded Abu Sayyaf in 1991. Born in the mid-1960s in Isabela, Basilan's only urban center, Janjalani studied theology and Arabic in Libya, Syria, and Saudi Arabia. He adopted the Saudi kingdom's extreme Salafist version of Islam and, with it, notions of global jihad, generally understood—some contend misunderstood—as "holy war."

Much has been written in recent years to explain the concept of jihad, not only to Westerners but to lay Muslims as well. Mainstream Islamic clergy go to great pains to define it narrowly as an individual's "striving in the way of Allah" against personal demons. But in popular understanding jihad has come exclusively to mean armed struggle against nonbelievers. The argument may be made that by using the term in this way Western news media and others are unwittingly applying an honorable religious standard to forbidden acts of brutality such as mass murder of innocents.

In the late 1980s, Janjalani joined the U.S.-financed mujahideen, or holy warriors, of Afghanistan in their ultimately successful war against the Soviet Union's Red Army. During that time, he is believed to have met Osama bin Laden, who allegedly gave him $6 million and instructions to return to Mindanao to establish Abu Sayyaf. By the early 1990s, the group was carrying out numerous bomb attacks and beheadings in the Philippines. Its crowning achievement was blowing up the interisland SuperFerry *14* on February 27, 2004, sinking the vessel off the coast of Manila and killing 116. By that time Janjalani was dead, shot in a battle with Philippine troops in 1998. He was succeeded by his younger brother Khadaffy Janjalani, who was later killed in a shootout as well.

For years, Abu Sayyaf was closely associated with confessed 9/11 plotter Khaled Sheikh Mohammed and with Ramzi Yousef, of 1993 World Trade Center bombing notoriety. The elder Janjalani worked with Yousef on the grandiose Operation Bojinka. He also cooperated with the Indonesia-based regional terrorist organization Jemaah Islamiyah, which killed 202 people, mainly Australian tourists, in the bombing of a nightclub on the Indonesian resort island of Bali in October 2002.

Diplomats and intelligence officers in the heavily fortified, colonial-era U.S. embassy on Manila Bay reported these and other Abu Sayyaf activities back to their State Department and CIA headquarters. Only after 9/11, though, did these missives finally ring alarms in Washington, signaling belated recognition that Muslim extremists in the Philippines were part of a global network. The Pentagon hastily cobbled together a plan to send several hundred civic action specialists to the southern Philippines. The planners required an "invitation" from the government of President Gloria Macapagal Arroyo, but the United States rarely has encountered insurmountable difficulty in winning official cooperation from a succession of corruption-riddled Philippine governments.

Beginning in February 2002, five months after 9/11, four months after invading Afghanistan, and thirteen months before unleashing Shock and Awe on Iraq, some six hundred U.S. Special Forces troops,

lightly armed for a training and civic action mission, were deployed
to Mindanao to launch the shoulder-to-shoulder, or Balikatan,
operation. Working alongside Filipino troops, they helped build
roads and drill wells, erect schools and clinics, and provide regular
medical services for the people of Basilan. The effort was largely
successful. It significantly helped reduce the image of Abu Sayyaf
from that of a romantic band of freedom fighters to a small, loosely
formed gang of kidnappers and murderers-for-hire.

Still, some residents complained that the Americans were also
gathering intelligence. This is a never-ending irritant for large
numbers of Filipinos, who consider the American military presence an insult to their nationhood. And, as is so often the case in
the Philippines, success inevitably engendered a perverse need
for failure: in September 2008, the Arroyo government unilaterally scuttled plans to sign a peace agreement, and the MILF
resumed fighting.

Mindanao remains threatened and threatening. The government and its armed forces on one side and the MILF independence
organization on the other have periodically broken the cease-fire
agreement agonizingly pounded out in 2001. And the military and
police are widely regarded as ineffectual and corrupt. According to
a chagrined Judge Bucoy, of nearly two hundred Abu Sayyaf members sought by the police for nearly a decade, only twenty-seven had
ever been arrested. Why so few? we asked. Bucoy flicked his thick
eyebrows toward his receding hairline in a Groucho Marxian facial
quirk many Filipinos use to respond inoffensively to the obvious.

He recounted in detail how in June 2001 a band of Abu Sayyaf
kidnappers had holed up at the Dr. José Maria Torres Hospital, in
the nearby town of Lamitan, with some two hundred hostages, among
them three Americans whom they had seized at a luxury resort three
months earlier. More than three thousand Philippine troops, backed by
U.S.-supplied technological support, surrounded the hospital and an
adjacent, open-walled Catholic church. A wild firefight erupted, and
military helicopters strafed the area with incendiary rockets. Among
the hostages, American Protestant missionary Martin Burnham and
Filipino nurse Ediborah Yap were killed, most likely caught inadvertently in the crossfire. Then, despite the presence of thousands

of armed troops, the Abu Sayyaf fighters slipped out of the hospital and escaped.

"How could that happen?" Bucoy rhetorically repeated our original question. "How could these kidnappers manage to roam around for three months before the hospital battle and then escape from all those troops and many are still on the move? Well, as an officer of the court, I cannot comment." Then he shot his eyebrows skyward again and smiled. *"Res ipsa loquitur,"* he said in his best law school Latin. "The thing speaks for itself."

Stories and rumors, what gossip-relishing Filipinos call *chismis*, of mutual back-scratching and palm-greasing between military and police with criminals and terrorists (Communists as well as Islamists) have been a coffee-shop staple for decades. Tales of armed troops on jungle patrol looking the other way as antigovernment fighters pass by unmolested abound alongside claims of cops selling guns to robbers. Local government officials and foreign diplomats, whose job is to track such accounts, say that some are true. And not just in the Philippines. Military and police corruption, to say nothing of political and judicial corruption, comprise an epidemic that sickens societies throughout the region. How the United States reacts, and should react, is dealt with in subsequent chapters.

A widely told but formally unconfirmed story that began making the rounds right after the hostage takers escaped from the Lamitan hospital had the Abu Sayyaf commander making a mobile phone call to a senior military officer outside the building at the height of the battle, confirming that there would be no shooting as he and his men slipped out the back. "Military careers are made here in the South," Judge Bucoy said with a smile. "And so are military bank accounts." And he flipped his eyebrows again.

3

The Lady in Black

Cababay Abubakar stood out among passersby as she hurried from her mud-splattered pickup truck to a coffee shop for a meeting with us in the Mindanao city of Cotabato. She was dressed, as always, entirely in black: a chic turban-tunic-and-trousers ensemble of her own design. While most observant Muslim women in tropical Cotabato cover their heads with airy scarves, they typically wear pastels, which suit the tropical environment, and almost never the enveloping black *chador* associated with the women of the Middle East. By creating her own outfit, Abubakar was blending her sense of Koranic obligation with her sense of style. "It's better to comply," she said. "My mother dressed this way, too. Despite what many people think, about the heat and so forth, it's really very comfortable, very easy."

Abubakar doesn't spend much of her tightly scheduled time discussing Islamic fashion. As one of the Philippines' better-known female Muslim educators, she runs her own madrassa, is chairman of a regional religious education accrediting association, raises funds for schools, and negotiates with government agencies to improve acceptance levels of madrassa graduates by Catholic and public colleges and universities as well as to public service and armed forces jobs. A wife and mother, she was completing a doctorate in education.

Education is to Abubakar the key to advancement opportunities for Philippine Muslims. For decades, contributions from charitable groups and wealthy individuals in Saudi Arabia had been a major source of funding for Islamic education in Southeast Asia, including Mindanao. But after 9/11, under pressure from Washington, which insisted that madrassas were training camps for young terrorists, the kingdom cut off the flow of cash. Although some funding continued to leak through the banking barriers that the United States and other governments put in place, the bottom line shriveled. In Mindanao, this meant that of more than a thousand religious boarding schools that operated before 9/11, fewer than seven hundred remained.

Not surprisingly, Abubakar denied categorically the charge that madrassas in the southern Philippines were associated with terrorism. U.S. diplomats in Manila supported her claim and, more broadly, so did government officials, non-Muslim and Muslim, across Southeast Asia. Still, in the Philippines, where Muslims are a suspect minority to begin with, the deep-seated suspicion persists that madrassas are hotbeds of evil, adding another layer to their burden.

"A religious education has always been a problem for Muslims in this country," Abubakar said over tea and cookies. "If you're a madrassa graduate, you can't even apply for a civil service job. Even if you've graduated from Medina or Cairo, from the best Islamic institutions in the world, your accreditations aren't recognized in the Philippines." Parents who are ambitious for their children to succeed in the larger society are stymied by government school regulations, which require that Muslim students participate in Christmas pageants and other religious celebrations, that Muslim girls take part with Christian girls in dances that are considered haram, and otherwise disobey Islamic tradition.

This often results in pressures on young Muslims attending government school, eroding parental control and demeaning the Islamic community. Girls balk at wearing head scarves and succumb to the allure of social life. So parents who fear the cultural loss choose to send their children to madrassas, which often lack facilities or faculty to teach such career-enabling courses as English, mathematics, and sciences. In what Muslims see as a sop, the central government recently launched a program to teach limited

Islamic studies at public schools in Muslim-dominated areas. But not many are particularly interested in taking such jobs, since they pay less than a third of standard teaching salaries. "The system," said Abubakar, "is designed to fail."

Abubakar's defense of madrassas had serious merit and was rational, they being the primary source of her income. At the same time, she insisted that the MILF was never a terrorist outfit. "I visited Camp Abu Bakar [an important MILF installation] and it was much less a military training camp than a social experiment in a pure Islamic community," she said. U.S. and Philippine experts have evidence that Abu Sayyaf and the Indonesia-based Jemaah Islamiya terrorist organization have undergone training, including bomb making, at the camp. These two groups, insisted Abubakar, "are a creation of the Philippine military" and have never existed. As startling as that might seem, we heard it widely in Islamic communities in the Philippines, Indonesia, and elsewhere.

Indeed, vast numbers of Muslims throughout the world dismiss even the possibility that fellow Muslims could commit acts of terrorism and certainly would not have carried out something so grossly un-Islamic as the 9/11 attacks. Understanding the genesis of these denials is critical to undertaking any reformation of U.S. policy in the Muslim world, not simply because they fly in the face of so much evidence, but also because they are so broadly accepted.

U.S. public relations efforts largely have been unable to counter such claims. A substantial piece of the problem is generic: one person's terrorist is another's freedom fighter; your thug may be my martyr; one's insurgency is another's war of liberation. To the British of the 1940s in Palestine, the Zionists of the Haganah, the Irgun, and the Stern Gang were terrorists. To their Redcoat ancestors in the American colonies of New England so were the Sons of Liberty, who opposed the Stamp Act in 1775. But to their own, these fighters were and always will be heroes and patriots.

The disconnect between Americans and Muslims is based almost entirely on Americans' certainty that they stand in defense of freedom and human decency and Muslims' equal assuredness that Americans adhere to a double standard that is wholly biased against them. These antagonistic convictions, taken together, constitute powerful glue that holds organizations such as the MILF together and draws them into closer contact with Muslims of the worldwide *umma*. Muslims in the Philippines have no doubt that the governments in Washington and Manila connive against them simply because they are Muslims. If U.S. foreign policy were evenhanded, they argue, Washington would help the Moros reclaim their "ancestral domain." In return, the Moros would be delighted to help the United States rebuild devastated bridges to the Middle East.

While some of this thinking is flawed, there is much to be said for the argument. Nothing would better represent American good-will than American volunteers working in Moro hospitals, on Moro farms, in businesses, industries, and schools. These same Americans could help reeducate—in the best sense of that abused term—the people among whom they would work and live. But before reaching that point, Americans have a long way to go and many pitfalls to sidestep in learning about the Moros.

Eid Kabalu is the official public face of the MILF. When a bombing takes place somewhere in the southern Philippines, Kabalu appears on TV to deny that the MILF played any role. When peace talks between the MILF and the government in Manila bog down in an impasse, he tells reporters that the fault is the government's and that the Moros are still abiding by the truce. As designated spokes-man, Kabalu periodically brushes aside government allegations that the group provides succor to Jemaah Islamiya or to Abu Sayyaf.

His credentials include years of combat during the 1970s and 1980s, first with the original Moro National Liberation Front and then with the breakaway MILF. For all his self-acknowledged youth-ful involvement in armed struggle, Kabalu projected an unlikely image as a terrorist, with his close-cropped, graying hair, sparse mustache, and comfortable waistline. As we discussed the future of the southern Philippines one day in Cotabato, he picked uncertainly at a *merianda*, an afternoon snack, of miso soup and fried shrimp at a quasi-Japanese restaurant we had chosen. "I know nothing about this kind of food," he confessed shyly.

Kabalu was circumspect and measured in responding to questions, clearly wanting to leave the impression that the MILF does its best to cooperate with the government. Despite its fearsome reputation and its acknowledged onetime financial links to al-Qaeda, the organization had lowered its expectations, he said, and taken a pragmatic approach toward the terms for autonomy it would accept "from Malacanang," the presidential palace, in Manila. "The Moros dominate only about 20 percent of Mindanao today," he said. "That's the reality, no matter how much we claim. We've become aliens in our own land and we now accept that."

In addition to non-Muslim Filipinos and foreigners, most hurtfully their own communal leaders have outsmarted ordinary Moros for centuries. Ever since Spanish times, tribal chiefs, known as *datus*, have sold off tribal land and pocketed great sums, building palatial residences for themselves and their relatives while their people live in extreme poverty. Noel Ruiz, a Filipino who represents the U.S. Agency for International Development in Mindanao, said that in the early days of their assistance programs, unsuspecting Americans dealt directly with some of these datus and a great deal of money disappeared.

While nearly all Muslims in the Philippines dream of a fully independent Bangsamoro, a Moro homeland, most acknowledge that it is not feasible and that they would happily settle for a prolonged period of calm and economic development. The MILF today claims a membership of twelve thousand, half of them armed, some still fighting. But, said Kabalu after draining a glass of orange soda, "most of us now are employed, farming, in school, or trying to return to normal life. We can still respond when necessary, but pretty much we've hung up our weapons."

While Kabalu sounded concessionary, a prominent associate of his, Michael O. Mastura, took a more aggressive approach in setting forth the MILF position. "We're talking autonomy and not independence—for now—but we're aiming for something more than just autonomy," Mastura had told us at lunch in a halal (sanctioned by Islamic law) restaurant in Manila. "In the end we may have to settle for something less than independence but we're not going to allow anyone to foreclose any of our options, our legitimate grievances."

Mastura, who bears the hereditary title of datu, is married to a Roman Catholic and is an attorney and a former member of the Philippine National Congress. His principal occupation these days is providing legal representation to the MILF as it tries to work out the best deal it can get from President Arroyo's government. To this end, he contended that the United States, because of its history in Mindanao, owes a historical debt to the Moros, which it is ignoring in its short-term obsession with Islamic terrorists.

"You Americans lack any sense of history," Mastura chastened us, an allegation repeated widely throughout the region. "That's why you're in such trouble in Iraq and the rest of the Middle East. All you know and care about is what you consider the moment's reality on the ground. But that's all wrong. Muslims today are trying to project their history onto their future, and if America doesn't understand that, you don't understand anything." Intriguingly, it was the Hispanic-American poet-philosopher George Santayana, the son of a nineteenth-century Spanish colonial official who wrote a history of Mindanao, who coined the cautionary aphorism "Those who cannot learn from history are doomed to repeat it."

Mastura was anxious to teach untutored Americans a Southeast Asian history lesson: Muslim and non-Muslim alike, the region's people are irritated by the fact that they have no choice but to consider the whims of the United States in practically everything they undertake in their national lives. By contrast, Americans pay no attention whatsoever to them. Their memories are long; Americans', fleeting. Their countries' histories trace back to the mists of time; America's is barely older than yesterday. Without an understanding and an appreciation of history, how can a world power expect to make wise decisions?

One historic decision that the Moros consider particularly misguided was passage by the U.S. Congress in 1916 of a piece of legislation known blandly as the Jones Act. The act was designed to serve as a preliminary constitution for the Philippines until the United States ended its sole experiment with colonialism and formally granted it independence on July 4, 1946.

The Jones Act, which clearly distinguished between the Muslim islands of the South and the Christian North, did not transfer responsibility for the Moro territories to the new legislature in Manila. But the Moros saw well ahead of time what was coming: more Christians, migrating south every day, taking over their ancestral lands; economic exploitation; no legal recognition of Moro customs and traditions; and, in a short time, total domination. In desperation, a tribal datu wrote to President Franklin D. Roosevelt in March 1935, pleading that "the American people should not release us until we are educated and become powerful because we are like a calf who, once abandoned by its mother, would be devoured by a merciless lion." Roosevelt ignored the appeal.

In no less poignant a rerun of this history, on January 20, 2003, prior to a state visit to Manila by President George W. Bush, MILF leader Salamat Hashim sent a letter suggesting that if the United States were not willing to make the Moro islands a U.S. protectorate it should at least help restore the ancestral rights of the Moros to their land. On June 18, 2003, the Moros received a polite reply from Assistant Secretary of State James A. Kelly, stating in part, "the United States will not mediate" between the government of the Philippines and the MILF.

When Bush addressed the Philippine congress in Manila the following October 18, he referred to Hashim's letter and said, "the United States supports President Arroyo's campaign to establish a lasting peace with the Moro Islamic Liberation Front. . . . I call on all the members of the MILF to reject terror and to move forward with political negotiations. When a lasting peace is established, the United States is prepared to provide development assistance to Mindanao."

Mastura brushed off Bush's assurance as biased toward the central government. He bitterly attacked Washington for more recently offering the Arroyo government $30 million in development funds for the South, to be used to entice the MILF to sign a peace settlement it considered inadequate. He likened the offer to the $20 million the United States paid Spain for the southern territory more than a century earlier—initially insulting and, over the longer term, counterproductive. "This is a slap in the face to us. Twenty million then; 30 million now; is that all that Mindanao is worth? The reason we've never grown up here in the Philippines is that we're always the little boy, the little brown brother, waiting for Uncle Sam's goodies."

As is so often the case in the Filipinos' lingering and largely unrequited love-hate affair with the United States and despite the slap in the face, the MILF in November 2003 officially welcomed the $30 million offer. But by the summer of 2008, the peace talks had slipped back into an impasse. Bombings resumed in Mindanao, along with other Muslim-related violence, and three hundred thousand people were driven from their homes. "What this shows," said Mastura, "is that, yes, the U.S. should intervene, but not just with the military and not just by throwing money. You should intervene through education. That's the key to everything. Provide scholarships for madrassas." (Mastura owns a religious school in Cotabato). He went on, "Americans need to interact with us here on a people-to-people basis, not just government-to-government. If not, many Moros will continue to go to the Middle East and Pakistan for advanced Islamic study. Then they come back with extremist notions and there's no place for them in the Philippine economy. What can you expect them to do?"

The desirability of nonofficial Americans teaching and working alongside local people, imparting skills sorely needed in local economies, is a theme we heard again and again as we traveled around the region. Many successful academicians, business executives, and government officials credited their English-language ability to positive experiences they had decades ago with teachers from the Peace Corps and wished that they'd return. Peace Corps volunteers, who at one time operated in strength throughout Southeast Asia, are now found only in the Philippines and Thailand, and their numbers are so depleted that few local people ever get to meet them. The murder of volunteer Julia Campbell in April 2007 in a mountainous area of the northern Philippines revived concerns at Peace Corps headquarters in Washington that dispatching more Americans to the region would be too dangerous to be seriously considered. She had been on vacation in the area, and investigators found no political implications. We believe that risks Americans might face in the Philippines are no more serious or threatening than they would encounter back home.

The Obama administration appears to be thinking along the same lines. In February 2009, Secretary of State Hillary Clinton announced in Jakarta that Peace Corps volunteers would soon return to Indonesia for the first time since 1965, as would scholars from the Fulbright Program.

4

The Family Man

A drive over the sharply etched Basilan hills, on a two-lane road recently paved by the U.S. Agency for International Development and the Philippine government, brought us to the tidy town of Lamitan. This was where the hospital fiasco, which Judge Bucoy had mentioned, occurred in 2001. On a concrete wall at the rear of the hospital someone had daubed in green paint and approximate spelling ROUTE OF WFDROW BY ABU SAYAF and an arrow pointing to a low brown door in the wall. In the spacious, semifinished Catholic church next door to the hospital, Mass was full-throatedly in session. Lamitan's population is fifty thousand, some 55 percent of whom are Roman Catholics. The rest are Muslims.

We pulled up at a substantial stucco and stone residence behind a tall steel gate. A child's pink bicycle stood to one side of the driveway. On the veranda, lined with upholstered cane chairs and sofas, sat the homeowner, forty-year-old Donel Ramos, a member of Lamitan's municipal council and the son of a former mayor.

Tipping his chin toward the driveway, Ramos quickly began unfolding a convoluted story: the bicycle belonged to his ten-year-old daughter, Donna Mae. She was presently visiting her grandmother in another town. She was away because she was "traumatized and afraid of returning home and going back to school." And the reason for that was that ten days earlier, Donna Mae had been kidnapped.

At about four-thirty on the afternoon of May 10, Ramos recounted, two men on a speeding motorcycle knocked his daughter off the bicycle as she pedaled on the quiet street in front of the house. Then they roared away with her clasped between them. Ramos, who was out of town, received a frantic call from his mother and rushed home. He immediately telephoned a number of contacts, seeking information and assistance. Among those he called were the officers in charge of the local military and national police garrisons, fellow members of the town council, and a member of the MILF.

After three days, during which Ramos heard nothing from Donna Mae's kidnappers, a locally based army officer called him. The officer was interested in collecting ransom money—for himself. Ramos refused to pay. In an illustration of how intertwined the web of presumed good guys and bad guys is in Mindanao, Ramos, a Catholic, said that this officer, a Muslim, had been a member of the MILF's estranged parent organization, the MNLF, before joining the army.

Ramos said he didn't identify the officer to the army or the police because he didn't want to cause further problems for his family, and "I know he'll receive his punishment from God." On the fourth morning, Ramos got a telephone call from the MILF member he'd contacted the first day. This man, to add another layer of complexity to the story, was the uncle of the ransom-seeking army officer. "He told me they had found my little girl," he said, suddenly choking, his eyes glistening. "He said she'd been captured by Abu Sayyaf and that the MILF had succeeded in a no-money negotiation. He said he did this for me because he owed a debt of obligation to my father." Nine hours later, Donna Mae was returned to Ramos and his wife.

To understand the power of the MILF in Mindanao it is essential to realize that the ancestors of the Muslims represented by the MILF today were among the first people in the Philippines to convert from animism to Islam, beginning in the late 1380s. Muslims have been fighting for independence from the bulk of the Philippine islands for nearly five centuries. Their early wars, beginning in the mid-1500s, were against Spain, which would rule the islands for 327 years, eventually converting 85 percent of the people to Roman Catholicism and creating the first of only two Christian-majority nations in Asia. The other is East Timor, which recently won its independence from Indonesia. The Moros remained wedded to Islam.

Following the Spanish departure in 1898 and the arrival of the new colonial master, the Moros, without missing a beat, went into battle against the U.S. Army.

In a particularly infamous incident, known as the Moro Crater Massacre, on March 10, 1906, a unit of 540 American troops slaughtered 600 mostly unarmed Moros, including women and children, on the rim of a dormant volcano. Mark Twain, a Missourian who at the time was a well-known journalist, wrote scathing commentaries on the incident. Twain saved special wrath for the American commander on the scene, Major General Leonard Wood, for whom a huge U.S. Army base has been named, also in Missouri. "'Slaughter' is a good word," wrote Twain. "Certainly there is not a better one in the Unabridged Dictionary for this occasion."

The Moros have been embroiled in contentious and erratic peace talks with the Manila-based government since the mid-1970s. The latest round of negotiations, the fourth, dragged on from 1997 to 2008, with Washington playing an observer role through the non-partisan, congressionally funded U.S. Institute of Peace. When the talks collapsed, Washington stepped back even further. Ironically, if the MILF could write its own dream ticket, an autonomous Bangsamoro would secede from the Philippines and become a protectorate of the United States, once its bitter enemy.

Weighing the nightmare of his child's kidnapping and eventual safe return along within the broader security picture on Basilan, Ramos said that the overall situation had shown some improvement. Until his daughter was snatched off her bicycle, there'd been no local kidnappings since the hospital siege in 2001, almost five years earlier. But now violence was rising again and there had been "a lot" of killings, including the recent murder of a senior police official. Still, Ramos interpreted the MILF's helpful participation in his daughter's case as a sign that the group was serious about reaching a permanent settlement with the Arroyo government. Abu Sayyaf, conversely, was in a state of decline, doing whatever was needed for its leaders to survive. "Theology is not the issue anymore," he said.

Father Bert Layson, a Filipino Catholic priest at the Church of the Immaculate Conception in the nearby town of Pikit, agreed. "The problem here is not simply religion," Layson said. "It's much more complex than that. People here have at least six different loyalties and, more or less, they fall in the following order: family; clan; datu; 'we Muslims'; the umma; and, last and least, the Philippines." And those divisions are just the basic ones. At the tribal level alone, Mindanao contains thirteen Moro tribes; eighteen pre-Islam indigenous tribes, whose members are animist, Muslim and Catholic; and nine Christian tribes.

Layson, a diminutive, studious man deeply supportive of the Moros, said that the plight they faced could be somewhat alleviated by development but that this alone would not restore peace. "It's an identity crisis and it's been infinitely heightened through globalism by the international Islamic revival. This is leading the Moros back to their old belief that they must live in an Islamic environment in order to truly practice Islam."

Like many people we met in Mindanao, Christians and Muslims alike, Layson said he believed that Americans, if only for historic reasons, should play a leading role in defusing the explosive situation. But he cautioned that the circumstances were too touchy and too nuanced to be handled entirely by soldiers, even if they were limited to civic action. But they're not, he said. "I know that the U.S. military is collecting intelligence with drones. I've seen the drones. But I don't say anything because I don't want to inflame the situation." He recalled that in 2006, one of the drones, termed an unmanned aerial vehicle (UAV), with a wingspan of about six feet—not much larger than a toy plane but capable of capturing and transmitting a broad range of electromagnetic wavelengths—crashed on the nearby island of Jolo during an operation against Abu Sayyaf. The local mayor tried to return it to the U.S. ambassador in Manila, who initially denied it was American before finally acknowledging ownership.

Many local residents are ill at ease about the presence of armed Americans in uniform. Anti-American Web sites in Tausug and other Mindanao vernaculars play off this unhappiness. "This is a terribly sensitive, grassroots problem," said Layson, "and it requires a long-term commitment of care and attention from those with deep-seated understanding and patience."

5

The Warrior

Colonel James Linder came on like a casting director's dream
come true of the archetype American soldier—rugged, take-
charge, optimistic, forceful yet controlled. There was a lingering
touch of small-town South Carolina and a hint of Tommy Lee Jones
as the sheriff. At forty-seven, he had led Special Forces operations
teams around the world, including Iraq, for twenty years. He
was the real deal.

Yet all was not as it appeared. As is often the case among
American soldiers dropped into hard-to-pronounce places, Linder
seemed conflicted between his image of himself as a warrior and
the actual reason he was in Mindanao. The irritant was that he was
under orders not to wage war but to win Muslim converts for Uncle
Sam. So, to rationalize, much like many GIs in the midst of ferocious
fighting in Vietnam, who had best expressed their circumstances in
terms of John Wayne movies, Linder turned half-seriously to a hoary
Hollywood scenario: "It's like the stranger walking into a saloon for
the first time. You know if you spit your tobacco juice wrong someone's going to get shot. We walk a fine line here, somewhere between
confidence and arrogance, between compassion and weakness."

Although Linder obviously relished the man-of-action veneer, he
seemed pleased to reveal a scholarly layer as well, citing master's degrees
in international relations and strategic studies, but only after emphasizing his warrior's credentials. Action—kinetics is the Pentagonese

term currently favored—is still job one in today's army. American soldiers assigned to duties other than killing other soldiers tend to feel shortchanged, as though what they were doing was somehow unmanly. Left to their instincts, they would attack, kill, and move on. So Linder bridled at what he considered a hurdle placed in his way: the Moros' "hang-up" with their past. "I refuse to be held hostage to history," he said. "If you spend your time complaining about the past you'll never advance. That's their problem here."

Foreigners often are bemused by Americans' evident lack of interest in history, including their own. Getting on with it; worrying about today and tomorrow but never yesterday; looking ahead, never back—these are qualities that provide Americans with the confidence to move perpetually forward. They also are shortcomings that preclude learning from past mistakes. Thus we marched boldly into Vietnam, never deigning to consider the humiliation the Vietnamese handed the French; into Afghanistan, despite the bitter lessons the Afghans taught the Communist Russians, the imperial British, and all other invaders as far back as Alexander; into Iraq, despite the Mesopotamian quagmire the British had fallen into there.

It is by now clear that American exceptionalism will not forever shield us from history's harsh lessons. To come to terms with the world's Muslims, we're going to have to learn from and pay respect to their history.

Under the Balikatan plan, Linder and his forces were making progress. We met in Linder's headquarters, a spare, cinderblock room in a tight cluster of stucco and wood buildings on the outskirts of Zamboanga. A pleasant enough city of some 602,000 people, Muslims and Christians, Zambo, as Filipinos call it, is at the southern tip of a narrow peninsula cleaving the Sulu and Celebes seas. It advertises itself to the scant tourist trade as the "City of Flowers." Near the U.S. headquarters buildings, adjacent to a small golf course, a leased white and green helicopter fluttered into and out of a vacant pasture. Its principal task was ferrying Linder and his men to the small and dangerous island of Jolo. Midway down the southern island chain, Jolo (pronounced "holo") was moving up the scale of danger from where it had stood when Linder and his Special Forces originally shifted there from Basilan.

At that time, early in 2006, Jolo was in the midst of what the Pentagon termed a Phase One insurgency, meaning that the Islamists were preoccupied with recruiting fighters and sabotaging minor government programs. That was essentially how anti-American forces in Iraq got their start after Saddam Hussein's overthrow. By the middle of 2006, Abu Sayyaf fighters on Jolo pressed the fight to Phase Two standard, claiming victims with explosive devices and sudden ambushes. By late August, they were openly fighting against Philippine troops, an indicator that the struggle was advancing toward Phase Three—all-out warfare.

And in mid-December, although the government claimed to have the insurgents bottled up, President Arroyo unexpectedly postponed a three-day summit of the ten-nation Association of Southeast Asian Nations (ASEAN) set for the southern business hub of Cebu. Being forced to make this last-minute change of plans humiliated Arroyo, with security sources saying privately that she put the summit on hold out of fear of a terrorist attack. Arroyo protested that she acted because a devastating typhoon was about to hit Cebu. As it happened, the storm missed Cebu, and the conference was reset for mid-January. The day before the ASEAN heads of government began arriving in Cebu, explosions in the nearby cities of General Santos and Kidapawan killed six people and injured dozens. The conferees hastily signed a pro-forma antiterror agreement and left for home.

Jolo, which has a population of eight hundred thousand, 97 percent of whom are Muslim, is Abu Sayyaf's principal remaining stronghold in Mindanao. Linder had to resist his soldier's instinct to impose a "kinetic solution" on the terrorists, hunting them down and killing them. Were he free to do so, he said, the Americans could "clean the place up in ten days." But Linder recognized that simply killing the terrorists on Jolo would produce extremely limited positive effects. "The enemy is not Abu Sayyaf or Jemaah Islamiyah or even al-Qaeda," he said. "It's an idea, an idea of intolerance, subjugation, and eventual elimination of America's way of life."

The notion that this enemy was something less corporeal than an army was not peculiar to Linder, but through Balikatan he was in a unique position to test it. The core of the plan was to help separate susceptible Muslims from those spreading the "idea" and to help provide the population with some cause for optimism. In the mirror of Islamic public opinion, however, whether in Southeast Asia, South Asia, or the Middle East, the U.S. military faces an opposing idea: that Muslims are America's victims. Under the 2002 military assistance agreement that established Balikatan, the Americans in Mindanao were restricted to "building capacity" of the Philippine armed forces to counter terrorism through civic action. Prior to Linder moving his troops onto Jolo, his predecessors spent three years slogging alongside Filipino soldiers and marines on Basilan. Working also with USAID and several international nonprofit organizations, the joint forces concentrated on waging peace.

No Americans were killed, and when they left Basilan in 2006 it was, while not free of terrorists, certainly much calmer than they had found it. Although Abu Sayyaf was still a presence, its fighters no longer were able to rove at will, and the armed forces of the Philippines wound down its strength on the island from fifteen battalions to two. Building on this achievement, Linder was using the Basilan model in Jolo as part of the continuing effort to pacify all Mindanao.

The tainted "hearts and minds" psychological-warfare approach of the Vietnam War era has been replaced in Mindanao by what is known in Defense Department argot as IO—influencing others. If the system continues to net positive results, the Pentagon anticipates trying it in other countries challenged by Islamic terrorist organizations. A key element of IO thinking is not simply to give assistance but also to use development projects to provide jobs for local people, paying them for their sweat equity, what aid specialists refer to as "teaching them how to fish," rather than just giving them fish to eat. Senior U.S. officers in Iraq acknowledged belatedly that they had paid insufficient attention to this approach there. It has netted some, but as yet not nearly enough, success in Afghanistan.

Americans began operating on Jolo in September 2005. The going was slow and frustrating. "What we're doing here is harder than taking a scalp," Linder told us, falling back into cowboy-movie mode. "It takes enormous patience because our Type A personalities are programmed to achieve solutions on our watch. It's much more satisfying to shoot the enemy in the face."

He disavowed any comparison between what he was doing and the U.S. pacification program in Vietnam. Rather, he equated his mission with the British counterinsurgency begun in 1948 against Communist guerrillas in Malaysia, or Malaya, as it was then known. The Malayan Emergency lasted twelve years and was one of the very few antiguerrilla wars anywhere to result in victory. He also compared himself with the lone-wolf British officer T. E. Lawrence— Lawrence of Arabia—who lived and fought with Arab irregulars against the armies of the Ottoman Empire in the run-up to World War I. Unlike the idiosyncratic Lawrence, though, who exchanged mundane army khakis for flowing Arab robes, Linder very definitely had not gone native on Jolo. He spent hours walking through villages of thatched houses in U.S.-issue jungle-camouflage fatigues, with a large, gold-framed U.S. flag patch on the right shoulder.

Chatting with the locals through an interpreter, he concentrated his attention on mothers and young children. He explained to us that he considered it an important part of his job to show the flag to those who would someday influence the future of Moro society. He hoped to assure them that he, his soldiers, and the United States were there not to kill or destroy but to help improve their lives. "If I can get that six-year-old boy to pause and look at that flag, when he's sixteen he'll remember that a friendly American warrior helped him go to school. That's a big deal."

Although villagers smiled, shook his hand, and shyly thanked him, the sell was not always an easy one. Long skeptical of U.S. motives, some Filipinos suspect that the United States, in placing troops in Mindanao, had a hidden agenda. At the top of that agenda, many were convinced, was America's unending desire to regain forward deployment bases in the Philippines. And each time a drone crashed or was spotted flying overhead, residents were reminded that the Americans had yet another reason for being there: spying. Linder laughed off the importance of the little drones, calling them "my model airplanes." "I don't mean to be glib, but I could do the intel mission with half a dozen Special Forces guys bucknekked and a butter knife," he said glibly. The implication was that the Americans were reluctantly restraining themselves, tying one hand behind their back.

"We try to be good guests," he said. "We build friendships and trust, and we hope that people will give us information." Some do. Several weeks earlier, two young brothers from a Muslim family with seventeen children led soldiers to an improvised explosive device hidden along a road in Jolo. The IED, an infamous weapon perfected in Iraq, turned out to be a new type for Mindanao, apparently built by Abu Sayyaf with signature Jemaah Islamiya technology. The discovery was taken as a sure sign that the Indonesian group was stepping up the level of its involvement on Jolo. To express gratitude and to help encourage the flow of information, Linder raised scholarship money so the two brothers could attend school.

We had joined Linder and two junior officers on a helicopter trip to Jolo one morning in June 2006, after he gave us a standard military PowerPoint briefing in his Zamboanga office. Speaking over linked headsets above the piercing clatter, Linder pointed down to an immaculate white vessel, ringed by a necklace of smaller Philippine Navy boats, anchored in the glittering Sulu Sea. It was the American hospital ship USNS *Mercy*, in the midst of a five-month tour of Islamic communities in Mindanao, Indonesia, and Bangladesh. Because of security worries, the *Mercy* remained well offshore, and local residents who required major surgery and other intensive care were ferried aboard for treatment. Ever since a Filipino physician was beheaded on Jolo, a few years previously, most doctors had stayed away and the population had suffered. The mission of the *Mercy* was considered a great success, and the navy made plans to send the USS *Peleliu* on a similar cruise soon afterward.

After forty minutes, the helicopter thumped down onto a jungle clearing outside Panamao, one of the only two towns on Jolo. A short walk on a muddy path took us to the district hospital, a low, cream-colored concrete building. Dr. Silak Lakkian, in a white clinician's coat and Muslim head scarf, conducted a brief tour of the small, frayed facility: fifteen beds, a refrigerator for vaccines, a few aluminum walkers, a defibrillator, and some desks and chairs, banged up and scratched but serviceable, provided by American charities. Along one wall stood a stack of cartons filled with donated patients' and surgeons' gowns and disposable diapers. Lakkian seemed delighted. "Before the Americans came we had almost nothing," she said. "They gave us these things because they want to improve life for us. Eventually, we hope it will lead to greater security."

Outside, facing the hospital, rows of slender concrete pillars sprouting rusting steel rods poked from the red mud like scrawny palm trees. This bare patch was being developed into the Panamao Municipal Center. Down another shoe-squishing path, bracketing a grassy playing field, three simple, single-story buildings arranged in a horseshoe were nearing completion. This was the town's new school, built with U.S. military assistance. Inside one of the structures, ten new desktop computers, supplied and linked to the Internet by USAID, were lined up on folding office tables. They were powered by solar panels on the roof. Arguably even more impressive to the local residents, adjacent to one of the buildings stood a pink-painted "comfort room," said to be the first indoor flush toilet on the island. Cost to the American taxpayer: $200.

The population of Panamao is thirty-nine thousand, everyone a Muslim. Like all cities and towns in the Philippines, it is divided into neighborhood administrative districts called *barangays*. Laba H. Obang, the captain of the barangay across the road from the school, a neat row of wooden houses on stilts, came rumbling along atop a bright red tractor. He clambered down from the machine, on loan from the regional government, and shook hands all around. Deeply browned, stocky, and powerful-looking, with a red kerchief knotted around his brow, Obang readily and effusively praised the American soldiers operating on Jolo. Indeed, he volunteered, he'd be willing to take a bullet for Colonel Linder, should the threat arise. Why would he do such a thing? "Because the colonel and his men want our people to be happy. They have helped cure the sick. They've contributed medicines and computers and built the school. They've improved our lives." Bearing in mind that Filipinos tend to be ebullient and that this impromptu interview was conducted with Linder and his officers smiling on, he nevertheless seemed genuinely grateful.

A few miles' drive from Panamao by military truck, along a newly paved road, American soldiers and Philippine marines were working side by side in the sweltering heat, conducting a Medical Civil Action Project (MEDCAP) in the tiny village of Tuup. Two hundred or so villagers, mainly women and children, squatted on their haunches in the scant shade along the edges of a schoolyard, waiting to see a Philippine Marine Corps physician and several American medics. Some MEDCAPs, in larger settlements, drew as many as three thousand people. Inside a stifling schoolroom, Dr. Abdul Keram Yusup, wearing an olive drab uniform and a white Islamic skullcap, sat at a teacher's small desk, writing prescriptions. The medicines came from nongovernmental organizations and American troops who routinely turned over their own personal medications when being rotated out of the Philippines.

Nearly all the women lined up before Yusup were gaunt, cheek-bones protruding sharply beneath faded cotton head scarves, and frail-looking. Many peered around the dim room through fogged eyes. "Mostly, they're suffering from vitamin deficiencies and glaucoma," Yusup said as he scribbled furiously. "There also are abundant cases of tumors, cleft palate, and goiter. The worst cases we're sending to the *Mercy*." In another airless classroom, temporarily converted to a surgery, Staff Sergeant James Jackson, from New Orleans, was operating on patients with a variety of cysts, many grown to hideous proportions from having been left untreated for decades. A solid-looking man in a sweat-drenched brown T-shirt and a .45 holstered at the hip of his camouflage cargo pants, Jackson recently had completed a tour of duty as a combat medic in Afghanistan, where he provided emergency care to fellow soldiers.

"This is much more gratifying," he said without hesitation. "I love what I'm doing here. These people have suffered for years with these terrible disfigurements. I can make them feel better and look better. They can function in society for the first time." Earlier that morning, he'd removed a growth from between the eyes of a young man. "It was the size of a grapefruit and his face looked more like a lion than a human being. Now he looks normal. I think that's just great."

In the dusty schoolyard, the midday sun baking the red dirt, Philippines Marine brigadier general Juancho Sabban was gnawing on fried chicken and coleslaw out of a white Styrofoam box. His stiffly starched fatigue tunic dropped straight from his shoulders, razor-creased trousers folded over gleaming black combat boots. Sabban flashed a brilliant smile and accepted congratulations for his recent promotion to brigadier. "Much of my career has been built here in the South," he explained. "I owe this region a great deal and I am committed to it." Earlier that morning, Linder, like Judge Bucoy a few days previously, had said that some Philippine officers made considerable money by selling military weapons and ammunition to terrorists. Sabban acknowledged that the illegal trade was "a serious problem for us."

As is common among many Filipino officers, Sabban did not hesitate to vent his political views. While the Philippines once had taken justifiable pride in its professional officer class, the late President Marcos began politicizing the armed forces when he imposed martial law, which remained in effect from 1972 to 1981. The politicization process worsened in 1986, when Lieutenant General Fidel Ramos and Defense Secretary Juan Ponce Enrile, turning on Marcos, conspired to join the successful "People Power" overthrow of the regime and installed Corazon Aquino in the presidency. Ramos was elected to succeed Aquino as president in 1992. Coup attempts, coup threats, and coup rumors have been standard Philippine political fare ever since.

Sabban complained that neither members of the Congress nor "Gloria"—President Arroyo—considered Mindanao a priority. "They're focused on pork and their own political interests," he said. Two weeks after our conversation, Arroyo paid an official call to the *Mercy* and visited the troubled Sulu area, the first time since she had taken office five years earlier.

6

The Veteran

Old terrorists, like General Douglas MacArthur's fabled old soldiers, seem to fade away slowly. In local government offices and on small farming homesteads scattered around Mindanao, we met men who a few years earlier had foraged for just enough food to keep them lean and mean enough to kill. Now they were going soft, spreading through the midsection, and turning gray. "I lost too many years out of my life at war," said Commander Zaide Taup, who asked us to call him Eddie. "Too many nights sleeping in the jungle, cold and wet. Too long without a wife and family. Now I'm fifty-three, and my guys and I just want to live a normal life. We farm in the daytime and we sleep well at night."

The aging ex-guerrillas and their families were benefiting from a USAID program known as Livelihood Enhancement and Peace (LEAP). They had purchased small lots, built small bungalows, and were raising grain and seaweed for market. Life was good.

"But," Eddie claimed as we spoke in the sparse shade of an open-sided shelter, "if something happens . . . we're ready." To illustrate, he patted a well-worn .45 tucked into the waistband of his blue jeans, not quite hidden beneath a roll of belly flab as thick as a bicycle tire. From a cord around his deeply suntanned neck dangled a universal badge of middle age, a pair of reading glasses. Seven of his "guys," sitting on benches and, like Eddie, packing heat and readers, nodded their heads and tossed off that characteristic Filipino eyebrow flip, silently acknowledging their willingness to answer a call to arms should it come.

Widespread possession of firearms adds to the difficulties of law enforcement in Mindanao. This has long been true throughout the Philippines. Years before 9/11 made high-intensity security examinations the norm in much of the world, Filipinos were being patted down and asked to check their weapons at the doors of hotels, banks, and government buildings.

Looking at Eddie Taup and his guys, it was evident that for them the war was over. But their story remains alive, its details still inspiring to younger Muslim men fighting today. Eddie's title of commander was a holdover from the two decades during which he had led guerrillas of the Moro National Liberation Front into battle against government troops. He held on to that identity with pride, insisting that in their day he and his men were principled, that their struggle for a Moro homeland was just.

Like other firebrands of the time, Eddie left his village in coastal Mindanao in 1978, sailing in a small boat to Sandakan, in the nearby East Malaysian state of Sabah. From there he slipped into Indonesian Borneo, where he readily obtained an Indonesian passport. "Back then, in every Muslim country, all you had to say was 'Moro' and that was good enough," he said. "Everyone supported Moro independence." With the forged passport, Eddie joined a multinational group of Muslim men who shared a cause and wanted to learn how better to fight for it. They shipped out to Libya, where for the next eighteen months Eddie learned how to use a broad range of weapons. Libyan leader Muammar Qadaffi, who fancied himself a revolutionary and a visionary, was sponsoring Islamist terror movements around the world.

Training alongside Eddie were Pakistanis, Yemenis, and various Africans, among others. For the first time in his life, Eddie learned that he and Muslims whose languages he did not understand could make common cause. The feeling was exhilarating, liberating.

After completing the course in Libya, Eddie was sent back to Sabah and worked in a "rear operations center." Then, in 1981, he returned to Mindanao and became a field commander. For the next sixteen years he led MNLF fighters in combat against the Philippine armed forces and police. He rejected any suggestion that he had been a terrorist. "In those days we didn't even know the term." But he acknowledged that he and his fighters commonly infiltrated villages and used residents as shields during battles. "I have to admit that there was collateral damage," he said.

Eddie's time as a field commander came to an end in 1996, when the MNLF signed a peace accord with the Manila government. The agreement was the climax of negotiations that had dragged on for some twenty years. In the end, the organization gave up its long-cherished goal of Moro independence. In acceding to the government's insistence on limited autonomy, the MNLF lost its appeal among younger fighters. They accused their leader, Nur Misuari, of selling out for peace.

Realizing that the accord did virtually nothing to alleviate poverty in the South, the young guerrilla leader Salamat Hashim formed the "New MNLF," which soon became the MILF. Hashim received what he termed "significant" funding from Osama bin Laden, and several hundred of Hashim's followers underwent training at al-Qaeda camps in Afghanistan prior to the U.S. post-9/11 invasion.

The original MNLF has functioned as the dominant Moro organization since coming to terms with Manila. Its representatives occupy seats of power in local governments, and seventy-five hundred former fighters have been integrated into the army and national police force, on occasion fighting alongside government troops against the offshoot MILF. The competition has caused bad blood between the two groups of onetime comrades.

The MNLF's days in power now seem numbered. Militant Muslims in the South are infuriated with the old order, convinced it caved in to Manila, wittingly or otherwise, ceding what they refer to as their "ancestral domain." Simultaneously, as the MILF squeezes Manila for guarantees in reclaiming these ancient land rights and future development, including oil and gas rights, its popularity rises. Its leadership senses clearly that today's younger Moros feel much more a part of the umma than did their predecessors. Once it takes power, the likelihood is that the southern Philippines will evolve toward greater Islamic fundamentalism. Whether that fundamentalism necessarily will lead to extremism and terrorism is another matter, and a critical one.

But in Cotobato, the MNLF secretary-general and mayor, Datu Musilmin G. Sema, warned us that because he doubted that Manila would ever grant autonomy to the Moros, "I'm afraid that some of our brothers, the less sober ones, from Jemaah Islamiya, Abu Sayyaf, and al-Qaeda, will go back to war. They're trying to establish themselves here right now." Although he didn't say so specifically, his clear implication was that these organizations cooperated with the more radical MILF. Sounding very much like Eddie Taup, Sema said, "I'm fifty-seven, I have children, and I don't want to go back to war. I'm very jealous of the peace I helped build and I'm very sensitive to anything that could destroy our peace." Whether MILF interaction with other terrorist and separatist groups, particularly al-Qaeda, Abu Sayyaf, and Jemaah Islamiya, continues to grow is a matter of contentious debate throughout Mindanao. Most MILF supporters dismiss allegations that the organizations cooperate or contend, as educator Cababay Abubakar had told us, that Abu Sayyaf and Jemaah Islamiya never existed.

While we were in Cotabato, three Muslim professors from local colleges telephoned and said they wanted to discuss these same issues. They came to our small hotel late one evening, and we sat around a table in the darkened, concrete-paved "garden," munching fried chicken and slapping mosquitoes.

The men described themselves as MILF supporters and echoed the organization's desire that the United States support an independent Moro state. Beyond that hope, which they conceded was at best remote, they disavowed terrorism as a legitimate tactic. But—and this should provide guidance to the United States in determining how to change direction in its approaches to the Islamic world— they understood why fellow Muslims turned to terror.

Dr. Mustapha Salih, a soft-spoken specialist in Islamic studies at Cotabato City Polytechnic, put it this way: "Abu Sayyaf and Jemaah Islamiya are our enemies. We're one with the United States and the rest of the world in fighting terrorism because it really affects our lives on a daily basis. They're extremists and we don't agree with what they do. But terrorism is their reaction to unjust treatment of Muslims, here, in the Middle East, and elsewhere. The majority of Moros feel the same way—we don't agree with them but we understand."

Salih's colleague Dr. Abdul Pagayao, a health and nutrition expert at Mindanao State University, had another subject on his mind: U.S. policy toward the Palestinians and how that spills over into the rest of the Muslim world. "The United States must change its policies on the Palestine-Israel conflict because, otherwise, the Moros and the other Muslims of Southeast Asia will become yet another of your enemies. The Palestinians are our brothers and we see the Israelis bombing their children. The United States must give justice to the Palestinians; that's the focal point of Muslims everywhere."

Here then, in the backyard of a no-star hotel on a small, sweltering island in the southern Philippines, was the crux of the argument the world's Muslims have with Americans: You have chosen to stand against us, to humiliate us, to dismiss us as fellow human beings. Some of us have chosen to lash back at you with the weapon of terrorism. Terror is the ultimate symptom of our degradation at your hands.

This is a huge and a bitter pill for Americans to swallow. Many will reject it outright. But unless we consider that this is the way the world's Muslims see Americans and that no amount of warfare is going to change their minds—quite the contrary—they will continue to be our enemies. Again and again, wherever we traveled, in Mindanao, southern Thailand, Malaysia, Singapore, and Indonesia, in villages and cities, wherever there were Muslims, the outrage and bitterness were inescapable, refueled daily by the news from Palestine and Israel, from Gaza, the West Bank, the Golan, Jerusalem.

For decades, the only news available to them originated in the West and was carried on a current of Western biases and assumptions. Now, Internet users in Mindanao and Borneo have access to the same information as those in Milwaukee and Buffalo. And they can view another kind of reality through an Islamic lens on al-Jazeera TV. As a result of this flood of information and propaganda, Southeast Asians who no more than twenty years ago had barely heard of many places in the Middle East other than Mecca, who certainly never had seen a Jew and probably wouldn't know a Palestinian if they bumped up against one, are obsessed with even the minutiae of daily events there.

Palestine symbolizes in high relief everything that is wrong with the United States. It comes first and foremost, ahead of their fury with the former George W. Bush administration's actions in Iraq. But that is a constant irritant as well. "Saddam Hussein was truly a bad man," said Dr. Maguid Makalingkang, the dean of graduate studies at Mindanao State University. "But the way the United States chose to overthrow one evil man was simply unjust and evil itself. Let's give President Bush the benefit of the doubt and say that his motivations for invading Iraq and his intentions there were noble. The result was the killing of tens of thousands of innocent people. That level of killing cannot be justified; it is not 'collateral damage.'

"Look, the United States is the world's great power, the only superpower. There is no doubt about that. But your foreign policy is hated by millions of Muslims and you cannot afford to kill us all. Surely there is a more subtle way for the United States to project its power? What we see are American people who would rather waste billions of dollars than admit a mistake. A little sincerity on your part would be helpful."

Complaints were legion that U.S. policy, through a succession of administrations reaching deep into history, has been inconsistent, based on multiple standards and lacking honesty in its dealings with Muslims. Americans may argue with such judgments. We may dismiss them as ignorant or ill-informed. But while that may help us let off steam, it won't achieve what we need it to—peace. Only ground-level help, prolonged and sincere, will accomplish that.

Sincerity is much more a measurable value in Asia than it is in the West. Chinese business negotiators complain that their American counterparts demonstrate insincerity by smothering even the simplest agreements in thick blankets of legalese when, they say, a handshake would do. Chinese and Muslims move vast sums of money around the world on the basis of a single cell phone call. The North Koreans, of all people, regularly accuse the United States of lacking sincerity in the infrequent and contentious meetings between the two governments. Even the Japanese, America's closest Asian friends, frequently question their ally's ingenuousness in diplomacy and business negotiations. Americans seem to distrust such emotional approaches. If metrics can't be applied, the exercise is a waste of time. Worry about perception, and we bog down. But each time we ignore another nation's sentiments, we leave more people bruised and angry. What we see among Muslims today is that collected anger, heaped to a level that is explosive.

The indirect U.S. role in the Mindanao settlement negotiations illustrates our obsession with moving forward at the cost of refusing to glance back. Following 9/11, the Bush and Arroyo governments worked exceptionally closely, their focus almost entirely on counterterrorism and intelligence-gathering. The United States more than tripled military assistance to the Philippines, from $38 million in 2001 to $115 million in 2005, the fourth-largest grant of its kind in the world. The United States placed Green Berets, Navy SEALs, and Air Force combat controllers on the ground in Mindanao under Operation Balikatan. But because U.S. involvement in the Philippines has so often come and gone, nationalists worry about America's sincerity—its motivation and willingness to stay the course. They welcomed increased aid, but wondered when it would be cut.

The Moros, for their part, are locked in a moral dilemma with themselves: wanting to believe that they can count on the Americans this time, while unwilling to forgive the United States for killing fellow Muslims elsewhere in the world. So fierce has been the blowback from America's Israel/Palestine policy and its wars of intervention that no matter when U.S. forces leave Iraq and Afghanistan, it will be a much longer time before the Moros and millions of other Muslims consider themselves at peace with us.

7

The President

Meeting her for the first time, in Manila's imposing two-hundred-year-old Malacanang Palace, one could not help but be startled by how petite Gloria Macapagal-Arroyo is. Under five feet tall, she wears a size zero dress. But elfin stature hasn't kept her from achieving an outsize political career and facing enormous criticism. A Georgetown University classmate of former President Bill Clinton, with a Ph.D. in economics from the University of the Philippines, she was twice elected to the Senate and in a 1998 landslide victory became the country's first woman vice president. Three years later, President Joseph Estrada, a onetime film star, was expelled from office following a watered-down rerun of the 1986 People Power street rebellion that had toppled the Marcos clan. Estrada was jailed on a charge of "economic plunder."

The military shifted its allegiance to Arroyo, and she was appointed president. In 2005, she ran for the office and was elected, defeating one of Estrada's former movie colleagues, Fernando Poe Jr. Then a secret tape recording of a telephone conversation between Arroyo and an election official was leaked, purportedly revealing her attempt to fix the outcome. Arroyo eventually confirmed the conversation but denied the intent. Poe refused to concede the election. He died of a stroke a few months later, but Arroyo never fully recovered from the election scandal.

Arroyo came to the much-abused presidency of the Philippines with considerable promise. Her father, Diosdado Macapagal, had served one term as president until Marcos defeated him in 1965. Macapagal, an intellectual and reformist, made a serious attempt to clean up government corruption. But he also adopted an ill-advised fiscal policy, which bled the economy white, and he paid the political price. His daughter campaigned on promises to deliver calm and order. It didn't happen. In addition to the never-ending Islamist tensions in the South, guerrillas of the Communist New People's Army, who had been relatively quiet for a decade or so, staged a comeback near the end of the 1990s. In response, between 2001 and 2006, some six hundred left-leaning political activists and journalists were kidnapped, "disappeared," or flagrantly murdered. Officials of the powerful Philippines Catholic Church blamed the Arroyo administration.

With general elections set for 2010, rumors of military coups against Arroyo's administration continued to come and go. Rumors of corruption, some more likely than others, at the highest levels of government, continued unabated. Arroyo's husband, José Miguel "Mike" Arroyo, exiled himself from the Philippines in June 2005 after being unable to deflect accusations of taking bribes from illegal gambling interests and using his role as "first gentleman" to influence government decisions. Following this embarrassment, the American head of an "International Board of Advisers" that Arroyo had formed, multibillionaire Maurice "Hank" Greenberg, resigned from the panel. Greenberg, former chairman and chief executive of American International Group, the world's largest insurance and financial services company, had immensely successful business interests throughout Asia. AIG itself fell on hard times in the 2008 Wall Street collapse and was bailed out by the Bush administration.

Despite these and other pressures, including threats of impeachment, Arroyo continued to hang tough, both in regard to her domestic constituents and her relations with the United States. She carried on the long-standing tradition of bending to most of Washington's demands. However, newly armed with economic support from a burgeoning China, she introduced a sense of realpolitik for the first time in Manila's dealings with U.S. leaders. Well on its way to becoming a major investor throughout Southeast Asia, Beijing undertook financing a light rail project north of Manila and helping revive the Philippines' flagging mining industry. When visiting American legislators and government officials pressed Arroyo, as they regularly do leaders of developing nations around the world, to clean up corruption and make government more transparent if she wanted to attract more American investors, she snapped back at them.

In a meeting with Bond, she responded bitingly that China made no such demands. The implication was clear: if you don't back off, we've got somewhere else to turn. This threat came at a time when the United States' reputation was being battered by the war in Iraq and other incidents. Among them was a scandal surrounding World Bank president Paul Wolfowitz, who had obtained a job promotion and excessive salary increase for his girlfriend. Exposed in April 2007, the deal registered badly because Wolfowitz had denied loans to allegedly corrupt governments. Furthermore, the neoconservative Wolfowitz, a former U.S. ambassador to Indonesia, was intimately identified with the Iraq war.

How was Arroyo playing her cards now? we wondered. Over a small, informal dinner in the presidential residence overlooking Manila's badly polluted Pasig River, she stressed her cooperation with U.S. counterterrorism demands while seeking to downplay her responsibility for the Philippines' disappointing political and economic performance.

She acknowledged that the romanticized hopes that had captured the imagination of the world and of millions of Filipinos with the overthrow of the Marcos kleptocracy twenty years earlier had failed to materialize. The Philippines remained bogged down in a host of economic, political, and social problems. The reason, as Arroyo explained it, was self-seeking dissension among the nation's elites. While implicitly absenting herself from this class, she charged that members of Congress, in particular the Senate, were more interested in retaining power than in working for the common good. "It's as though we're two countries, economic and political. When the economy is on the verge of takeoff, the other side, the destructive, political side, drags the economy back down."

Filipinos alternately laugh and weep over this irresistible tendency to pull back into the squirming basket those on the verge of successfully extricating themselves. They call it society's "crab complex." Observers of the Philippines, for decades pitied or mocked as the pathetic sick man of Southeast Asia after failing to rise to its potential following independence, have fruitlessly puzzled through the causes of its failures. Among them is Lee Kuan Yew, the stern paterfamilias of Singapore, who has studied his neighbor intensively and gratuitously offered unsought and ultimately unaccepted advice. Lee says that the problem stems from Filipino elites divorcing themselves from the population—except at election time, when they renew their marriage vows. He traces this division of interests to Spanish colonialists, who intermarried and established an upper crust of fair-skinned Spanish-Filipino mestizos. The American colonialists continued to operate through them, and so has the U.S. government in the post-independence era.

Our reliance on the elites, many of whom are blatantly corrupt, largely explains the hostile side of the love-hate many ordinary Filipinos feel for the United States. Thus, when then Vice President George H. W. Bush publicly told the widely reviled Marcos in 1981 that "we love your adherence to democratic principles and to the democratic process," millions laughed bitterly.

The elites have long exercised their political will as well as control over the economy through large-scale agricultural, industrial, and commercial domination. "The mestizo ruling class feels no obligations to the peons down the line," according to Lee, and Arroyo expressed no doubt that this indictment, although simplistic in its sweeping breadth, was based on fact. Whether she or any other Philippine leader can or is willing to do anything about it is entirely another matter. "What it requires is the most fundamental changes in our society," she said, "our values, our education, our religion, the entire culture of corruption."

In place of complete and unattainable societal restructuring, Arroyo had spent recent years maneuvering for a more limited but still potentially meaningful political shift: a change in the national constitution from the U.S.-style presidential setup to a parliamentary system. The Institute for Popular Democracy, a Manila-based nonprofit research and advocacy organization, backed the change. "With few exceptions," it said in a report, "the system continuously produces corrupt and incompetent politicians. The best way to get better politicians is to change the whole system of representation, starting with the electoral system."

This so-called Charter Change, which the irrepressible Philippine news media inevitably headlined "Cha-Cha," went nowhere. Senators and members of the big business oligarchy, who would be major losers in a newly decentralized government and economy, reacted by circling their wagons into crippling gridlock. In addition, nationalists worried that a revised constitution also would reverse the current Philippine ban on foreign (read American) military bases.

At the height of the Vietnam War, the United States operated two of its largest overseas military bases at Subic Bay and Clark Field, near Manila. The Pentagon in those days claimed that the bases were "irreplaceable" and, for that reason, a succession of U.S. administrations turned a blind eye to the Marcos regime's corruption and brutality. In return, millions of Filipinos came to see the United States as complicit in this behavior. So it came as no surprise when demand for closure of the bases swept through the Philippine Congress in a patriotic surge after Marcos fled Manila for exile in Honolulu. The departure of the Americans in 1991 was highly popular, even though it cost the Philippines dearly in U.S. economic assistance and base-related jobs. In 1998, the Congress partially altered course, granting U.S. forces visiting rights. Periodic outbursts, such as a contentious trial in 2006 of an American Marine, Lance Corporal Daniel Smith, found guilty of raping a twenty-two-year-old Filipina while his buddies cheered him on, keep the nagging issue in limbo. Three years later, the alleged victim, Suzette Nicolas, who by then had emigrated to the United States, recanted, acknowledging she had been a willing participant. Women's rights groups and other protestors immediately smelled a fix by the two governments. Smith had been held on the grounds of the U.S. embassy, despite a Philippine Supreme Court order that he be transferred to a domestic prison. This American flouting of the country's highest court further stoked Filipino fury. The entire affair amounted to a sordid metaphor for relations between the two countries.

Hobbled by multiple forms of paralysis, it's little wonder that the Philippine government pays insufficient attention to Islamist pressures in the South. It is a country with one of the world's highest population growth rates, almost 2.4 percent. Unemployment and underemployment total 30 percent. Ten million people—11 percent of the population—are forced to travel to the Persian Gulf and other parts of the world, including, embarrassingly, some of its better-off Southeast Asian neighbors, to find menial work. Under the circumstances, Mindanao and its restless Muslim minority can seem much farther from Catholic Manila than a one-hour airplane ride.

PART TWO

Ring of Fire:
Indonesia

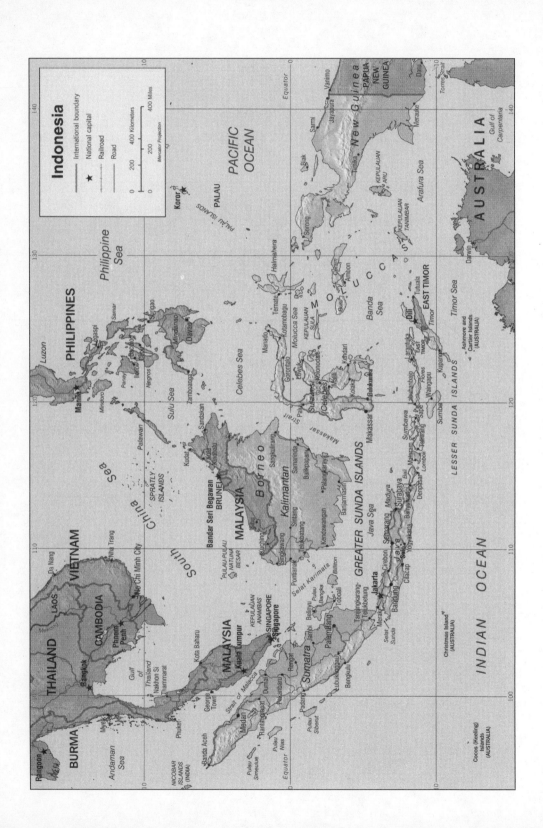

Indonesia

- —— International boundary
- ★ National capital
- ┼┼┼ Railroad
- —— Road

0   200   400 Kilometers
0   200   400 Miles

Mercator Projection

8

The Preacher

Traveling eastward across the bottom petal of the orchid-shaped island of Sulawesi, from the thriving port city of Makassar to the impoverished fishing and coconut-plantation district of Bulukumba, was like driving in reverse through Indonesia's recent economic development. To the limited degree that Americans follow events in the country with the world's largest Muslim population, the story is an optimistic one of a new democracy growing stronger. But beneath the surface is a growing demand for fundamentalist Islamic rule, and our 180-mile drive gave us an exceptional opportunity to observe how it threatens the nation's hard-won gains.

Makassar was once a backwater known to the outside world, to the extent that it was known at all, for the eponymous hair oil manufactured there, popular among fragrant Edwardian dandies. The oiled-hair fashion spun off a demand among fastidious housewives in the West for a way to protect the backs of upholstered parlor chairs from unsightly stains—crocheted doilies called antimacassars. As recently as fifty years ago, few self-respecting households in Europe or America were without them.

Today, pomade and doilies are passé and Makassar, now a city of 1.2 million, has moved on. Its port bustles with cargo vessels; its vast dockyard is stacked high with containers bound for and coming from every point on the globe. Gated communities shelter the families of prosperous port executives and government officials, the streets lined with elaborate, red tile–roofed McMansions and private schools. On velvety weekend evenings, downtown streets rumble with young couples on motorcycles, the boys' faces obscured behind tinted, Darth Vader helmets, the girls with more modest versions perched atop head scarves. Families snack and swim off palm-fringed beaches. Multistory, air-conditioned malls and well-stocked chain supermarkets with names such as Makromart, Hypermart, and Matahari are packed day and night. One evening, we attended a wedding reception for a thousand guests at the best hotel in town, where buffet tables were so overloaded that enough food was left behind to feed another large party.

But within an hour's drive out of the city, heading east along a two-lane, blacktop road, we left the flow of late-model sedans and vans and joined first a stream of motorbikes, then *becaks*, the ubiquitous, pedal-powered passenger tricycles of Indonesia's Everyman, and finally tiny wooden carts hauled by clip-clopping, picket-ribbed ponies, sharing the right-of-way with plodding water buffalo. Now we passed wooden houses teetering on stilts, with rusting roofs of metal sheeting and windows without glass. Open-front stalls offered gleaming, chromed, onion-shaped domes in assorted sizes, some no larger than coffee urns, to be popped atop the roofs of mosques under construction everywhere. Just off the roadside beach, dainty outrigger canoes skittered like clusters of water bugs. Constant was the jumble of scarecrow TV antennae and satellite dishes that sprouted from every structure and hand-drawn signs advertising mobile phone services such as "Nokia Cell Global."

The poor might be scrambling to survive, but they are plugged in. They know Teletubbies, Mickey, and Goofy. They read online that al-Qaeda number two Ayman al-Zawahiri has dismissed Barack Obama as a "house Negro" and a "hypocrite"; that an enraged Iraqi journalist has thrown his shoes at George W. Bush; and that the Indonesian terrorist mentor Abu Bakar Ba'asyir has once again damned the United States. They view the map of Israel, and to them it looks like the fabled *kris*, the wavy bladed Indonesian dagger, plunged into the heart of Islam. They know what the rich among their countrymen possess—and what they themselves do not. They know to question, as they never would before, why them and not us?

Because, their clergymen tell them, we are not living by Allah's law, by Sharia. Because Islam is the perfect religion and the laws of the *kafir*, the infidel, under which we live in this system of democracy, are wrong for a Muslim society. And so, they think, maybe Sharia will make our lives better.

They're finding out in Bulukumba. With 350,000 people, 98 percent Muslim, most of them peasant farmers whose landholdings are shrinking as their numbers increase, Bulukumba is one of the most densely populated and poorest parts of Sulawesi. This makes it an ideal model "Islamic village," where *radikal* local clergy and politicians have imposed Sharia over secular law.

The seventeen thousand islands of Indonesia stretch along the Pacific Rim's so-called ring of fire and are subject to volcanic eruptions and earthquakes. At nearly 240 million people it is the world's fourth-largest nation (after China, India, and the United States). It also has the largest Muslim population, 220 million, and for most, Sharia has always been the final word in personal and family matters. But in mid-2006, Bulukumba became one of four districts in Sulawesi and more than two dozen across the country where Sharia quietly took precedence over civil law. In these places, the fundamentalist clergy was brazenly challenging the government and the constitution of Indonesia. And the government was not responding.

The process was being implemented subtly, step by step. First, all women in Bulukumba were required to wear the *jilbab* (head scarf); all wage earners were required to contribute 2.5 percent of their income as *zakat* (alms), which traditionally had been an individual's voluntary decision. This was proving burdensome to low-income people, who were now subject to both religious and government taxes. By age seven, children were required to prove that they could read the Koran in the original Arabic, which Indonesians do not speak, as a precondition for admission to elementary school, as were couples seeking approval to marry. Civil servants also had to demonstrate Koran-reading proficiency to be promoted. Street signs in the Roman alphabet, common in Indonesia, were replaced with Arabic-based Jawi script. Beer, which had been available at a few guesthouses and eateries catering to foreign visitors, was banned.

The point was made: Sharia was now the law, not only of Islam but of local government as well. Since many of the strictures were already part of Muslims' daily personal life, the effect was only gradually sinking in. Furthermore, the most severe traditional punishments for infractions of Sharia, such as stoning, flogging, and amputation, had not been implemented, though they were anticipated.

We soon learned that how the changes were being accepted depended on the nervous state of the person we asked. Two couples looking to be in their mid-thirties stood chatting in the early evening cool alongside the main street as we drove into town. The men wore T-shirts and trousers, the women simple, sleeveless housedresses. We approached and after exchanging greetings asked why the women weren't covering their heads. They blanched, then word-lessly turned and slipped into their small houses. In a larger house down a quiet dirt lane, Arifin Umam, a teacher in a government elementary school, said that he and "most people" in Bulukumba welcomed the aspects of Sharia that had been introduced so far. Now, alms collection was better organized and distribution of funds after a recent flood much more equitable and efficient. In fact, he'd be pleased if Sharia were to replace all the existing district laws. Seated on a plastic-protected sofa, Arifin cast a sidelong, fleeting glance at the friends from Makassar with whom we were traveling and said that "only outsiders, elites, and intellectuals" opposed the changes.

A few doors away, a Muslim preacher with the single name Mardianto (indicating that he was a migrant from Indonesia's main island of Java) offered a more worrisome take on developments. He said that politicians and clerics working together to impose rules that Muslims were expected to abide by of their own free will were endangering the future of the republic. In 1945, the constitution of Indonesia rejected Sharia proposals and established *pancasila* as the national philosophy. Derived from the Sanskrit meaning "five principles" and based on ancient Hindu-Buddhist codes of ethics, pancasila was adopted by lawmakers in an attempt to neutralize the Islamic nationalism that had blossomed when Indonesia won its independence from the Netherlands. Its tenets are: belief in one God; just and civilized humanity; national unity; democracy derived through open-ended deliberation; and social justice for all. Pancasila has been the backbone of the country—and a bone in the craw of Islamists—for the past half century. "Indonesia is supposed to be flexible and permit everyone's aspirations," said Mardianto. As head of the Association of Indonesian Islamic Preachers of Bulukumba, he said that he was the only cleric in the district unafraid to speak out. "The others are intimidated and so are most ordinary people." Mardianto worried that unless the administration of President Susilo Bambang Yudhoyono summoned up the nerve to rein in the Sharia movement, "it could fragment Indonesia into a bunch of disgruntled districts, something like what happened in the former Yugoslavia." Like Mardianto, many Indonesians consider Yudhoyono a tentative, nervous leader, even though he won the presidency in 2004 in a landslide. It was the nation's first direct election.

The driving force behind the pro-Sharia movement in Sulawesi is an eight-year-old organization based in Makassar that goes by the initials KPPSI, from the Indonesian for Preparatory Committee for the Implementation of Islamic Law. The KPPSI is one of many new political organizations that took wing when Suharto was toppled in 1998. Its stated ambition is to overcome poverty and corruption through the application of Sharia. In fact, the group, which shelters behind a cover of intellectualism, has close relations with a number of mujahid-style gangs, and its unstated goal is to end constitutional law throughout Indonesia.

Many young KPPSI members are country boys from places such as Bulukumba who have graduated from Indonesian madrassas, called *pesantren*, and then moved to Makassar to attend college. The organization's appeal to these young students is that it takes "anticrime" and "anti-immorality" stances and lectures that only religious law can "purify" Indonesian politics. Despite these claims, three KPPSI members were serving seventeen-year jail sentences in the Philippines, where they were arrested in 2002 after being found in possession of C4 plastic explosive. They had been found guilty of bombing attacks in the Philippines and Indonesia. The arrests and follow-up publicity exposed the KPPSI to public scrutiny.

In the past few years, the KPPSI has gathered strength based on the adoption of fundamentalist laws in the newly autonomous province of Aceh, on the distant island of Sumatra. Aceh was at the epicenter of death and destruction from the 2004 Indian Ocean tsunami. Two years later, Indonesia granted the province unprecedented autonomy, thereby ending thirty years of warfare between the central government and the Free Aceh Movement. Sharia police now patrol the streets of Aceh in trucks, hunting down unmarried couples appearing in public without chaperones and women showing their hair. Caning has been instituted as punishment for these and other indecent acts. Offenders, among them adulterers, gamblers, and thieves, some of them non-Muslims, are arrested, dressed in white gowns, hauled before jeering crowds outside mosques, made to stand atop elevated platforms so that the crowds and TV cameras get an optimal view, and lashed with a long, rattan cane by a masked man in a red gown.

The caning variety of corporal punishment has long been meted out in Muslim Saudi Arabia, Pakistan, Malaysia, Brunei, and in secular, Chinese-dominated Singapore for a variety of offenses, civil as well as religious. Authorities in Malaysia and Singapore administer the beatings out of public view. Aceh's Sharia authorities say they have no plans to impose such Saudi- and Taliban-style punishment as stoning adulterous women to death, cutting off the hands of thieves, or decapitating murderers.

The Aceh example is spreading to other districts of Indonesia, where self-styled morality enforcers and municipal police are cracking down as they see fit. In one well-publicized case, zealous police in the industrial suburb of Tangerang, just outside the capital city of Jakarta, seized Lilis Lindawati, a married mother of two, who was waiting for a ride home outside the restaurant where she worked in February 2006. Her hair was uncovered. When the brown-uniformed police, known as "tranquillity and public order officers," found lipstick and powder in her purse, they charged her with prostitution and sentenced her to three days in jail.

The head of the KPPSI is Aswar Haswan, a husky, good-looking man of forty-four. He said that he has a master's degree in communications but goes by the honorific "Doctor." We called on him after our return from Bulukumba. Aswar received us in a large reception room of Makassar's central mosque, an imposing, geometrically complex structure of gray stone and glass with green wood trim, surrounded by broad lawns where teenage boys were practicing soccer moves. He said he was "certain" that the majority of Indonesian Muslims favored a theocratic state, and that if the minority who opposed Sharia better understood how it would improve their lives they would change their minds. Indonesia, he argued, with its vast Muslim majority, was never meant to be secular.

The majority was entitled to rule, he told us, though, like in America, without violating the rights of the minority. "Indonesia is not a secular country. It is an Islamic democracy, a theocratic democracy." When we asked which nation he looked toward as a successful example of this kind of duality—Malaysia, perhaps? Iran?—Aswar smiled thinly and shook his head. "No, there is no model. Indonesia is unique." He acknowledged that non-Muslims feared that the imposition of Sharia in districts such as Bulukumba, let alone at the national level, which is the KPPSI's long-term goal, was a threat to their civil rights. "It's true that they see themselves as outsiders and they have no feeling of ownership in Muslim law. It's a real problem. But now that our society is more open, everyone has the right to demand justice and soon they will find that Sharia is the only way to save Indonesia from its current crisis."

A few days after our discussion with Aswar, we met at a noisy Jakarta Starbucks with Marzuki Wahid, an official of the central government's Religious Affairs Department. He, too, fears a crisis. But he sees the KPPSI and organizations like it as the cause, not the cure. He also believes that his own agency shouldn't exist in Indonesia, where separation of the state and religious institutions is constitutionally guaranteed. "The very existence of the Religious Affairs Department is a compromise between religion and nationalism," he said. "Now religion is definitely increasing its role in national life and in politics."

A few weeks before this conversation, Marzuki had spoken to a gathering in Bulukumba, where he criticized the imposition of Sharia. KPPSI toughs barged into the meeting, cutting him short, and later attacked the headquarters of the nongovernmental organization that had invited him. The experience had left him shaken. "These so-called Islamic villages, like Bulukumba, are a serious threat," Marzuki said. As he explained it, the KPPSI and other Islamist groups adopted the strategy of confronting government at the district level because earlier attempts to impose Sharia from the top down had failed. "They're going in through the back door," he said. "If they succeed in changing Indonesia into an Islamic state, this will lead to demands for a Christian minority state. That would mean civil war and the disintegration of the nation." Christians, many of whom are ethnic Chinese, are 7 percent of the population.

There is no doubt that with the spread of religious-political groups such as the KPPSI, fundamentalism and piety are growing. Some two hundred thousand Indonesians make the hajj to Mecca each year, far more than ever before; TV stations are carrying more religious programming, and it is growing in popularity; Islamic Arab-style dress is becoming more common, for men as well as for women. Criticizing these developments is a touchy matter, because those who take the religious approach claim to be travelers on the moral high road, and others fear that by opposing them they'll be condemned as infidels. "Think of it in the current American context of growing Christian fundamentalism and it becomes clear," Marzuki suggested.

There is no way to prove that increased religiosity is linked to increased radicalism, but, Marzuki said, "I can feel it. There's definitely more intolerance, and it's not just between Muslims and Christians. The radicals are intolerant of anyone with different ideas. If you're a Muslim but not one of them they attack you as a heretic and a kafir." Marzuki was deeply disturbed by the failure of the Yudhoyono administration to move against the ultrareligious groups. "Their slow and weak response makes it clear to the public that they don't take these things as seriously as I do," he said. "That is an important error and we're going to suffer for it."

9

The Minister

There can't be many countries where the official charged with national defense is more obsessed with eliminating poverty, educating children, and finding jobs for young people than with building troop strength and modernizing the arsenal. But that is the case in Indonesia.

Defense Minister Juwono Sudarsono is that rare, far-sighted government servant who recognizes that until social justice is established for the world's largest Muslim population, the young will remain susceptible to the lure of extremism and Indonesia will remain insecure. Sudarsono says that the hard-core terrorist organizations of Indonesia, the home-grown Jemaah Islamiya in particular, plus a growing list of ultrafundamentalist groups such as the KPPSI, are recruiting followers and building support by young people because governments past and present have done little to improve the lives of the masses.

The argument resonates broadly. After half a century of strongman rule under Presidents Sukarno and Suharto and a decade of more or less democratic leaders, only 10 percent of Indonesia's 240 million people have access to clean drinking water, electricity, basic education, and medicine. The great majority of Indonesians of all religions have made clear that they want to live in a democracy, but among the 90 percent of them who are Muslims, the notion that Islamic rule may be the solution to unremitting poverty is beginning to make sense, at the very least to some of the more frustrated among them.

Nor is the irony lost on many Indonesians that religion's greatest challenge to a nonsectarian state has flowed directly from the advent of democracy. SBY, as President Yudhoyono is widely known, is a former army general, a secularist, and a firm believer in the partitioning of religion and government, as established by the constitution. He also has expressed repeatedly his commitment to democracy. And that commitment has placed him in the awkward position of having to yield to the Islamists' insistence that they are free to condemn his government and to demand replacing what is essentially outdated European jurisprudence with Sharia.

Suharto, who died in January 2008, held the religious right on an exceedingly short rein throughout his thirty-two-year, hard-fisted rule. Like SBY, he was a former general. He, too, was utterly secular until, in his final months in office, in desperation and with his power evaporating, he draped himself in an Islamic mantle. Many Indonesian Islamists, threatened with arrest and worse during the Suharto regime, had fled to Malaysia and other more comfortable Muslim environments. With his removal from office in May 1998 and the budding of democracy, these hard-core preachers and terrorists returned home to resume their self-appointed mission of remaking Indonesia into a theocracy.

The character of Indonesia's government has always been an iffy thing, somewhere between fully secular, such as India's, and purely theocratic, such as Saudi Arabia's. When Sukarno declared the nation's independence, in 1945, he appealed to Muslims to accept that the state would be nonsectarian—based on "an agreement of fundamentals" acceptable to all religious, racial, and provincial groups and the three hundred ethnicities spread across the five-thousand-mile-long archipelago. That Indonesia has actually hung together all these years testifies to the neutralizing effect of opposing forces, in this case public open-mindedness versus dictatorial rule.

But the keystone supporting such an ambitious structure in such an exceedingly diverse set of cultures is pancasila. Ultimately it is the extraordinary willingness of so many people to buy into this vague and high-minded philosophy of mutual respect that explains

Indonesia's unlikely national survival. But lofty principle took a battering during the Suharto era, when the dictator perversely identified his repressive regime with pancasila. Today, with democracy seriously at work for the first time, that set of societal principles is under attack as seldom before and, with it, the very sense of what constitutes Indonesianness.

The challenge laid down by the Islamists contends that with such a lopsided majority, Indonesia's Muslims are entitled to an Islamic state. The minorities may like it or leave it. This is sharply at odds with pancasila, the constitution, and with Sukarno's 1945 independence declaration that "being Indonesian" meant that members of all religions would be united through a "sublime union of all Indonesian culture and tradition," including "the enrichment of Islam through understanding the beliefs and precepts of other faiths." Even though Indonesians have largely adhered to that thesis, they have periodically descended into grisly ethnic and religious chaos. Recent polls show that the great majority of Indonesians still support pancasila, but the pressure in favor of Sharia is building. That pressure was plainly on show in August 2007, when tens of thousands of people filled a stadium in Jakarta and rallied for the imposition of Sharia and a return to pan-Islamic structuring of government under a caliphate.

Most Indonesians, Muslims, Christians, and others, live with the gut-level fear that should the Islamists gain the upper hand and succeed in supplanting secularism with religious law, the result would be a bloodbath unprecedented in scope. Even though only 7 percent of the population is Christian, in a nation of 240 million that minority is about 17 million, more than enough to fight long and hard. Sudarsono fears that outcome and believes that the most direct way to avert it is by providing jobs to the young and disaffected.

Sudarsono, sixty-five, holds degrees from universities in Indonesia and the Netherlands, the University of California at Berkeley, and the London School of Economics. His career includes teaching at Columbia University's School of Public and International Affairs and a term as Indonesia's ambassador to Britain. He has honed a refined sense of how the West, and the United States in particular, can best assist disaffected Muslims join the globalizing world.

During an extensive conversation in a rococo reception room of the Defense Ministry in Jakarta, he told us that if Indonesians are going to avoid a nightmarish Islamist future they must move quickly from philosophical debate to pragmatism. In this, he said, the involvement of the United States was vital. As an example of what Americans could offer he suggested, "How about projects on interfaith employment, projects funded jointly by Islamic and Western multilateral aid agencies and donor governments?"

With the U.S. military presence in Iraq and Afghanistan an ongoing irritant to Muslims everywhere, Sudarsono said that the United States would do well to stake out a longer-term strategy keyed to offering more private assistance without expecting public recognition. "I know that the idea of low-profile, high-performance help is very difficult for Americans to accept. But over time, by helping us without making us look like you're paying us off for doing America's bidding, you will help us and help yourselves. When all is said and done, what poor young Muslims across the developing world really need is jobs, jobs, jobs. Jobs will help them regain their identity and dignity. Social justice and employment will reduce their feelings of marginalization and humiliation. Work will enhance their sense of individual self-worth."

Prior to the onset of the global economic recession in mid-2008, Indonesia's unofficial unemployment rate, concentrated among men in their late teens and twenties, was a crushing 10 percent, triple the figures in most of its neighboring countries, other than the Philippines. Sudarsono reasoned that defusing the appeal of Islamist extremism with jobs would also make his own task as defense minister easier, reducing the strains imposed on the security services. "Otherwise," he said, "they may have to crack down against those who are too desperate and too despondent to care or to be aware of the rule of law and human rights."

Sudarsono stressed that if the United States wanted to improve its perception among Muslims it would have to lower its profile while raising its performance. Leaders in other parts of Southeast Asia said much the same thing. While they unanimously expressed deep gratitude for the high-profile response by U.S. military ships, aircraft, and personnel to the tsunami disaster, they insisted that this was and would have to remain a rare exception. This is a classic reaction by leaders of weak states: forced to ask for help and then humiliated by their own helplessness. Reflecting that bipolarity, positive opinion about the United States among Indonesians spiked immediately after the tsunami, from a post-Iraq invasion low of 15 percent to a startling high of 79 percent, according to a Pew Research survey. By 2006, though, the positives had dropped to 30 percent.

Indonesia's relationship with the United States has always been an on-again, off-again affair. The chief reason is the lopsided interplay between the two nations: Indonesia desperately in need of all forms of U.S. assistance; the United States trading that assistance for military, and most recently antiterrorism, cooperation, even when such cooperation may not have been in the best interests of ordinary Indonesians. For decades the relationship has provoked a great deal of Indonesian bitterness. In 1964 an infuriated Sukarno publicly scorned U.S. ambassador Marshall Green: "Go to hell with your aid!"

Two weeks before our interview with Sudarsono, in June 2006, the minister met in the same room with then defense secretary Donald Rumsfeld, the men sitting on the same carved, gilded chairs we were occupying. In their public statements afterward, the two defense officials sounded mutually soothing and agreeable. But in our discussion, the Indonesian said he had told the American privately that the United States, with its "overwhelming" defense budget and its "omnipresence," couldn't help but cause resentment in Indonesia and in much of the world. "It's not just a matter of what you do, it's the very fact of your being," he told Rumsfeld. "The more powerful you are militarily, the less influence you have politically and diplomatically."

Rumsfeld, like so many U.S. government officials, more accustomed to lecturing than listening, was "taken aback" by this bluntness, said Sudarsono. But the Indonesian pressed ahead. He told his guest that the Bush administration's ceaseless pressure on the Yudhoyono government to run its counterterrorism program according to the White House's wishes was backfiring. The United States, he said, should back off. Coverage of Rumsfeld's visit in the Indonesian news media reported that the American was there to

complain about the imminent release of the extremist cleric Abu
Bakar Ba'asyir. Ba'asyir had been jailed for three years on charges
of involvement in the deadly bombings of a nightclub popular
with Western tourists on the resort island of Bali in 2002 and of a
Marriott Hotel in Jakarta in 2004. He was, in fact, released just after
Rumsfeld left town, on June 13, 2006.

"If you insist that we rearrest Ba'asyir," Sudarsono said he told
Rumsfeld, "we'll be seen by our own people as America's lackeys.
It's far better that we do things our own way. Even if we try and fail,
it's better." In December 2006, Indonesia's Supreme Court cleared
Ba'asyir of all charges. This action infuriated the Bush administration as well its allies in Australia and Britain. Among the 202 victims
in Bali, 88 were Australian, 26 were British, and 7 were American.

To ensure that a repeat of Bali and the Ba'asyir fiasco didn't occur,
the State Department invested $20 million in helping Indonesia
train and equip a counterterrorism police unit known as Special
Detachment 88. Indonesia chose the "88" designation to honor the
slain Australians, the largest number of victims from a single nationality. The CIA, FBI, Secret Service, and Army Special Forces conducted
the training. They developed teams expert in investigations, explosives, and precision attacks. The unit has since been credited with
capturing or killing more than two hundred suspected members of
Jemaah Islamiya. As may be expected of any law enforcement organization closely associated with the United States, Special Detachment
88 also has been accused of human rights abuses.

Indonesia's political leaders, like those in other Muslim countries
with sensitive ties to Washington, walk a risky tightrope stretched
between the often-conflicting demands of the United States and
their own people. The results often are frustrating for Americans
as well as taxing and dangerous for the cooperating leaders. If the
United States is to succeed in helping cement democracy more
firmly in these countries, it will have to, as Sudarsono put it, "provide discrete, background help." It must accept that the leaders it is
dealing with have their own problems and that these at times may
have to take precedence.

A key priority in Indonesia's case falls into Sudarsono's baili-
wick: reforming the nation's armed forces. The behavior of the

1.6-million-member Tentara Nasional Indonesia, or TNI, which comprises the army, navy, and air force, has long been at issue in the overall relationship between the two countries. Under Sukarno and Suharto, who maintained power through close personal ties to top military commanders, the armed forces took a direct and frequently brutal hand in maintaining order as they saw fit. The military and the nation's elected officials were equal partners, with retired officers holding prominent cabinet positions and seats in parliament and active-duty officers playing dominant roles in regional and local governments.

Because Indonesia has not faced a significant external threat since the 1963–1965 *Confrontasi* with Malaysia, the armed forces were free to concentrate on running the country. They pursued a policy of "dual function," meaning that they were responsible for national security as well as overseeing the economic development of the country. This duality led to infamy when, in 1965–1966, the army took it upon itself to slaughter between 160,000 and 500,000 ethnic Chinese Indonesians. Some the military suspected of being Communists, while others merely had aroused the financial envy of their Muslim neighbors.

A decade later, on December 7, 1975, the armed forces invaded the neighboring former Portuguese colony of East Timor. The military annexed and held the tiny half-island enclave under bloody occupation until 1999. During that quarter century, Indonesian soldiers massacred between 100,000 and 200,000 Timorese, nearly all of them Roman Catholics. In a heavy-handed example of U.S. intervention in Indonesia's military affairs, President Gerald Ford and Secretary of State Henry Kissinger met with Suharto in Jakarta the day before the East Timor invasion and gave him a thumbs-up. This was eight months after the fall of Saigon, and the United States was still nervously anticipating the collapse of the "domino" states of Southeast Asia to the Communists. Kissinger believed it was vital for the United States to continue propping up Suharto's Indonesia, in theory the largest and most vulnerable domino of them all.

Because the United States was Indonesia's chief arms provider, it was critical to Suharto that he have Ford's assurance that supplies would not be interrupted by the invasion. "We will understand and will not press you on the issue," Ford told the Indonesian dictator. "We understand the problem and the intentions you have." Added Kissinger, with just a pinch of caution, "It is important that whatever you do succeeds quickly [because] the use of U.S.-made arms could create problems." In fact, the United States continued to supply Indonesia with weapons through the East Timor bloodletting and until 1999, when President Clinton, under intense political pressure from human rights activists, suspended the supplies. The embargo held for five years.

But the previous decades of close identification with the rampaging armed forces, while mouthing platitudes of democracy, lastingly damaged the United States' reputation among numerous Indonesians and other Southeast Asians. There was a simple lesson to be drawn from this experience: When Americans back a dictator hated by his own people, they inevitably will be tarred by the same brush. As is evident from U.S. support for a succession of military dictators around the world, most recently Pakistan's Pervez Mushareiff, the lesson has not sunk in.

In the aftermath of the 2004 tsunami disaster, the United States lifted its embargo on nonlethal equipment and military vehicles to help support the Indonesian military's humanitarian efforts. Fourteen months later, the Bush administration announced that it would resume admitting Indonesian officers to the International Military Education and Training program, known as IMET. Some members of Congress, most notably Democrats Patrick Leahy of Vermont and Russ Feingold of Wisconsin, remained staunchly opposed to the reversion, after fighting it throughout the years during which Christopher Bond led the Republican effort in the Senate to restore Indonesians to the program. But by then, most lawmakers in Washington agreed that under Yudhoyono, the military was cleaning house.

Sudarsono, who was pushing hand for military reform, made no attempt during our talk to minimize the armed forces' squalid record over more than fifty years. But, he said, "It's just unrealistic to expect that in a country like Indonesia we can adhere to U.S. anticorruption and human rights standards. We simply can't afford that level of accountability." Conversely, he offered the judgment that, "If the military was out of the picture, the record of human rights violations would be much worse. And we're getting better, that's undeniable." Discussions with a variety of Indonesians in widespread parts of the country indicated that this substantially was the case, though none claimed that the armed forces had fully disengaged from civic affairs or was likely to do so soon.

The reality is that there is as yet no viable substitute for the military. It has always been the only organization with the discipline and the skills to control the archipelago. Consider that the islands stretch as great a distance as from San Francisco to Bermuda and are inhabited by people speaking more than 730 languages and ranging in development from post–Stone Age to postmodern. This dispersed, disparate population makes America's seem condensed and homogeneous by comparison. Unlike the British imperialists in India, who established a large and competent native civil service long before it left, the Dutch colonialists, during their 350 years of harsh occupation, never prepared the indigenous people to rule themselves. The Dutch, whom Americans tend to think of as those adorable, rosy-cheeked folk tending tulips beneath their windmills, turned out to be particularly cruel masters of their darker-skinned fellow humans. The only institution Holland left with the capacity to inherit control was the native military. And the colonialists had trained it to be harsh. Further complicating matters, from the start of independence until the present, the military never received a budget sufficient to maintain itself. This led the officer corps to establish a host of for-profit businesses, opening the way to widespread corruption involving domestic and foreign investors.

With news media now free to take on all comers, an article in the *Jakarta Post* reported in 2005:

> For years, the [military] has been accountable only to itself. It raises and spends large sums of money completely outside government control. It is involved in a vast network of military-owned business enterprises, shady deals with private entrepreneurs, criminal activities such as illegal logging, and corrupt practices like inflating the price of weapons purchases. Foreign

corporations operating in Indonesia can easily become linked to
lawful and unlawful military business activities.

In one well-publicized case, the U.S. mining giant Freeport-
McMoRan Copper and Gold, Inc., hired entire army units, paying
$60 million through 2004 for security for its huge gold-mining
operation in remote West Papua. At least one-third of the money
was doled out directly to individual commanders. Not coincidentally, late in 2006, Freeport provided helicopters to the army
to ferry thousands of troops into the province. The troops were
dispatched to quell an uprising by Papuan separatists armed with
bows and spears. The tribal warriors were raising Papuan flags as
a sign of defiance to the central government. While emphasizing
that he opposed symbiotic relationships between companies such
as Freeport and the military, Sudarsono rationalized it as an example of Adam Smith's famed invisible hand. In this thesis of capitalism, an individual pursuing personal wealth tends inadvertently to
promote a broader good in the community. "That's why, since the
early 1950s, all commanders have been given leeway to find their
own way," he said.

For similar reasons, the People's Liberation Army of China
likewise came to own some six thousand enterprises, from disco-
theques to dairy farms to commercial satellite launching, employing
more than half a million civilians. Both the Chinese and Indonesian
forces have begun selling off some of their holdings. A considerable number of Indonesian military businesses, including luxury
hotels and airlines, collapsed in the 1997–1998 taming of the sto-
ried Asian Tiger economies. With the region once again gradually
building up a head of steam, prior to the onset of global recession
in 2008, private-sector investors have moved into many of the former military-controlled companies. But as anyone, foreign or local,
seeking to do business in Indonesia quickly learns, this does not
mean that military corruption has been appreciably reduced.

While its democratic and economic trajectories undoubtedly
are pointed upward, there is no getting away from the reality
that a country as sprawling and complex as this is bound to suffer
future setbacks. Yet it is for that very reason that if Americans are

to play a well-reasoned, proactive role in Southeast Asia—a role that could produce lasting, positive results for the United States and for Muslims everywhere—the most effective start would be in Indonesia. And the most effective thing to do is to begin teaching Indonesians to learn so they can earn.

10

The Inspector General

Poverty, according to Ansyaad Mbai, the chief of Indonesia's counterterrorism operations, is the most devastating of four conditions behind the rise of Islamic radicalism in the country. Along with corruption, globalization, and history, poverty has created "the rich soil in which terrorists have sunk their roots. Unless the great moderate majority has its way, the future of Indonesia will be with the radicals."

We spoke with Mbai at his office in police headquarters in Jakarta, huddled around the head of a large U-shaped conference table. He is also inspector general of the National Police. He cautioned that the chances of such a future would be heightened if the United States were to continue pressing the Yudhoyono government to use its heaviest weapons on Islamists. Rather, he said, Americans would be well advised to study the underlying causes of extremism in Indonesia and recognize that their interaction produces radicalism no less certainly than the blending of certain chemicals produces explosions.

In emphasizing the role of poverty, Mbai agreed with what Defense Minister Sudarsono had told us. What distinguishes their assessment from similar views in the United States is that they do not see poverty as the only cause. Soon after the 9/11 attacks, American analysts, all too many searching for a one-size-fits-all explanation for the cause of Islamist terrorism, initially singled out poverty. Then they abandoned their own thesis as being overly simplistic.

The search for a single, black-and-white provocation misses the point. While poverty in Indonesia accounts for the vulnerability of millions, it is but one agent interacting with others. Islamic terrorism has no single cause, and it has no single remedy. Recognizing this complexity and the importance of penetrating it, Indonesian authorities have taken an enlightened, respectful approach to many of the terrorists they arrest. Trusted clergymen meet frequently with prisoners to discuss their understanding, or misunderstanding, of Islam. Some have even been invited to barbecues hosted at the homes of their jailers. The thinking is similar to that of American intelligence professionals who argue against the use of torture to extract information: demonstrate genuine interest in them as human beings and they're far more likely to cooperate.

Second on Mbai's list of four contributors to radicalism was history. Most Indonesians, undereducated at best in both religious and secular history, are easily aroused by the Islamist provocations they hear during street demonstrations spreading across towns and cities. "The terrorists don't think in terms of the unitary Indonesian nation-state," said Mbai. "They think only of the umma; that the Muslims of Indonesia and the Middle East are together one umma. As they see it, Islam once achieved a golden age and then went into decline—not for any of its own failures, but because of oppression by the West. The Crusades are the cornerstone of this interpretation. Islam was attacked and destroyed, and that's still the situation today. That's what they're fighting to change."

To the poor and the young, this is rabble-rousing stuff. Playing off the ancient animosity, leaders of Islamist groups continually warn of attempts by Indonesian and Western Christians to proselytize and otherwise "Christianize" the country. U.S.-based Pentecostal and charismatic sects are the most rapidly growing religious institutions in Indonesia, winning converts from established Christian churches and from Islam, often through promises of miraculous health cures. Mainstream Indonesian Catholic and Protestant pastors with whom we met told us they worry more about challenges from the evangelicals than from Muslims. Conversely, Islamist hyperbole has contributed to brutal religious fighting in the provinces of Aceh, Ambon, Central Sulawesi, and East Timor and in the Maluku Islands over recent years.

Mbai's third reason for trouble was globalization and, more to the point, how ordinary Indonesians and people in developing countries perceive it: They are the losers and Americans are the winners. They consider major U.S. and other Western corporations such as Freeport-McMoRan and ExxonMobil to be drains on their country's natural resources, providing limited, low-paying jobs to a few while paying vast sums to foreigners and their corrupt Indonesian political-military partners. "To the average person," said Mbai, "globalization is just another facet of the U.S. government's power to destroy their Islamic identity."

It is corruption, the final component on Mbai's list, that is perhaps the most pervasive of Indonesia's chronic socioeconomic afflictions. Of 180 countries monitored by the Berlin-based organization Transparency International in its annual Corruption Perceptions Index, Indonesia regularly fares poorly. In its 2008 listing, TI rated Indonesia at 126, tied with such countries as Eritrea, Libya, and Uganda. By comparison, Somalia was most corrupt, Denmark the least, along with New Zealand and Sweden. The United States stood at eighteen, tied with Japan and Belgium.

In a system of governance like Indonesia's, in which the police, the armed forces, the civil bureaucracy, and the national leaders are all grossly underpaid, corruption is the lubricant required to keep the machinery turning. If an automobile driver doesn't cross the traffic cop's palm with a few rupiah, not only will the driver be subjected to time-consuming harassment, but also the policeman and his family may not have enough to eat that evening. If an entrepreneur doesn't factor bribes into his expansion plans, he may as well forget about being granted the required licenses and permits—and the department clerks he ignored might not be able to pay their children's tuition bills. Government ministers and generals, judges and doctors, homeowners and schoolteachers: everyone pays or receives.

Everyone, that is, except the peasants and impoverished urban dwellers at the bottom of the heap—which is to say most Indonesians. They are underfed, undereducated, underemployed. Those charged with providing relief refuse to act without a bribe. Where can they turn for help or hope when all of those they're supposed to respect are on the take? In the United States, people who have reached the end of a fraying rope, who are bitter, sick, and frustrated, commonly turn to Christ. In Indonesia, the answer is to fight for Islam.

In an attempt to decrease if not eliminate corrupt practices as well as to streamline operations and enhance the public's sense of democracy at work, President Yudhoyono early in his administration decentralized government, spreading power outward from Jakarta to the provinces, based on the notion that this would build local economies and reduce corruption. The results have been disappointing.

At a meeting in 2006 of the nonprofit United States–Indonesia Society in Washington, D.C., Douglas E. Ramage, the representative in Jakarta of the San Francisco–based Asia Foundation, reported that while democracy was "now a given" and that the country was for the first time in years stable, decentralization had provided local officials with the power to make antibusiness decisions to promote bribes for themselves. In other words, corruption was now decentralized, too. "Doing business is difficult for Americans and other foreigners as well as for Indonesians," Ramage said. "This is mainly because of new local regulations, legal as well as illegal." And at a meeting with Bank of America officers, Frans Winarta, a leading Indonesian lawyer, said that because new reform laws had not been seriously implemented, bribery and other social evils remained rampant. "The legal system is corrupt, neither independent nor impartial," he said. He pointed out that the chief justice of Indonesia was paid an annual salary of $24,000. Winarta said that the level of remuneration throughout the courts gave judges little incentive to hear potentially threatening cases.

The radicals' answer is the Sharia legal system and eventually an Islamic state. Aided by illegal cash flows from Wahhabi organizations in Saudi Arabia and more broadly by the ascendant pan-Islamic movement, with its anti-American focus, Jemaah Islamiya and other extremist Indonesian organizations are making a case for restoring the caliphate, first in the archipelago and eventually across much of the rest of Southeast Asia. Their first concrete move has been to impose Sharia in susceptible places such as Bulukumba, aided by some of the same local government officials who are making life difficult for would-be investors. Concurrently they are pressing the central government for dialogue, the intention being to establish their legitimacy. The government has so far held back.

The notion of a reinvigorated caliphate was a dead letter for more than a century. But it was reinstated by Osama bin Laden when he referred to it in an early condemnation of the U.S. war in Iraq. "Baghdad, the seat of the caliphate, will not fall to you, God willing," bin Laden warned the Bush administration in a statement broadcast by al-Jazeera in 2003. Bush and Rumsfeld tried briefly to evoke the specter of the caliphate to build support for the "global war on terror." But few Americans knew the term or fathomed the concept of the caliphate, and most Western analysts did not give the likelihood of its reestablishment much credence.

Nevertheless, Mbai said that the Indonesian National Police have recovered documents from Jemaah Islamiya in which leaders stated that the caliphate is their goal and that they intend to achieve it by replacing the present legal system with Sharia step by step, one locality after another. Mbai considers this process, which is well under way, a serious threat to Indonesia's future as a diverse nation. "The majority of Indonesian Muslims are moderates and they oppose turning our country into a religious state," he said. "They acknowledge the importance of Sharia in their personal and family lives, but their Sharia is within the context of an Islam based on Indonesian values. Indonesian culture comprises all of our cultures. If Sharia were implemented here as it exists in the Middle East, it would not be possible for us to maintain a unitary state. Indonesia is built on diversity. Without diversity we would not be Indonesians."

Indeed, the national motto, Bhinneka Tunggal Ika (Unity in Diversity), must be taken as something more than a truism in a polyglot, multiethnic, multi-religious country of Indonesia's scale. It is ironic that as Indonesia seeks to solidify the hard-won democracy that evaded it for more than fifty years, democracy itself has opened the country to the very challenges that its strongmen held in check. The gradual ratcheting back of military control of politics has had the unintended effect of opening doors to radical Islamists.

This raises critical questions of what the United States can and should do—and not do—if it wants to see a democratic, nonsectarian Indonesia survive.

The answer, in Mbai's judgment, is to start small and start now: help young Indonesians get jobs here, through small business and similar job opportunities, so they don't have to go to the Middle East or elsewhere outside Indonesia for work. American investors in the developing world tend to be large-scale and corporate. They often lack ground-level sensitivity to social and cultural factors. Freeport-McMoRan, for example, naturally enough employs mainly Papuans in its Papua mining workforce of eighteen thousand. This has created a no-win situation for the company: Papuans accuse Freeport of being a pariah, aligning itself with the military in the brutal crackdown on separatists. Muslims, in turn, charge it with being anti-Islamic because it hires Papuans, who predominantly are Protestants. Freeport finally has undertaken a thorough and remarkably open examination of its policies.

Similarly, in Aceh, ExxonMobil operates the massive Arun natural gas deposits and an associated liquefied natural gas plant, for decades a major source of profit for both the company and the Indonesian government. The company reportedly has extracted $40 billion worth of gas during the past decade alone. But for years most of the revenue went to Jakarta, where it helped enrich Suharto and his cronies. Now that political power has been decentralized, Jakarta-based big business leaders have simply redrawn the map, supporting their own district-level political cronies in return for favorable legislation.

This is how Michael Renner, of the environmental research group Worldwatch Institute and the United Nations–monitoring Global Policy Forum, described the scene:

> Arun's fruits have been exceedingly bitter—ranging from expropriation to exploitation, and from pollution to savage repression. After natural gas was found in the early 1970s, the Suharto dictatorship took hundreds of acres of land in the area from villagers without compensation. Hundreds of families were displaced, many condemned to poverty. . . .

[S]urrounding communities have lived in the shadow of arrogant
corporate behavior . . . ExxonMobil has the trappings of a state
within a state. Its facilities are fenced off from surrounding communities. Expatriate management and engineering staff enjoy luxurious
living quarters. The company has its own landing strip. . . . Then
there is "Exxon's Road" . . . the only paved road. For many years, it
was off limits to ordinary Acehnese, who have to travel on narrow
dirt roads. . . . Natural gas flaring and chemical spills have caused a
range of health problems in nearby villages and industrial waste has
polluted rice paddies and fish ponds.

Beginning in 1976, joint exploitation by Mobil, as the company then
was known, and the central government helped spark the emergence
of the separatist Free Aceh Movement, known by the Indonesian
acronym GAM, and twenty-four years of bloody rebellion. Acehnese
living in the area of the ExxonMobil operation tell of brutal assaults by
military forces. With five thousand of these troops deployed to protect the company, and with the company making its equipment and
facilities freely available to the troops, villagers made no distinction
between the American firm and the Indonesian military. From their
perspective, there still is little reason to see American and multinational
companies as anything other than direct successors to Indonesia's old
colonial masters. In 2005, following the tsunami, GAM and the central
government signed a peace accord, with Acehnese settling for greater
autonomy rather than the full independence they had sought. The
peace agreement, which grants Aceh 70 percent of its natural resource
revenues—up dramatically from 5 percent—has, to some extent, let
ExxonMobil off the hook.

Still, said Mbai, many Acehnese anticipate that the money will
end up benefiting government officials, this time at the local level,
and once again doing little for them. "That's why I stress that the
best way for Americans to go is small person-to-person projects."
He pointed out that Jemaah Islamiya documents and interrogation
of its trainers and foot soldiers showed that "many more of them are
interested in getting a job than in following a radical ideology."

This sounded very much like what the young terrorists had told
Filipino judge Bucoy in his Mindanao courtroom.

11

The Jihadi

When he reminisces about his years in the al-Qaeda military academy on the Afghanistan-Pakistan border, Farihin Ibnu Ahmad's brown eyes glow and his soft voice takes on a timbre that any graduate of West Point would recognize as the pride of a career officer. That's how he sees himself: a professional military man and the son of a military man, a committed soldier who fights for the cause in which he believes. For Farihin, that cause is the struggle to rejuvenate Islam. The war he trained for is jihad against America. His army is Jemaah Islamiya.

In 2000, Farihin drove across the island of Java to Jakarta with components of a massive car bomb, which he delivered to Jemaah Islamiya colleagues. On August 1, they detonated the bomb outside the Philippine embassy in the capital. The blast killed two people and severely injured more than twenty others, among them Ambassador Leonides Caday, the intended target. Jemaah Islamiya had chosen the diplomat to avenge an attack by the Philippine armed forces three months earlier at the MILF's Camp Abu Bakar, on the southern island of Mindanao, under orders of then Philippines president Joseph Estrada. The MILF was playing host to Jemaah Islamiya trainees and instructors, six of whom were killed in the attack.

Farihin's involvement in the embassy bombing went undiscovered at the time. Two year later, however, Indonesian police arrested him after linking him to murderous attacks on Christian residents of

Poso, a violence-racked city in the province of Central Sulawesi. He was found guilty, imprisoned for two and a half years, and released in 2004. Now that he was out of jail and under police surveillance, his role in the jihad was to continue the struggle against "U.S. hegemony," but rather than with bombs or guns, through what he termed "propaganda and persuasion."

Had the United States rather than Indonesia seized Farihin, he almost certainly would have been locked away at Guantánamo Bay. But Indonesian police officials say that monitoring activists such as Farihin, which they combine with their own ample doses of propaganda and persuasion, is more effective than keeping them in prison, where they are able to spread their views to other inmates. All but a handful of U.S. specialists disagree sharply with this tactic.

During his interrogation, Farihin had told the police that Jemaah Islamiya was planning "something big." But apparently because of the al-Qaeda system of compartmentalizing information, he knew nothing more. Ten days later, on October 12, the big thing happened: 2 of his colleagues blew themselves up at Paddy's Bar and the Sari Club, two popular nightspots on the tourist-haven island of Bali. The coordinated blasts killed 202 people and injured another 208. The bombers had anticipated killing mainly Americans, but most of the victims turned out to be Australians. It was the deadliest terrorist attack in Indonesian history.

Farihin sees himself not as a terrorist, but as one of Allah's warriors, struggling against crusaders. His enemy is the United States. "I regret what happened on Bali," he told us. "It was an act of terror, not jihad. I know that now, and it hurt our reputation among many Indonesians. It was a big mistake." What made the bombing a mistake, from the Jemaah Islamiya viewpoint, was not that it killed innocent bystanders but that it took place outside a predetermined area of conflict. Had it occurred in, say, southern Thailand, where Muslim-Buddhist killings are a daily event, it would have been acceptable under jihadi rules of engagement. Farihin remained convinced that the United States is the enemy. "President Bush declared a crusade against Islam. That means the United States considers all Muslims to be terrorists and intends to kill us all," he said.

Over glasses of sugary, milky iced coffee at an open-air market near central Jakarta, Farihin recalled what had drawn him to the jihad as a boy. He was born into a deeply conservative Muslim family in the Javanese town of Pasig Malaya. His father was a member of Darul Islam, a precursor to Jemaah Islamiya and other militant Islamist organizations. In the early days of the republic, because Darul Islam fought against Indonesian Communists, it received covert support from the CIA, in much the same way as the agency backed the anti-Soviet mujahideen of Afghanistan, only to see them change into the violently anti-American Taliban.

Farihin's father was implicated in a failed attempt to assassinate President Sukarno in 1956. One of his brothers also became a Jemaah Islamiya member. Beefy at age forty-one, with gray strands creeping into his wispy chin whiskers, Farihin, who sometimes goes by the alias Yasir, recalled the pride he felt as a boy about his family's association with the extremist organizations. "They were true leaders," he said, a quick smile revealing a broken front tooth. "They had clear concepts about the jihad and the struggle for Islam. They knew what had to be done and they knew how to go about doing it. That clarity of purpose appealed to me."

Sons following their fathers into extremist groups is a traditional pattern in Indonesia. Farihin's father sent him as a teenager to study religion at a madrassa in Karachi, a seething Pakistani port city of violence, crime, poverty, and religious extremism. There he met members of his own generation from throughout the umma who shared his devotion to Islam and to the jihad. Some of these friendships would stay with him through his career. After briefly returning home to Pasig Malaya, Farihin went back to Pakistan and, in 1987, began military training at a jihadi military academy. It was operated by a Pashtun tribal warlord, Abdul Rabb al-Rasul Sayyaf, who was alleged to have committed war crimes in Afghanistan in the 1990s. A decade later, Abdul Rabb became a member of the U.S.-backed government of Afghan president Hamid Karzai.

The academy was in Sadda, on the Afghan side of the fluid border with Pakistan. Saudi Arabian Wahhabis, including Osama bin Laden, funded it. They moved their money through Abdul Rabb's organization, Ittihad-i Islami Barai Azadi Afghanistan, the Islamic Union for the Liberation of Afghanistan. Farihin never saw Osama, "but every-one knew he was staying there and helping the struggle. We called him 'the rich Saudi.'" One celebrity Farihin did see at the academy was Pakistan's then president, General Mohammed Zia ul-Haq. Zia, whose elaborate mustache, slicked-down hair, and deep-set eyes gave him a remarkable resemblance to generic silent-movie villains, had seized power from the secular, scotch-drinking civilian prime minister Zulfikar Ali Bhutto in 1977. Zia then oversaw Bhutto's hanging and launched Pakistan onto the path of radical Islam and Sharia, which it treads dangerously today.

Zia was a quiet ally of the United States, working closely and behind the scenes for years with maverick Texas Democratic representative Charlie Wilson in funneling clandestine arms, cash, and personnel from the CIA to the mujahideen. Shortly before Zia died, in a still-mysterious air crash on August 17, 1988, he visited Sadda. He met there with representatives of seven Afghan mujahid factions, which then were on the verge of a stunning victory over the Soviet Red Army. Farihin described the visit to us and said Zia was fully aware that future officers of the international jihad were undergoing bomb-making and other terrorist training at the site. "Of course the Pakistani military knew," he said with a shrug. Presumably the United States also knew and failed to act or failed to understand the significance of the academy operating with the knowledge of its Pakistani friend. That failure is an indelible stain on U.S. intelligence, for which Americans still are paying the cleaning bill.

During his three years of training at the academy, Farihin learned tactics, weapons, explosives, and other military subjects and underwent tough physical training. The cadets, nearly four hundred to each class, some fifteen hundred in all, wore standard military fatigues. Students came from such diverse places as France, Pakistan, India, Yemen, Egypt, Saudi Arabia, Iran, Mindanao, southern Thailand, Malaysia, Singapore, and Indonesia. Classes were conducted in Arabic and English and translated as required. In 1993, the academy at Sadda was abandoned and replaced by a similar facility near Turkham, on the Pakistani side of the border, between Peshawar and Kabul. Since then it, too, has been shut down, and no comparable training facility is believed to exist in the region.

Farihin graduated as a second lieutenant in 1991 and was sent back to Indonesia, where he rejoined Jemaah Islamiya. For the next two years he taught physical training to recruits in jungle and mountain camps around Java. "We trained our men to go anywhere in the world where there was jihad," he said. "We sent about twenty to Mindanao and a few to Pattani [southern Thailand]." Indigenous fighters were not brought to Indonesia for training and still are not because, under Jemaah Islamiya's interpretation of jihad as purely defensive, Indonesia is not a "war zone."

Since his release from prison, the splintering of Jemaah Islamiya in the aftermath of the 2002 Bali bombing and the subsequent arrest of some 300 of its members, Farihim has been working for Abu Bakar Ba'asyir, the radical Islamist cleric. Although under police surveillance, as long as he remains nonviolent he is free to work for the eventual Islamist takeover of Indonesia. "We're arguing with the government for the implementation of Sharia and struggling against the anti-Islamic propaganda of the United States," he said. The violent wing of Jemaah Islamiya, under the command of Noordin Mohammed Top, a Malaysian national accused of masterminding the Bali assault, continues to plot terrorist attacks under orders from bin Laden, according to Farihin. "My faction doesn't agree with Noordin, but he is a Jemaah Islamiya leader and we can't stop him. He has soldiers who are ready to die."

As we finished our by now tepid drinks, Farihim conceded that Jemaah Islamiya had suffered grave losses in public support since the Bali carnage. "We're trying to recover and that's why I advise members of my faction not to follow Noordin and conduct terror actions. We don't want to strengthen the American argument that Indonesia is a terror nest."

12

The Lawyer

Operating from the opposite bank of Indonesia's yawning socio-economic divide, a well-to-do lawyer named Adnan Wirwan shares with Farihin a close association with, and high regard for, the radical Islamic clergyman Abu Bakar Ba'asyir, the outspoken mentor of the Bali bombers. When we first sat down to speak with Adnan, it seemed unlikely that the polished lawyer and the Jemaah Islamiya jungle fighter could have much in common. Certainly they had begun their lives headed in opposite directions.

A few years before Farihin's father had shipped him off to study at the Karachi madrassa, where he learned that Americans were his enemies, Adnan's parents had dispatched him from the sweltering tumult of Jakarta to the tidy, blue-collar orderliness of Suitland, Maryland. He spent a year as an exchange student in the Beltway suburb of Washington, D.C., and the experience profoundly influenced his attitudes about Americans. "Ever since, I've had nothing but good to say about the American people. Even my mother, after she visited the United States, said that 'Americans are more Islamic than we are.' Believe me, coming from my mother, that's high praise, indeed."

But as we continued speaking, it became clear that some of the more obvious differences between the terrorist and the lawyer didn't run very deep. Their mutual admiration for Ba'asyir made that clear.

Adnan was now forty-nine and a successful defense attorney. Ba'asyir, his most notorious client, was high on America's (and the United Nations') list of designated Islamic terrorists. But Adnan referred to him, the so-called spiritual leader of Jemaah Islamiya, only as "my client."

"He's not a terrorist, a radical, an extremist, or even a fundamentalist," he told us. "He's just a Muslim, with the Koran and the Hadith [the record of Mohammed's maxims] as the basis of his life." That benign description bore no resemblance to what law enforcement authorities in Indonesia, Australia, and the United States say about Ba'asyir. They accuse him of being the guiding light and inspiration of the Jemaah Islamiya bombers who struck the Marriott Hotel in Jakarta and the two tourist clubs in Bali. They consider him a fanatical follower of Osama bin Laden who forged operational links between al-Qaeda and Jemaah Islamiya; a fiery preacher of hateful antigovernment, anti-American, anti-Western, anti-Israeli, anti-Semitic, and antisecular vitriol; and a teacher of terrorists. Some of the allegations are indisputable, acknowledged and even boasted about by Ba'asyir himself. Five of the eleven Jemaah Islamiya members accused of planning and carrying out the bombings were former students at Ba'asyir's thriving Islamic boarding school on Java, where anti-Americanism is a required course.

Ba'asyir spent four years in prison after the Suharto regime found him guilty of subversion in 1978. In 1985, he fled to Malaysia, spending seventeen years helping build Jemaah Islamiya there and in Singapore. He returned to Indonesia in 1999, a year after Suharto was overthrown, and renewed his campaign to establish Islamic law in the country.

Although Indonesian prosecutors accused him of masterminding the Bali and Marriott bombings as well as a series of assaults on Christian churches in 2000, they were remarkably sloppy in organizing their case, and the evidence they assembled was no more than a flimsy patchwork. Among their few specific charges was that he gave the bombers his "blessing." The government was unable to make any substantive charges stick. Ba'asyir served twenty-six months in a prison outside Jakarta after the court found him guilty on minor charges. During his time behind bars he had cell-phone access to his associates and periodically made inflammatory statements to the press. On October 1, 2005, while he was in prison, three suicide bombers carried out another set of coordinated attacks on restaurants popular with tourists in Bali, this time killing 20 and injuring 129. Ba'asyir was not charged. Six months after his release in June 2006, expectation of which had brought an irate defense secretary Rumsfeld to the office of Defense Minister Sudarsono, Adnan succeeded in having his client exonerated, even further infuriating the U.S. and Australian governments.

Considering the corrupt nature of the Indonesian judicial system and its Supreme Court in particular, it is reasonable to conclude that in clearing Ba'asyir, the nervous Yudhoyono administration was bowing to the extremist religious establishment. Ironically, it was Yudhoyono who as minister of security had led the investigation of the Bali bombing, which gave him bragging rights in his successful presidential bid.

As Adnan explained it, the greatest fear of the Yudhoyono and Bush governments related to the resurgent power of Islam in Indonesia was financial. Ba'asyir and other extremists subscribe to an elaborate conspiratorial thesis that contends that Zionists operating out of Wall Street and the City of London control the Western financial system. This cabal dreads the return of the caliphate and Sharia, which would destroy the entire international banking order. Sharia forbids the use of *riba*, a term that incorporates usury and other forms of interest. "My client," said Adnan, "believes that banks are cruel; they are there not to develop society but to suck the people's blood." Accusing Ba'asyir of the bombings, he told us, was nothing more than a desperate attempt to ruin a man of religious conviction who disagrees with the Indonesian system of governance and has the courage to say so in public. "Trying my client on charges of terrorism was just an excuse. It was as if you jailed me without evidence because I happened to disagree with you and your legal system."

While Ba'asyir exploits Muslim bitterness over the United States and Israel as an important motivational device, the Indonesian legal system is at the core of his battle with the government. Like others in the struggle to replace the Dutch-based constitution with Sharia, he argues that both the old laws and the new democracy have failed the country and that only God's rule is relevant. Ba'asyir's demands receive a certain amount of support in the broader legal community. Indonesia's criminal code has remained intact since the Dutch imposed it in 1838. While the Netherlands has amended its own laws numerous times, Indonesia has not. Thus even those who oppose Sharia can claim, and they do, that the law as it now stands is the same colonial instrument that the Dutch used to repress Indonesian freedom fighters. "My client believes that all the systems we've been through in Indonesia have not worked," Adnan said. "He wants Sharia because this is the law given to us by Allah. If Allah says that only men, and not women, should lead us, then that is that. If Allah says that adulterers should be stoned to death and thieves should have their hands cut off, who are we to question Allah?

"My client opposes liberalism, which he sees as a license to do whatever one wants. He says, 'Just because that is your wife doesn't mean you can have sex in front of us.' To him, sex means even kissing or holding hands. Others may call this fundamentalism, but it adds up: first there's holding hands, then kissing, then who-knows-what. You may call this intolerant, but my client wants only what is written in God's law." The lawyer claimed that a number of these strictures were comparable to those followed by certain Christian fundamentalists in the United States. But rather than using them as commonalities to defuse mutual antagonism, "Americans" (a reference Adnan used interchangeably with "Christians") hurl them as barbs against Muslims. "This is American hypocrisy at its best. This is just one example of your Islamophobia, of how you demonize Muslims." American Christians and Jews countercharge, of course, that Muslims are the hypocritical demons, since it is they who use violence as a religious tool.

Obviously there is plenty of hypocrisy to go around, and true believers of all faiths indulge freely. What, other than hypocrisy, explains the standard rationalization, continually offered on all sides of religious fault lines: Because (fill in the blank) is a religion of peace—except when it is a religion of justifiable war—those who engage in violence are not true followers of (fill in the blank).

Many Muslims with whom we spoke in Southeast Asia used this line of analysis in explaining why fellow Muslims could not possibly have carried out the 9/11 attacks. They, along with other Muslims throughout the world, had no doubt that the attacks were plotted and conducted by agents of the CIA and Israel's Mossad. Similar thinking explains their insistence that the bombings in Bali were carried out by Australia.

Adnan discussed his views and those of his client during a relaxed, lengthy conversation at the poolside of a luxurious resort hotel where he was staying in the Javanese city of Solo. The hotel was outside the village of Ngruki, where Ba'asyir runs al-Mukmin, a *pesantren*, as Islamic boarding schools are known in Indonesia. It was the day after Ba'asyir had been released from prison and the lawyer was making arrangements for his client's triumphal return home. Ba'asyir had driven with his lieutenants for fourteen hours, from his prison in Jakarta, across the Javanese countryside, in a convoy of dark Toyota Kijang vans.

Despite his advocacy, Adnan's personal devotion to fundamentalism seemed less convincing. In appearance, he was utterly distinct from the scraggly-white-bearded Ba'asyir, who was never seen in public without a skullcap, signifying that he had made the hajj; an Arab-style *dishdash*, or tunic; and a shawl. Adnan—with a salt-and-pepper mustache, in slim black jeans and white golf shirt, wrist adorned with a gold and steel Rolex, gold-framed reading glasses low on his nose, cell phone close at hand, speaking American-accented colloquial English—gave every indication of being a man of the world, the very essence of modernism and moderation.

His legal practice over twenty-two years had given him a comfortable life. But he anticipated that Sharia eventually would become the system of law, not only in Indonesia but also across a borderless, worldwide caliphate, putting secular lawyers like him out of business. "Not in my lifetime, but it will happen. I share my client's belief that Islam will prevail. Many of today's leaders may be killed, but others will come."

Following our interview with Adnan, we drove the few minutes from his hotel to Ngruki. There we found Ba'asyir holding forth on what lay ahead. He was addressing a thousand or so cheering followers at the school, a substantial compound of well-kept buildings and neatly swept streets guarded by sturdy-looking young men in black masks and black windbreakers with "Mujahidin" embroidered in Roman letters yellow across the back. Painted in back and red on a classroom wall was this slogan, in Arabic and English: "Al Qur'an [the Koran] is our way of life, Jihad is our way. Death in the Way of Allah is our biggest [sic] Aspiration."

Ba'asyir, deceptively frail-looking at sixty-nine, stood on the front veranda of his house and lectured to the crowd in a strong, clear voice. "I say to the kafir that it will be useless to be at war with Islam. You definitely will be destroyed. . . . No matter what, Islamic law must be imposed. For centuries, while Islam reigned, the world was safe, with prosperity and justice everywhere. After the fall of Islam, infidels reigned, and the world is now in darkness and full of injustice."

Ba'asyir, whose protruding teeth and thick lips gave him an unsettling, wolfish grin, lauded the Bali bombers as devoted warriors of Islam. Their only error, he said, was in carrying out their attack in the wrong place, echoing the same point that Farihin had made during our interview at the Jakarta snack shop a few days earlier. "The mistake is, why did they use bombs in nonconflict areas? However, they are Islamic fighters because their intention is purely to serve Allah and their goal is to defend Islam and Muslims, who are treated with injustice by kafir everywhere."

After Ba'asyir finished his remarks and went into his house, the crowd began dispersing. A few of the students hung around, though, excited by a rare opportunity to stare at real, living Americans. One exchange offered us an insight into the conflicted thinking of some of these youngsters. "Call me Ronnie," said a skinny young man in cutoffs, the faintest feathering of a mustache shading his upper lip. He said he had graduated from Ba'asyir's pesantren two years earlier and now was attending a nearby university, majoring in English. Why English? "It's the best way to earn a good living," he replied.

What would he like to discuss? "It's a fact that kafir hate Muslims."

Was he taught that at the pesantren? "Yes, it's in the holy Koran."

Did he believe that Ba'asyir was involved in Bali and other bombings? "Of course not; he's a holy man. The U.S. government forced Indonesia to put him in jail."

And what were his plans for the future? "I would like to go to America to improve my English and get a good job. But it's impossible for graduates of this pesantren to get a visa."

The next day, we flew from Solo back to Jakarta, where we looked up another of Adnan's clients, Habib Rizieq Shihab. Born in Yemen and educated in Saudi Arabia, Rizieq claims direct descent from the Prophet Mohammad. He also is the leader of the Islamic Defenders Front, known by its Indonesian initials FPI, formed by a group of army generals and senior police officers in 1998. It began recruiting street thugs and petty criminals to act as a militia in opposition to emerging prodemocracy activists following the fall of the Suharto regime. Membership in FPI and its related extremist groups is believed to total two million. More threatening is their ongoing association with military and police officials. As a sideline, the FPI extorts owners of nightclubs and other businesses.

Rizieq was jailed for seven months in 2003 for inciting his young, white-shirted followers, who often hide their faces bandit-style behind kerchiefs, to attack nightspots in Jakarta with clubs and stones. Rizieq keeps up a steady drumbeat of vitriolic verbal assaults on those who oppose his demands for an Islamic state, comparing them with Hitler and the "big lie" propaganda tactic he ascribed to Jews in his 1925 autobiography, *Mein Kampf*.

We followed attorney Adnan's directions to a basement auditorium in a central Jakarta skyscraper, where Rizieq had called a meeting. Speaking to a rapt crowd of about 250 men and 100 or so women, he lashed out at the governments of Indonesia, the United States, and Israel and issued a blunt warning to moderates, or as he called them, "liberal" Muslims. "The fact that the liberals are trying so hard to get rid of us shows how frightened they are about the growing demand for Islamic law in Indonesia. We should prepare for confrontation, for war, because that's what the liberals want. If they form a paramilitary that's ready to die, we will form one that's ready to kill. Yes, the FPI is violent; we're violent defenders of Islam."

The crowd, men in the center of the spacious room, women to one side, interrupted Rizieq repeatedly with cries in Arabic of *"Allahu akhbar!"* (God is great!) Most members of the audience appeared to be middle-aged and middle-class. All the women were fully covered. Most men were dressed in shirtsleeves, a few in neckties. A handful wore Afghan-style cloaks and mushroom-shaped hats, hinting that they had been mujahideen.

Scenes like this in the world's largest Muslim country can mislead Americans. Even though such naked hostility represents the mind-set of a small minority, it's all too easy for us to equate it with all Indonesians and, in turn, with all Muslims. This misinterpretation had led senior figures in the Bush administration and the State Department to apply unrelenting pressure on Yudhoyono to be more aggressive in fighting back. But as Police Inspector General Mbai told us earlier, "The U.S. and the West don't understand that after we've lived so long under authoritarian government we're now fully committed to democracy and we don't want do anything that might harm the new and still-delicate system. So, the government not only has to be democratic, it must appear democratic. It must take soft measures and avoid violence. We must dare to uphold the law. Unfortunately, this creates an image of Yudhoyono as slow and soft. I myself often feel frustrated and nervous."

The Islamists would like nothing more than for the government to take repressive steps. Americans would do well to recognize that Yudhoyono is squeezed in a triple-jawed vise. He is under great stress from the United States, from Indonesian radicals, and from moderates as well. It won't take too much more pressure to crack the eggs on which he treads.

13

The Headmaster

While Al-Mukmin, Abu Bakar Ba'syir's pesantren in Ngruki, is at the furthest extreme of Indonesia's radical Islamic boarding schools, students at more moderate institutions may not be crazy about America either.

During our visit to another pesantren in another city on another day, a seventeen-year-old named Abdullah rose sheepishly from the cool tile floor, where he and his classmates were seated cross-legged, taking a test, to respond to a question we had just asked: What was the first thing that came to his mind when he thought of America? Abdullah glanced quickly around at the two dozen or so other boys and then fixed directly on the questioner's eyes. "It is a superpower that uses its power only for its own purposes." His classmates burst into enthusiastic applause.

Abdullah was studying at Pesantren Dar Al Tauhid Arjaninangur, in the small, tree-shaded port city of Cirebon, on the northern coast of Java. Al Tauhid is one of the more liberal and respected Islamic schools in the country. The headmaster, Hussein Mohammed, was born at the school in 1953 and inherited it from his grandfather. Hussein speaks frequently at settings in Indonesia and abroad on the need for equality for Muslim women and is a progressive thinker on a broad range of social issues. He is a graduate of the elite Al-Azhar University in Cairo, and is well versed in scripture and law.

Those Americans who equate Indonesia's pesantren with Ba'asyir's or with Pakistan's radical madrassas need only hear Hussein to recognize that educators like him, far from those who should be feared, are the West's best hope in the Muslim world: "Our philosophy is simply to provide religious education and create people with religious morality," he told us. "My own thinking is to teach progressive Islam. Muslim culture today is stagnant, unable to face contemporary challenges. There's a need for reconstruction. We can't be trapped any longer in the past, in the Middle Ages. Too many interpretations of Islamic law are stuck in the time of the Crusades, and that's what is behind the widespread negative view of Christians. Islam needs to adapt, to change. Islam is tolerant and egalitarian. That's what we teach."

The unwillingness of some educators, Ba'asyir among them, to give up their medieval worldview lies at the root of Americans' suspicion that Islamic religious schools are training grounds for terrorists. But according to terrorism experts such as Inspector General Mbai, no more than thirty pesantren teach hatred of the United States and Israel. Nearly all were established and funded by Saudi Arabian Wahhabists, whose interpretation of Shia Islam demands a return to the puritanical life that Mohammed himself led fourteen hundred years ago. The vast majority of the country's forty thousand pesantren, at which some 20 percent of young Indonesians are educated, attempt to prepare their graduates to function in an integrated world. As a U.S. diplomat with decades of experience in Indonesia and Malaysia put it, "Most pesantren are as malevolent as 'Our Lady of Mount Carmel.'"

In fact, comparing Islamic fundamentalists in Southeast Asia with fundamentalist Christians or Jews is a worthwhile exercise for Americans. Certainly, the preponderance of religious fundamentalists in the United States do not believe in or resort to violence to achieve their ends. They may preach, pray, blog, complain to newspaper editors, rail in the public square, or strive to influence legislators. But they do not detonate bombs or fire guns. Only a handful blow up government buildings, shoot abortionists, or plot the destruction of others' shrines. And that's pretty much the way it is with most of Southeast Asia's Muslims. But make no mistake: Hussein and his staff are certain that the United States is biased against Muslims, and they teach that to their students along with other lessons that some Americans would find flawed.

On Israel-Palestine: "We teach that the land has always belonged to the Palestinians and that because the Jews lost their homes in Europe the United States gave them a homeland in Palestine. That is injustice."

On Iraq: "By trying to impose democracy, the United States is exhibiting a double standard, one for itself and another for Iraq. Imposition of an ideology on another country is anti-democratic."

As Hussein, a slender, intense man in a skullcap, brown-and-blue-checked sarong, and loose plaid shirt, showed us around the school, he expressed optimism that the current surge of extremist thinking in Indonesia would fade. "I believe that the progressive forces will win," he said. "Radicalism is a temporary phenomenon. We're now in a global community based on democracy and rationalism. Most Muslims realize that and welcome it."

Although this is very likely true, Hussein and other Indonesian educators concede that unless developed nations can help ordinary, mainstream Muslims alleviate poverty and overcome lack of opportunity, radical Islam could become their last resort. Explanations of, and excuses for, Muslim impoverishment are varied and include corrupt leadership and histories of foreign exploitation. But there are powerful indicators that the chief underlying issue is lack of education.

Here are some relevant statistics: The 57 member countries of the Organization of Islamic Conference have a total of 500 universities, or 1 for every 3 million Muslims. By comparison, the United States has 5,758 universities, or 1 for every 52,000 Americans; and India has 8,407, or 1 for every 134,000. In 2004, China's Shanghai Jiao Tong University compiled an "Academic Ranking of World Universities," and not one from a Muslim-majority state was in the top 500.

Here's where such dispiriting circumstances lead: According to the United Nations Development Program, literacy in Christian-dominated countries stands at nearly 90 percent, and 15 Christian-majority nations have a literacy rate of 100 percent. Muslim-majority states average about 40 percent literacy, and none has 100 percent.

And here: Muslim-majority countries have 230 scientists per 1 million population, while the United States has 4,000 per 1 million and Japan, 5,000. The Muslim world spends 0.2 percent of its gross domestic product on research and development, while the Christian world spends about 5 percent.

And here as well: The combined annual gross domestic product of the 57 OIC countries is less than $2 trillion. The United States alone produces goods and services worth $10.4 trillion; China, $5.7 trillion; Japan, $3.5 trillion; and Germany, $2.1 trillion. India's GDP is estimated at more than $3 trillion. Saudi Arabia, the United Arab Emirates, Kuwait, and Qatar collectively produce goods and services, mostly oil, worth $430 billion. The Netherlands alone has a higher annual GDP, while Buddhist-majority Thailand produces goods and services worth $429 billion.

Put another way, Muslims are 22 percent of the world's population and produce fewer than 5 percent of its goods and services, and that figure is declining annually. Most succinctly, many of the world's poor countries are Muslim. There are exceptions, notably the oil-rich sheikhdoms and upwardly mobile Malaysia, but they are few.

With Indonesia and its huge population poised between moderation and extremism, educators in need of funding for their pesantren are caught in a sensitive, highly politicized trap. "If I accept American money I'm labeled pro-U.S.," said Hussein, "and that's the kiss of death."

The central government, which would like to diminish the power of the radical schools, continues to try to choke off the flow of Wahhabi funds. But President Yudhoyono also is anxious to maintain strong relations with Saudi Arabia. And because any distinction between Saudi government funds and money contributed by private religious sources in the kingdom is murky at best, Indonesian authorities have restrained themselves from cracking down.

On the government-to-government level, Saudi Arabia has responded to Indonesian appeals resulting from Bush administration pressure after the 9/11 attacks and shut down official cash flows along with several so-called private charities. But Saudi money continues to seep into the country, much of it brought in by individuals.

In March 2004, at about the time of Ramadan, Indonesian news-
papers reported that a staff member of the religious section of the
Saudi embassy in Indonesia, Ibrahim Qamasyi, hand-carried a suitcase filled with $200,000 through Soekarno-Hatta International
Airport into Jakarta. In 2005, the secretary-general of a Saudi organization known as the World Islamic League traveled to the great
Javanese Buddhist stupa of Borabodur, a major tourist attraction, and
reported—not to the police, but to the Ministry of Religious Affairs—
that a suitcase containing $290,000 was stolen from his hotel room.
The Saudi left the country the next day, and the money was not recovered. Over a three-month period in 2006, Fahad al-Harbi, the Saudi
director of the league's Jakarta office, made three cash transfers—
$230,000, $320,000, and $930,000—to a newly opened personal bank
account in Jakarta. Indonesian police authorities told us that they did
not know where these funds ended up, but they assumed the money
was intended for Wahhabist pesantren and mosques.

Toward the end of the George W. Bush years popular sentiment
was running strongly against the United States, and Headmaster
Hussein had to ratchet back his unending quest for funds. With
four hundred boarding students, boys and girls aged fourteen to
twenty, each paying about $22 a month, money was always short.
Several of the simple beige stucco buildings we walked through had
broad cracks in their walls, and one heavy, red tile roof, propped
up by bamboo poles, swayed dangerously close to the ground.
Hussein quietly accepts funding from the American nonprofit Asia
Foundation for a pro-human rights, profeminist, anti-corruption
advocacy group known as Fahmina, which he founded in Cirebon.
"But I can't take any for the school, or parents would quickly label
me the enemy and pull their children out," he said.

So he tries to be even-handed in doling out criticism. "In my
view, we need to criticize whoever commits injustice—Muslim
and non-Muslim. But we need to criticize their actions, not their
ethnic or religious background. For example, the 9/11 attack was an
injustice; it was disproportionate to whatever the United States had
done before."

In the spring of 2006, Hussein had attended a meeting in
Jakarta, where he told then World Bank president Paul Wolfowitz

that fundamentalism was on the rise because Indonesian Muslims resented American pressure to comply with its "war on terror." Wolfowitz responded that fundamentalism was part of a complex set of issues, including poverty. "I think we're both right, in part," Hussein told us. "But the bottom line is that there is a need to rebuild the lives of Muslims. Americans need to come here to see for themselves how best to do it."

Education is the key. "You can bring pesantren teachers to America," he said. "They would study and at the same time help to change the prejudices of Americans about what we teach here. The problem in Islam lies with the weakness of civil society. So, we must give space to civil society to grow. Americans can help facilitate improvement of human resources, but avoid government-to-government funding. Form alliances with nongovernmental organizations and pesantren. That way, you can come to understand us and we can learn more about you."

14

The Publisher

Luthfi Tamimi publishes one of Indonesia's most radical, anti-American, pro-Islamist magazines, *Sabili*, which means "My Way" in Arabic. So it is hardly surprising that his advice differed widely from that of Headmaster Hussein. But what he had to say was surprising nonetheless. "You must take a long, hard look at your good friends, the Wahabbist Saudis. They're not what you think they are. They've been taking your country for a ride for a long, long time." He had concluded years ago that the Saudi royal family was "playing you guys for suckers. The Bush family in particular thinks the Saudis are your friends. But look what they're doing here in Indonesia: pumping in tons of money to convert us to Wahhabism, building mosques and madrassas where they teach anti-Americanism. What are you thinking about?"

Luthfi came by his cynicism firsthand. Before launching *Sabili*, he spent eighteen years working in Saudi Arabia. And not just at any job, but as an employee of the U.S. embassy in Riyadh, including a stint in the defense attaché's office during the 1990–1991 Gulf War. One of the first things he did after welcoming us to his office was pass around snapshots of himself posing with General H. "Stormin' Norman" Schwarzkopf, Ambassador Charles W. Freeman Jr., and Secretary of Defense William J. Perry, taken during their visits to the embassy. Luthfi, fifty-seven, said he enjoyed his work with the U.S. mission in Jiddah and was paid well, including an annual home-leave trip to Indonesia to see his family. "The Americans in Saudi were good guys; kind of clueless, but good guys," he said with an easy grin.

Luthfi was a walking, talking contradiction. He came on in a strong, uniquely American way, with a hearty handshake, a loud welcome, and an offer of cigarettes and coffee. Within minutes he was arguing that Indonesia should be administered under Sharia, though Indonesian-style, not the Saudi interpretation. He said he admired Jews, and Israelis in particular, for their "intelligence—far smarter than Muslims" and their success in "making the desert bloom." Moments later, he flipped to a scathing article in his magazine's latest issue on the history of Israeli attacks on the al-Aqsa Mosque and another on "Jewish sins," based on Koranic quotations.

He nonchalantly waved the back of a hand past framed *Sabili* covers hanging in the entry hall of the gracious, cream-colored villa that houses its offices. One, a *Time* look-alike, was of Abu Bakar Ba'asyir as "Man of the Year." Another was of President George W. Bush under the headline "Expose American Propaganda." Yet another pictured a combat scene from Afghanistan and was titled "Fighting against Infidels."

Glossily turned out in a deep purple shirt with spread collar and coordinated Italian silk tie, he served us a traditional Arab lunch of roast lamb and rice, which we ate in the traditional way, with the fingers of the right hand. When he spelled some unusually long Indonesian words for us he had fun using the U.S. military phonetic alphabet, "alpha, whiskey, golf . . . "

So what's a smart, friendly Indonesian who benefited for so long from U.S. government generosity abroad doing running an anti-American Islamist publication now that he's back home in Indonesia? The answer was at once straightforward and tangled. The initial attraction was financial, he said. Like hundreds of thousands of Indonesians, Luthfi had gone to the Persian Gulf to make money. He'd spent all those years living alone in Saudi Arabia until, in 1995, his daughter was about to enter high school. Separation had badly damaged his marriage. In addition, he had long since grown bitter about what he saw as Saudi arrogance and intolerance. It was time to leave. Soon after returning to Jakarta, he met a wealthy entrepreneur who wanted to launch a magazine and was looking for a savvy publisher who could run it for him. Luthfi was his man. "The money was good and I was free to make the magazine anything that would sell," he said. Fundamentalism was beginning to sell. In a few years Luthfi built *Sabili*'s circulation to eighty thousand, and its owner was happy. So was Luthfi. "We're making money." Mohammed Iqbal, a scholar at Gadjah Mada University in Jogjakarta specializing in radical Islamist publications, told us that *Sabili* was the most successful and the most extreme of one hundred or so similar magazines in the country.

In about 2000, as *Sabili* was growing in prestige and earnings, Luthfi began thinking about another stream of money, this one from his former host country, pouring into Indonesia and upsetting the delicate social balance. This disturbed him. With huge amounts of oil-generated wealth available, the government in Riyadh was constructing mosques and madrassas throughout the country and staffing them with Wahhabis dispatched from Saudi Arabia. The Saudis translated Wahabbist books and tracts into Indonesian and distributed millions of free copies. Village youngsters were flocking to the madrassas, where they studied Arabic, in preparation for travel to Saudi Arabia and other fundamentalist Middle Eastern states. There they underwent further study and were infused with the most retrograde form of religious practice in the Muslim world. After graduating, some went on to Afghanistan and Iraq, to join the armed struggle against the United States.

From the Saudi perspective, it was the ideal moment to launch a concerted drive in the world's largest Muslim-populated country. The Saudis were spurred to take aggressive action in Indonesia and other parts of Islamic Southeast Asia by the Shia mullahs' 1979 revolution in Iran and the Afghan war against the Soviet Union, which began in the same year and concluded in triumph for the mujahideen. The importance of the mullahs' triumph throughout both Shia and Sunni Islam is comparable to the dramatic spark that the imperial Japanese struck in Southeast Asia early in World War II. Even though the invaders treated the local people brutally, they learned that supposedly inferior races could overcome the white man and rule themselves.

Luthfi told us that he didn't like what he saw happening when he returned home. "I found that Muslim-Christian relations had changed and there were new strains between them," he said. "The Saudis had a grand plan to build a new mosque or madrassa every thirty kilometers. When Indonesian students came back from the Middle East they went to places like Cirebon and Makassar and Surabaya and began setting up nongovernmental organizations and building more schools. The Saudis would come to Jakarta every June or July and conduct seminars on Wahhabism. They opened offices of the Islamic Relief Organization and the Muslim League. That was when I got back and I thought, 'Oh my God, this is a problem.'"

Luthfi's worries were well placed. The Saudi-based International Islamic Relief Organization (IIRO) is widely suspected of financing international terrorist organizations along with the Muslim World League. On August 3, 2006, the U.S. Treasury Department charged that their Indonesian and Philippine branches raised funds for al-Qaeda, Jemaah Islamiya, and Abu Sayyaf. Osama bin Laden's brother-in-law Mohammed Jamal Khalifah established the Philippine branch of the IIRO as a charity in the late 1980s or early 1990s. Its director, Mahmud Abd Al-Jalil Afif, was implicated in the 1992 assassination of a Filipino Catholic priest, Father Salvatore Carzeda, in Zamboanga.

In Indonesia, Luthfi observed that as the Saudis accumulated power and influence they began criticizing indigenous peculiarities of Islamic practice and disparaging Indonesian traditions. Because Indonesia's Muslims over the centuries have layered their earlier Buddhist and Hindu customs with late-arriving Islamic rules, they have ended up with a broad range of spirit-linked superstitions and customs, such as offering food to dead ancestors, accompanying the call of the muezzin to prayers with drums, and piercing their skin with sharp objects to demonstrate that they are protected by Allah.

The infuriated Saudis berated all this as haram and non-Islamic. They insisted that imams in mosques they financed be either Saudis or Indonesians educated in Saudi Arabia. Their demands grew more stringent with the return from Malaysia of Ba'asyir and other radical Islamists after the fall of Suharto's New Order regime.

These demands set off tensions and conflicts among Indonesian Muslims as well as between them and non-Muslims. Luthfi, disturbed though he may have been, opportunistically tapped into these differences as a means of promoting his new magazine.

Then, on January 19, 1999, an argument between a Christian bus driver and a Muslim passenger in the city of Ambon, in Indonesia's Moluccan Islands, exploded into rioting and what eventually would become five years of bloodshed between members of the two religious communities. Church bombings became commonplace around the country. At one point a hundred thousand Muslims demonstrated in Jakarta, baying for Christian blood, carrying a blood-smeared cruciform and banners that read, "Tolerance Is Nonsense, Slaughter Christians." By the time the carnage ended, in large part through the intercession of multimillionaire businessman Yusuf Kalla, who later was elected vice president under Yudhoyono, as many as ten thousand Christians and Muslims had been killed.

Luthfi said that the years of warfare in Ambon terrified him. Although he described himself as a fully observant Muslim, he said his Islam was of the broad-minded Indonesian variety. "I realized that if hatred was allowed to spread, then all of the conflicts between the Wahhabi, the Sunni, and the Shia in the Middle East would spill over into Indonesia." Now, with militant Islam marching across South Asia, from Afghanistan, through Pakistan, and into India, he said he was more alarmed than ever and claimed that he was trying to "gradually" tone down the Islamist fervor of *Sabili*. "But, you know, it's a business, and if we offend too many of our readers, we'll lose them. I can't afford to do that." It makes sense: imagine what would happen to Rush Limbaugh's ratings if he went soft on Hillary Clinton or to Jon Stewart's if he put George W. Bush on a pedestal.

The Saudi involvement that Luthfi said he deplored is widely accepted as a leading cause of social unrest in Indonesia. Another factor with even more damaging effect was the nation's monetary collapse in the summer of 1997. What became known as the East Asian financial crisis had begun that spring in Bangkok. Like avian flu, the Thai financial sickness flew across Asia and settled deep in Indonesia. The exchange rate of the rupiah collapsed.

In Southeast Asia, governments and businesses that had borrowed funds in dollars were unable to pay their interest and fell into bankruptcy. The Washington-based International Monetary Fund offered "rescue packages," but the conditions were onerous, causing many Indonesian as well as Malaysian Muslims to turn against not only the IMF but the United States as well, both of which they equated with Zionist control. The government of China, which had avoided most of the damage by manipulating its own currency with care, stepped adroitly into the breach, offering cheap loans and new investments to Indonesia and other stricken governments. This seemingly sympathetic posture continues to serve China's interests in Southeast Asia.

A major and long-lasting effect of this economic upheaval was that more young Indonesians flocked to the Middle East in search of jobs. Half a million work in Saudi Arabia alone, the great majority being women, employed as domestic servants. While their employers subject many of the women to sexual and other abuse, the men are exposed to Wahhabism. And, as is by now an established pattern, some return with new and fearsome understandings of their religion.

Like almost everyone on our Southeast Asian journey, Luthfi had advice for Americans. "First of all," he said, "stay out of religious affairs. That's none of your business, and anything you might do will cause a negative reaction. At the moment, any Muslim who stands up and attacks the United States is a hero. You have made too many mistakes for too long to be able to change that anytime soon.

"What you should do is concentrate on introducing more small business opportunities and help create jobs. Your government spends a lot of money in Indonesia, but too much of it gets into the wrong hands. Stop wasting your taxpayers' money. The problem here is poverty."

15

The Older Brother

S end vocational teachers," Rozy Munir urged us. "Send experts who can teach information technology. Send private-sector Americans who can help us with a whole variety of trades, crafts, agriculture, business. . . . We need all of them. Just make sure that we don't have to pay! And take more Indonesian students into your universities for advanced degrees."

Munir is vice chairman of Indonesia's ultimate mass sociopolitical organization, Nahdlatul Ulama (NU), which claims a staggering thirty-five million members. The group, whose name means Revival of Learned Men, is by far the largest Muslim organization in Indonesia and, almost certainly, in the world. NU speaks for religious and political moderation, and its strength is based on a network of ten thousand pesantren, along with mosques, orphanages, poorhouses, farmers' and merchants' unions, and small industries. While not itself a political party, its endorsement or condemnation will almost certainly make or break any candidate. It is the socioreligious base from which political parties draw their recruits.

A charismatic Javanese religious scholar named Hasyim Asy'ari, scion of an ancient line of Javanese kings, founded NU in 1926. Hasyim's son became independent Indonesia's first minister of religious affairs, and his grandson, Abdurrahman Wahid, a former president of Indonesia, is the current leader of NU. Indonesians know Wahid by the affectionate nickname Gus Dur (Older Brother).

He is nearly blind, and having suffered two strokes, which cause him to fall asleep at odd moments, he might leave unprepared foreigners with the impression of a pathetic, almost comic figure. But to millions of Indonesians he is a hero and a commanding presence in the realm of mainstream Islam.

In recent years, Wahid joined forces with a politically conservative American, C. Holland Taylor, a graduate of the University of North Carolina and Princeton and a former leading international telecommunications executive. After taking early retirement in 1998, Taylor, who had worked and lived in the Arab world for years, moved to Indonesia and immersed himself in its culture and language, which he now speaks fluently. He and Wahid cofounded an idealistic organization known as LibForAll, intended to counter the arguments of Islamist extremists and to diminish the influence in Indonesia of Saudi Wahabbism. With the blond, boyish-looking, and energetic Taylor behind the scenes of LibForAll, Wahid is its public face.

Wahid was a longtime outspoken opponent of President Suharto. This reputation helped get him elected president of the nation in 1999, during the chaotic period of flux following Suharto's fall. His presidency was tumultuous and short-lived, and he was impeached in 2001. Wahid, who states frequently and publicly "I am for Israel," was driven from office in part because he attempted to move Indonesia too far and too fast into liberalism. At the same time, his critics were fully justified in accusing him of inept, erratic leadership and of tolerating corruption among his government associates. His vice president, Megawati Sukarnoputri, a daughter of the dictator Sukarno, replaced him, thus completing a bizarre cycle in Indonesian history.

Although he'd been educated, reluctantly, he says, at universities in Cairo and Baghdad, Wahid opposed Arab interjection into Indonesia's affairs. Twice before he became president he made private, secretive visits to Israel. After being elected, he began agitating in favor of establishing diplomatic relations with the Jewish state, which neither Indonesia nor Malaysia has ever had. In January 2001 he met secretly in Jakarta with acting Israeli trade minister Reuven Horesh. This and other perceived un-Islamic behavior cost him the support of Indonesia's armed forces, leaving him in an untenable position.

In the wake of that unacceptably liberal drift, NU altered course, striving to regain a more traditional middle ground of moderation. "We oppose Indonesia becoming an Islamic state and we have ever since we were founded," Munir, a devoted follower of Wahid, told us during an interview in the organization's spacious, modern headquarters building in central Jakarta. "We support our multiple cultures. At the same time, we are a religious organization and that's why we build and operate thousands of religious schools. We reject Wahhabism because it has nothing to do with Indonesians' understanding of Islam and, for the same reason, we support pancasila."

Many moderates such as the sixty-four-year-old Munir, who holds a master's degree in economics from the University of Hawaii, insist that they don't seriously fear an Islamist revolution in Indonesia. But they worry about creeping Islamization and Shariazation, which are putting down roots at local and district levels and advancing toward the power centers. This gradual process is husbanded by a handful of small but vociferous and often violent groups with names such as the Islamic Defenders Front and the Council of Martyrs. These organizations, some led by Arabs born and educated in the Middle East, were able to set up shop because of Indonesia's newfound democracy, and now they are thriving despite it.

"We've had direct elections but poverty is still rampant," said Ahmad Suaedy, executive director of NU's prodemocracy think tank, the Wahid Institute. "In that sense the radical groups are right. But they're authoritarian, while we believe in pluralism as the basis of Indonesia. So we're going to have to continue fighting for democracy." By comparison with NU, the radical groups are small, meaning they range between five hundred thousand and two million members each. Their strength comes from close affiliations with powerful national and regional politicians and senior military officers. The great majority of Indonesians, having suffered through half a century of authoritarian rule, are put off by these links and, without doubt, want to press on with the democratic effort. But in addition to the gravitational pull of poverty and unemployment, they face the unassailable moral argument that Allah has already dictated the law. The moderates may turn to the constitution of Indonesia for legal backup, but the radicals have the Koran on their side: *To Him belongs the dominion of the heavens and the Earth. It is He who gives Life and Death. And He has Power over all things.*

Such an assertion is a difficult one for any Muslim to refute in any circumstance, but particularly so when the issue is an alien Western concept such as pluralism. Increasingly, this debate is taking place in sweaty meeting halls and in the streets of Indonesia's cities. After unflattering Danish newspaper cartoons depicting the Prophet Mohammed raced across the Internet in 2005, gangs from Habib Rizieq Shihab's FPI attacked the embassies of the United States and Denmark in Jakarta and ransacked bars and nightclubs.

Then came *Playboy*.

The first domestically published issue, licensed by Playboy Enterprises, Inc., in the United States, hit the streets of Jakarta and other major Indonesian cities on June 6, 2006. Although its photographs wouldn't raise so much as an eyebrow of an American used to nothing more risqué than a Macy's lingerie ad in the local daily, it triggered instant titillation and outrage.

Several hundred FPI toughs attacked the *Playboy* office, located, as fate would have it, in Jakarta's ASEAN Aceh Fertilizer Building. Police arrested no one. The frightened publishers fled to the more tolerant surroundings of Hindu-majority Bali, where real women lounging on beaches in bikinis are considered ho-hum. In fact, much racier fare had been sold openly at Indonesian newsstands for years. But *Playboy* was the perfect foil for the radicals: "pornographic" and American. Even before the Indonesian edition's initial publication, FPI and other violent groups had forced moderate members of Parliament to propose a vaguely worded bill that had the potential to ban not only pornography, but also do away with certain traditional Indonesian dances, swimsuited sunbathing, and kissing in public, including among married couples. This burning issue had been on attorney Adnan's mind when he spoke to us about his client Ba'asyir.

Some Americans resident in Indonesia told us that the pornography dispute affected few and closely paralleled the same-sex marriage controversy in the United States. "It's a wedge issue," said a businessman who'd worked in the country for nearly twenty years. "The extremists are pushing it in order to divide the public. And they're succeeding." Muslims by and large joined the fray on the extremist side, while Christians and nationalists pushed back. The face-off heightened religious tensions. Unsubstantiated rumors circulated that Yudhoyono's wife, Kristiani, was secretly a Christian. In a pointedly symbolic reaction, the first lady quietly let it become known that she would henceforth be known simply as Ani.

Into this breach stepped, or rather rolled, Gus Dur. In his late sixties, though appearing much older because of his illness, he was confined to a wheelchair, barely able to make out shapes through thick glasses, and liable to doze off, slack-jawed, in midsentence. In the midst of the *Playboy* brouhaha, he addressed a public meeting in western Java and took on all comers, vociferously assaulting the antipornography legislation, the radical organizations, the Yudhoyono government, and the police. Enraged FPI men stormed the gathering, shouted the sick man down, and shoved him off the stage. Their thuggish behavior breathed sympathetic new life into Wahid's reputation as a patriot and a religious scholar after spending the five years since his impeachment in the political wilderness.

The Yudhoyono administration, embarrassed by the assault, ordered police to arrest some of the usual FPI suspects—not for attacking Wahid, but for trashing a café—and pledged to crack down on all violent groups. But the government soon lost its nerve, giving rise to worries among moderates that Yudhoyono, like Prime Minister Abdullah bin Haji Ahmad Badawi in neighboring Malaysia, would succumb to political pressure to appear more Islamic than the radicals.

Yudhoyono's need to tread lightly reflected the fact that the Indonesian democratic experiment remained in delicate condition. Extremists were trying to press the president into dialogue on a range of Sharia-based issues, the anti-pornography bill being the one that most readily captured the public's imagination. By hanging back and allowing the radical groups to soil their own image, the timorous president was attempting to deprive them of any legitimacy they might gain through debate with his government. While Yudhoyono dithered, the unseemly assault on Wahid immediately reinstated him as the living symbol of Indonesian democracy and moderation. Suddenly he was lionized by the same news media that had mocked him or ignored him.

We visited Wahid in his Jakarta office late one morning. He'd been up until the wee hours, watching the World Cup soccer tournament, and apologized for being more tired than usual. During our interview in the dimly lit office, shades drawn against the scorching sun, he slumped in a chair behind his desk, his chin dipping onto his orange batik shirt. He seemed uninterested in discussing our concerns about Islamic fundamentalism in Indonesia and wanted to talk about how he learned English (VOA and BBC broadcasts) and his favorite American authors (Melville and Twain).

But then a pointed question about the current leadership provoked him, and he responded, in a barely audible voice, with a scathing assessment of Yudhoyono. "He is a weak president. He allows others to impose their will on him. He has lost the original intention of the constitution, for the state to provide prosperity and justice. He allows injustice to take place and poverty to continue." He paused for breath. Then he raised his head and uncorked the ultimate slap at the president: "He caters to the needs of the United States, but ignores the needs of Indonesia."

Shortly afterward, Yudhoyono announced that, as widely anticipated, he would run for a second five-year term. With more than 170 million people registered to vote for the 560-member legislature—and 11,000 candidates running from 38 political parties—the election, on July 8, 2009, went remarkably smoothly. Yudhoyono, who emphasized his secular credentials during the campaign, was returned to office easily. His opponents put considerably more emphasis on their religious credentials, and their campaigning leaned on Islamic symbolism. While Yudhoyono's wife pointedly appeared at his side with her raven bouffant hair uncovered, his opponents' wives took pains to never leave home without the jilbab. Although this helped spark a run on jilbab shops, most Indonesian voters, even austere Muslims, saw the religious fashion show for what it was.

The outcome of the election, which, coincidentally perhaps, became evident as Iran's mullahs were cracking down viciously on voters infuriated with the allegedly fraudulent reelection of

President Ahmadinejad, was a clear indication that religious political parties in Indonesia had reached a critical juncture. If they were going to remain a credible force, it seemed, they would have to wind back their stress on Sharia and identify themselves more closely with the daily lives and struggles of ordinary Indonesians. But just over a week after election day, deadly twin bombings struck a pair of American luxury hotels in central Jakarta, killing at least nine people and injuring more than fifty. The Islamists, or some of them anyway, had determined that they would not go gently into the night simply because fellow Muslims had voted for SBY's take on democracy and secularism.

Early analysis suggested that a splinter group comprising younger, unreconstructed JI members were to blame. But there seemed to be equal reason to question ardent followers of some of the reelected president's opponents, particularly those with intimate military ties. Whatever the investigation into the bombings turned up, the renewed violence smeared a haze of doubt over Indonesia's hoped-for period of peaceful promise. For the moment, at least, if Indonesia's fundamentalist-political leaders wanted guidance on how ultraconservative Islamic parties were coping elsewhere, they could look across the straits to Malaysia.

PART THREE

One Step Back: Malaysia

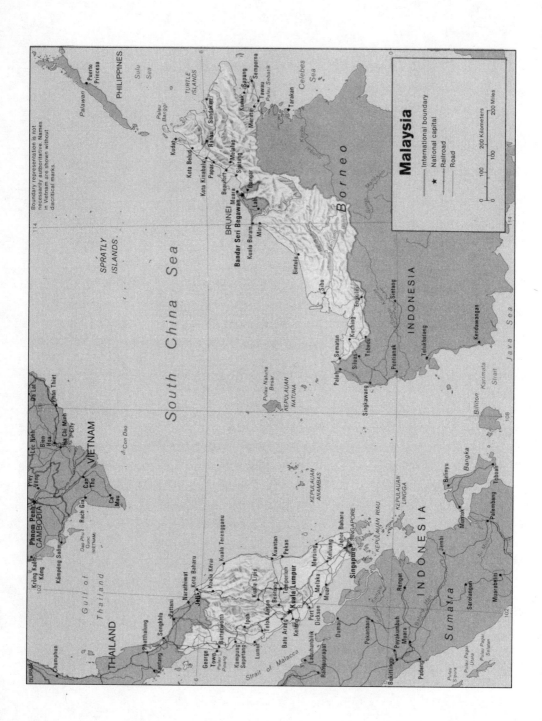

Malaysia

- International boundary
- ★ National capital
- Railroad
- Road

0   100   200 Kilometers
0   100   200 Miles

Boundary representation is not
necessarily authoritative. Names
in Vietnam are shown without
diacritical marks.

PHILIPPINES

Sulu
Sea

Palawan

Puerto
Princesa

TURTLE
ISLANDS

Pulau
Banggi

Celebes
Sea

Semporna
Tawau
Lahad Datu
Sandakan
Kunak
Kudat
Ranau
Beaufort
Papar
Kota Kinabalu
Kota Belud

Pulau Sebatik
Tarakan

Borneo

BRUNEI
Bandar Seri Begawan
Muara
Seria
Kuala Baram
Miri
Limbang
Bintulu
Sibu
Kapit
Sintang
Engkilili
Kuching
Sematan
Sibu
Siluas
Paloh
Tebedu

Kendawangan

INDONESIA

Teluk baeng

Pontianak

Singkawang

Java
Sea

Karimata
Strait

SPRATLY
ISLANDS.

South   China   Sea

Pulau Natuna
Besar
KEPULAUAN
NATUNA

Billiton

Bangka

Belinyu
Muntok
Palembang
Toboali

KEPULAUAN
ANAMBAS

KEPULAUAN
LINGGA

KEPULAUAN RIAU

INDONESIA

Sumatra

Jambi

Rengat
Pekanbaru
Dumai
Muara
Payakumbuh
Bukittinggi
Padang
Pulau
Siberut
Pulau Pagai
Utara
Pulau Pagai
Selatan
Sarolangun
Muarabungo

VIETNAM

Da Lat
Phan Thiet
Loc Ninh
Bien Hoa
Ho Chi Minh
City
P. Con Dao
Prey
Veng
Phnom Penh
CAMBODIA
Krong Koah
Kong
Kampong Saôm
Rach Gia
Dao Phu
Quoc
(VIETNAM)
Cap
Ca
Mau

Gulf
of
Thailand

THAILAND

BURMA

Chumphon
Phatthalung
Songkhla
Yala
Kantang
Narathiwat
Sattun
Kota Baharu
Kuala Kerai
Kuala Terengganu
Kuantan
Pekan
Mersing
Endau
Kluang
Johor Baharu
SINGAPORE
Singapore
Kuala Lipis
Benting
Temerloh
Melaka
Muar
Batu Pahat
Labuhanbilik
Rantauprapat
Port
Dickson
Kelang
Kuala Lumpur
Telok Anson
Kampung
Sepetang
Ipoh
Butterworth
George
Town
Pulau
Pinang

Strait of Malacca

16

The Jahil

As an international arms dealer, Jamaluddin Mansor lived large. He made a lot of money, rewarded himself with a luxurious home and fast cars, and maintained a string of girlfriends as some other rich men did polo ponies. Then middle age arrived, and with it, the inevitable crisis. He divorced his wife, a successful Malaysian businesswoman who operated a chain of cosmetics shops. He had lost his way. He felt emptiness where his heart should have been. "I had a Mercedes and a big house, but I couldn't fill the vacuum. I had plenty of money but, of course, I couldn't buy love or peace of mind."

Then epiphany struck: he was a *jahil*, a Muslim who was ignorant of the faith into which he'd been born.

So in 1994, at age forty, Jamaluddin launched himself on a quest. He studied Arabic and learned the correct way to pray five times each day. He quit drinking, left the weapons business, and went into gas and oil. He began publishing a group of successful magazines aimed at promoting Islam among young Malaysian men and women. He remarried, to an ancestor-worshipping ethnic Chinese woman, who converted to Islam for him. He grew even wealthier. The government of Malaysia bestowed on him the honorific title Datuk, in recognition of his service to the nation. Now, with silver beginning to glimmer in his black mustache, life was better than ever. Jamaluddin was a happy man. He had found Allah.

As we sipped tea in his modest second-floor office on the edge of Kuala Lumpur's Chinatown while listening to his story of rebirth and redemption, one of us asked teasingly if he knew of another man who'd been born again at forty and went on to fulfillment. "Bush!" he shouted, throwing his hands into the air in mock horror. About anything else he and the American president might have in common, he said, suddenly serious, "I know this. I wouldn't send an army into Iraq. And I'd have a balanced policy between Palestine and Israel."

Yet, in much the same way that George W. Bush's two election victories reflected the conservative needs and aspirations of a substantial number of Americans at the turn of this century, Jamaluddin was a metaphor for many Malaysians as two seemingly contradictory forces pull them in opposing directions. Malaysia today is an anomaly among Muslim nations, prospering, growing in international prestige, and at the same time becoming increasingly pious.

In twenty-five years, the country's financial, political, and cultural capital has blossomed from a sleepy backwater at the "confluence of two muddy rivers" (which is what Kuala Lumpur means in Malay) to a stunning metropolis of a million and a half people. One of the tallest buildings in town back then was a ten-story hotel with a creaky revolving restaurant on the top floor. Diners looked out over a tabletop-flat, overgrown village, its dim lights stopping abruptly at the black swath of rubber estates, palm oil plantations, and eroded tin mines carved from dense stands of virgin jungle.

Today the city is renowned for its futuristic architecture, highlighted by the eighty-eight-floor Petronas Twin Towers. Named for the national oil company, they are the tallest pair of skyscrapers in the world. The downtown flows with no boundary in sight into meandering suburban sprawl. Where strolling, parasol-toting pedestrians once found a touch of relief from steamy heat in the shade of sidewalk arcades, office workers now bustle through air-conditioned elevated skyways. Commuters travel in cool comfort between K.L., as everyone calls the city, and outlying technology and administrative centers on a superefficient, high-speed rail line. Dusty little shops and charcoal-fueled food stalls have given way to glittering department stores and restaurants offering the best of what the world has to offer. K.L. is tomorrow's city in the tropics.

The story of such remarkable progress unfolding in what had long been a drowsy corner of Southeast Asia has spread a cross the umma, inspiring Muslims around the world and earning their admiration. In 2006 Malaysia took over simultaneously the chairmanships of the Organization of the Islamic Conference, the Non-aligned Movement, and the Association of Southeast Asian Nations.

But something is out of kilter. While the skyline soars toward the future, Malaysia's Muslim Street is moving in a different direction. In the 1970s and 1980s, it was unusual for Malay women to cover their hair or to wear anything more modest than the traditional sarong *kabaya*, a hip-hugging, ankle-length skirt and snug blouse. Typical for men were lightweight trousers and loose batik shirt, a cool, relaxed style reminiscent of the Hawaiian aloha look. Arab dress was limited to the handful of traveling businessmen from the Middle East. Now more than 80 percent of Malay women wear a closely wrapped head scarf. Middle Eastern dress, popularized by the vast number of Arab travelers who now visit for business and pleasure, is gradually becoming more common for both sexes.

The nation's first postindependence prime minister, Tunku Abdul Rahman, a Malay prince, looked to the West for inspiration during his tenure. He was at ease on the golf course, at the racetrack, and the mah-jongg table, with a tall gin and tonic in hand. He married at least four times (the record is unclear), once to an Englishwoman and another time to a Chinese Malaysian. And he was wildly popular, reelected to office for thirteen years, until resigning in 1970.

The Tunku's successor, Tun Abdul Razak, from a privileged Malay family, was best known for being a dour workaholic. But in private life, he danced foxtrots and rumbas at parties with other men's wives—and his wife with other women's husbands. No one gave it a thought. None of it would be acceptable today. When one of us mentioned to Razak's son, Deputy Prime Minister and Foreign Minister Najib Abdul Razak, that he had danced with his mother at a party at the swank Lake Club back in 1970, a dark look crossed his face and he said nothing.

The government now fields a large religious police unit, and it is vigilant. In 2005, the police arrested two Muslim brothers, both factory workers in their thirties, for sharing a bottle of Guinness stout in a restaurant. A religious court judge subjected each to six strokes of the cane and fines of $1,316. The same year, a 150-member religious police squad swooped down on Zouk, a popular K.L. nightclub, and arrested scores of Muslims among the trendy young patrons. Dozens of women protested afterward that the police had harassed them sexually, made suggestive comments about their clothing, and taken humiliating photographs. The government's minister for Islamic affairs defended the arrests and the actions of the police.

Like the rehabilitated jahil Jamaluddin, people who used to define themselves by their ethnicity as Malays now are apt to refer to themselves foremost as Muslims. Attendance at mosques is rising sharply, along with Arabic-language classes, puritanical interpretations of public behavior, and the intervention of Sharia into civil affairs. Ethnic Chinese, who make up about a fourth of the country's twenty-five million population and are a mix of Buddhists and Christians, are, to put it mildly, uneasy. The much smaller Indian minority feels more marginalized than ever by the growing Islamization of what once was the most open-minded multicultural country in the region.

With the government fearful of the severe damage that communal struggle could inflict on Malaysia's promising future, based on the scarred memory of Malay-Chinese riots in 1969, it constrains public debate. The news media are self-censored, seldom airing discussion of underlying societal strains. Although government-sanctioned protesters in Kuala Lumpur mounted the largest anti-Western demonstrations permitted in years in response to the satirical Danish cartoons of the Prophet in 2005, major news outlets did not publish the drawings. One daily in the East Malaysian state of Sarawak, on the somewhat remote island of Borneo, did print them and was shut down. Law enforcement agencies monitor ethnic-based groups, instantly smothering the smallest spark of sectarian dissent.

As a result of all the discipline, serious racial violence has not recurred since 1969. On May 13 of that year, following a general election in which Chinese candidates made impressive gains, bloody rioting broke out in Kuala Lumpur. For a week, young Malay *amoks* slashed Chinese with *parangs*, a kind of machete; Chinese hacked Malays with meat cleavers. The outcome was several hundred corpses lying in the streets among burning cars, and police firing automatic weapons indiscriminately. The riots left the fragile social fabric sundered for years. Many educated Chinese and Indians fled to Australia, Canada, Britain, and neighboring Singapore, creating a brain drain that Malaysia couldn't afford. The brutality marked a watershed, comparable in impact with the race riots that erupted a year earlier in the United States following the assassination of the Reverend Dr. Martin Luther King Jr.

The causes and effects of religious and racial tension within Malaysia mirror those in Indonesia. But nervous leaders in each country attempt to play down their own problem, telling foreign visitors that they're more worried about the situation in the other nation. Malaysians say that poverty in Indonesia could produce a blowup; Indonesians say that Islamic fundamentalism is gaining ground in Malaysia. Each fears a spillover from the other. The majorities in both countries are Muslims of the same Malay stock (as are the people of Mindanao and southern Thailand), and their primary languages are closely related. Also, as has been worked out over time, the Malay *bumiputra*, or *pribumi* (sons of the soil), run both governments and fill the bureaucracies, armed forces, and police, while ethnic Chinese tend to business.

Left unspoken is the clearly demeaning implication that Malays lack entrepreneurial drive and ambition. Malays have long envied Chinese their commercial acumen and financial success; Chinese reflexively denigrate Malays as lazy. If this mutual finger-pointing and name-calling seem familiar to black and white Americans, it should. For similar reasons, the delicate topics are skirted in public, discussed only privately and with discretion.

In the aftermath of the 1969 riots, beginning in 1970, the then Prime Minister Tun Razak introduced a sweeping program of Malay affirmative action. This so-called bumiputra program granted special privileges to the majority community. Concurrently, Dr. Mahathir bin Mohamad, then struggling for his political life, published a highly controversial book, *The Malay Dilemma*. In it, Mahathir shocked the nation by openly acknowledging Malay indolence.

"In early Malaya, no great exertion or ingenuity was required to obtain food," he wrote. "Even the weakest and least diligent were able to live in comparative comfort, to marry, to procreate . . . the hot humid climate is not conducive to either vigorous work or even to mental activity." The British, recognizing the problem, brought in huge numbers of Chinese immigrants to run the colonial economy. Suddenly, Malays were second-class citizens of their own homeland. Wrote Mahathir, "[W]hatever the Malays could do, the Chinese could do better . . . before long the industrious and determined immigrants had displaced Malays in petty trading and all branches of skilled work."

Mahathir, a physician by training, became prime minister in 1981 and quickly stepped up the pace and scope of the bumiputra plan. He opened more doors of universities, the civil service, and high-profile, government-owned companies to Malays, lowering admission and hiring standards to boost their numbers. Chinese and Indian Malaysians felt discriminated against, though most also realized that they had little choice but to swallow their bitterness. Another Mahathir strategy put new emphasis on the Malay language, making it compulsory in schools while cutting back teaching in Chinese and English. Use of both had been widespread and gave Malaysians an invaluable leg up in globalized trade and diplomacy. Malaysians speculated that Mahathir, because his father was of mixed Malay-Indian ancestry, felt the need to continually reaffirm his Malay roots and that this accounted for his outspoken biases.

On the international stage, Mahathir assaulted the United States as a "state sponsor of terror." He baited American Jews and Israelis in return for Arab investment in Malaysia. Although Mahathir's anti-Semitism provoked a succession of American leaders during his twenty-two years in power, it didn't interfere with economic relations. The United States is Malaysia's leading trade partner, purchasing $34 billion worth of its goods in 2005, while selling $10 billion.

Malaysians, now well off in the emerging economic world, no longer seek U.S. government aid, though they would welcome more private investment. Actually, the two have done business in a big way for nearly 150 years: the Union Army bought tin from what was then

Malaya during the Civil War, and Henry Ford purchased rubber to make tires for his Model T. Today, ExxonMobil and Murphy Oil are the two largest foreign investors in the country. Scores of major American corporations, among them Motorola, which produces 95 percent of its laptops in Malaysia, Intel, and toymaker Mattel run profitable manufacturing operations in the technology and industrial parks that Mahathir developed. As U.S. ambassador Christopher La Fleur told us, "This is the country with which America has the best economic relations about which Americans know nothing."

By focusing so much attention on Malay rights, Mahathir was attempting a tricky juggling act, acceding to a less threatening set of demands for economic advancement while trying to hold back the "green tide" of Islamic extremists. Finally, in 2002, he gave in and declared that Malaysia was an "Islamic fundamentalist state" and that all Malays were "proud" of this. In the end, Mahathir's rhetoric succeeded only in bottling up frustration among true fundamentalists while stirring extremists toward further provocations.

Increased cultural cross-fertilization with Arabs, beginning in the early 1980s, led to great numbers of young Malay men studying in the Middle East and bringing their newfound asceticism back home to an impressionable audience. The Egypt-based Islamic Brotherhood inspired many Malays. Extremists from Indonesia, such as Abu Bakar Ba'asyir, who were given refuge during the Suharto years, furthered the process through their teaching and preaching. Four al-Qaeda adherents chosen to carry out an abortive plot to hijack a plane and crash it into the U.S. Bank Tower in Los Angeles in 2002 were Malaysians. With a no-visa welcome mat laid out for Middle Easterners, Malaysia became a safe house for men such as Khalid al-Mihdhar and Nawaf al-Hazmi, two of the 9/11 Pentagon bombers.

On the other hand, Mahathir's race-based policies helped meek, impoverished Malays achieve a level of self-confidence and prosperity they had never imagined. In a single generation, Malays whose parents scratched out a bare-bones existence raising tapioca and living in *attap*-thatched huts in rural kampongs owned concrete bungalows. They drove Protons, built by a national car company that

Mahathir had muscled into existence. Government-mandated low interest rates, favorable to Malays, made it all possible.

But at the same time, many villagers flocking to the cities in pursuit of higher education and better jobs found themselves dwelling in mixed neighborhoods, among Chinese and Indian neighbors. In such unfamiliar circumstances, they felt alone, rootless, and bereft. This urbanization and cultural dislocation contributed to Malays' identifying themselves for the first time with Palestinians, Iraqis, Iranians, and others in the greater umma. Like Jamaluddin Mansor, they turned with new interest to Islam and were convinced that their previous level of faith was inadequate, if not sinful. "People are looking for the correct path, for the truth," Jamaluddin told us. "They want to go back to true Islamic beliefs. You in the West may call this 'fundamentalism,' but that can have positive or negative implications. In the West, terms like 'fundamentalist' and 'conservative' can be applied as benchmarks. In Islam, we're all fundamentalists. Islam has no gradations, no direction toward greater or lesser orthodoxy. It's clearly defined in the Koran and it is very straightforward: you lead a good life on Earth and you go to Heaven."

Explicit in Jamaluddin's evaluation, which is widely held by Muslims whom most Americans would term fundamentalists, is a basic distinction between Islam and Christianity or Judaism: A Christian or a Jew may subscribe to any in a broad range of interpretations, from ultraorthodox to ultraliberal, and still be regarded as a "good" member of the faith. But there is no such thing as a "good" or a "bad" Muslim. There is no cherry-picking; for example, keeping dietary laws at home but eating haram in restaurants. One is either a Muslim or one is not. By this definition, a terrorist, who snuffs out the lives of innocents, is not a Muslim. "Moderates" fall back on this rationale to distance themselves from radicals.

Jamaluddin dismissed any suggestion that Islam was out of step with a rapidly modernizing Malaysia. Rather, he argued, since Allah was the absolute master of all that transpires, Islam was fully in sync with the amassing of great wealth as well as with the most advanced scientific knowledge. "Acquisition of knowledge is the foundation of Islam," he said. "In medicine, engineering, science, mathematics, it's all been basic to Islam since the time of the Prophet, peace be upon him. Over that knowledge are the Koran and the Hadith. They form the umbrella. Allah has given us water, sunlight, and air; seeds and earth; vegetables, fish, and animals. It is the responsibility of Muslims to care for these gifts. We may make money based on what we take from these gifts and how we use them."

He himself was an example of how Muslims may benefit from Allah's beneficence. "God put oil and gas in the earth. I extract it and make money. I use some of that money to publish magazines that advise men and women how to live a full Islamic life." What distinguished him from Western capitalists was his belief that he was simply a temporal steward of his wealth. "All the money in my pocket belongs to God. As a good CEO, I must use it to care for my employees and to protect the environment."

17

The Prime Minister

When Mahathir bin Mohammed resigned as prime minister in October 2003 at age seventy-eight, the Bush administration, along with many Malaysians, breathed a sigh of relief. Certainly Mahathir had performed economic miracles that in a very real sense confounded the antimodernist trend of radical Islam. But he had been a strident, divisive figure as well.

One particularly abhorrent step in his relentless drive to retain power over twenty-two years was the jailing in August 2000 of his deputy prime minister and longtime protégé Anwar Ibrahim on charges of sodomy and corruption, charges that many Malaysians and knowledgeable Americans considered trumped up. Anwar by then had influential friends in and around the Clinton administration. These advisers convinced President Clinton to cancel a planned White House meeting with Mahathir in reprisal.

In 1998, Clinton had dispatched Vice President Al Gore to Kuala Lumpur, where he went out of his way to encourage Malaysians to topple Mahathir. Speaking at a formal dinner of the Asia-Pacific Economic Cooperation conference, Gore said, "[W]e hear calls for democracy, calls for reform . . . we hear them today—right here, right now—among the brave people of Malaysia." Then he turned on his heel and stalked out of the hall. In Washington, Democrats and Republicans alike applauded Gore's candor. But whatever he had hoped to achieve, perhaps a Philippines-style People Power uprising, his clumsy intervention backfired miserably. Malaysians across the political spectrum rebuked him, charging that he had insinuated himself into their domestic affairs and had attempted to provoke rebellion.

Throughout the region, critics were quick to point out that American leaders didn't publicly stand up to great powers such as China or Russia, but felt free to insult small countries such as Malaysia or Burma. Gore's remarks also rekindled memories around Southeast Asia of then Vice President George H. W. Bush's 1981 paean in Manila to Philippines president Marcos, praising the dictator's "adherence to democratic principles."

That level of insensitivity by two U.S. vice presidents, a Democrat and a Republican, still causes people to shake their heads in wonder at Americans' stunning ignorance. Many Malaysians were pleased to see the younger Bush defeat Gore in 2000. And when the 9/11 attacks struck, Mahathir reacted swiftly, positively, and sympathetically, offering cooperation from Malaysia's intelligence services. Mahathir held his fire through the Afghanistan invasion. Then came Iraq. "We watched in awe as Bush became the most hated man in the world," Minister of Education Mustapha Mohammed told us.

But for all the repugnance Mahathir voiced publicly in the wake of the Iraq invasion, he still had his vanity, and in May 2002, seven months before retiring, Mahathir visited Bush in the White House. A one-on-one meeting in the Oval Office with the president of the United States, whomever he may be, confers a stamp of authentication that few world leaders are prepared to bypass. The get-together was meant to tone down the high-decibel discord between the two men and their nations. Instead, it backfired, further soiling Mahathir's reputation at the end of his reign.

The meeting was misbegotten from the outset. It had been arranged by the lobbyist Jack Abramoff, working through Bush's chief aide, Karl Rove. Abramoff charged the Malaysian a $1.2 million fee to set it up. When word of the payment leaked out during congressional investigations of Abramoff, it evoked irate public reaction among Malaysians. Mahathir was forced to acknowledge the payment, but he insisted that meetings with the president of the United States always were arranged by lobbyists, and for a fee.

"It is true that somebody paid but I don't think it was the [Malaysian] government," he asserted fuzzily. "I did not touch the money at all. In the U.S., it is a practice that if you want to meet their leader, you have to go through a lobbyist and the lobbyist has to be paid. That is their system. It is not corruption at all and it is very open, but they don't reveal names."

Mahathir said that the Washington-based Heritage Foundation, an influential, nonprofit, conservative think tank, had urged him to seek the meeting so he could help "influence [Bush] in some way regarding U.S. policies." The Heritage Foundation had for years denounced Mahathir for his anti-Americanism. But in the summer of 2001, it did an abrupt about-face, financing a trip to Kuala Lumpur for three members of the House of Representatives and their spouses. In preparation, Heritage put on briefings for the delegation titled "Malaysia: Standing Up for Democracy" and "U.S. and Malaysia: Ways to Cooperate in Order to Influence Peace and Stability in Southeast Asia."

If any goodwill came out of the Oval Office meeting it died aborning. Following the invasion of Iraq, Mahathir lashed out at the United States as a "rogue nation." And at a summit gathering of the Organization of the Islamic Conference, he slipped back into his comfort zone, charging that "Jews control the world by proxy." That earned him a sharp slap from Washington and put relations back in the deep freeze.

In 2003, Abdullah bin Haji Ahmad Badawi succeeded Mahathir as Malaysia's prime minister; the one clocking out on the punch-card system he had instituted for all government workers, and the other clocking in. The United States anticipated that Abdullah would tone down the anti-American, anti-Semitic rhetoric. Broadly speaking, he did. But he did not relent in open criticism of the Bush administration's policies in Iraq and the greater Middle East.

Unlike Mahathir, who had scrambled up through the rough-and-tumble of domestic party politics, Abdullah was a sophisticated government servant and diplomat. He came from a pious Muslim family and held a degree in Islamic studies from the University of Malaya, the nation's premier institution of higher learning. This background gave him unquestioned religious pedigree and credentials. But while

Abdullah was considered unambiguously pious, he also was known as a religious moderate, just the sort of Muslim whom the United States wanted to see in charge. At home, Malaysians called him "Mr. Clean" and looked to him to eliminate, or at least reduce, the corruption that had grown endemic during Mahathir's prolonged stay in power.

He got off to a promising start. Seeking to distance himself from Mahathir's identification with extremism, Abdullah quickly began advocating a uniquely Malaysian interpretation of the faith, known as Islam Hadari. Meaning "Civilizational Islam" in Arabic, it is meant to imply that Islam is a modulating influence on the world. The concept, established under another name by former prime minister Tunku Abdul Rahman in 1957, holds that the religion is fully compatible with modern development and with peaceful coexistence between Muslims and non-Muslims.

Abdullah took his program on the road, assuring foreign governments that under his administration Malaysia would work with the West in determining the root causes of Islamic terrorism and eliminating them. Speaking at New Zealand's Victoria University in March 2005, he said, "Malaysia has adopted Islam Hadari as the long-term national approach for providing socioeconomic justice and fairness to its citizens. . . . This approach has also been inspired by our firm belief that good governance, healthy democratic practices, empowerment of the citizenry through education, and equitable sharing of the benefits of economic growth will remove any attractiveness toward radicalism and blunt any tendencies toward extremism."

In Washington, the Bush administration and Congress were delighted, foreseeing Islam Hadari as a model for governments in other Muslim countries. Then Abdullah's wife, Endon Mahmood, died of breast cancer at age sixty-four, and his determination began to slip. She had undergone chemotherapy treatments in Los Angeles for two years, as had her twin sister. Abdullah often referred to Endon as his "number-one supporter," and friends said he was unable to bounce back once she no longer was at his side.

Much like President Yudhoyono in Indonesia, Abdullah seemed to lack confidence in facing down demands from extremists. The two men and the political circumstances they inherited were remarkably similar. Although Indonesia went through three short-term presidencies between the fall of Suharto and the election of Yudhoyono, both he and Abdullah were seen as understated, self-effacing leaders confronted by the daunting task of replacing strongmen who had defined their countries for a generation or more through the sheer strength of their domineering personalities. Both new leaders were expected to introduce democratic reforms. But in the increased space opened up by those reforms, Islamic puritans were empowered to challenge both to reverse course. Critics charged that they soon showed themselves to be slow-moving and indecisive and that they were losing control over rebounding corruption. A key difference in conditions in the two countries is that while Indonesian extremists feel that they have little to lose by conducting their protests in the streets, Malaysians are unwilling to put their financial gains at risk. Malaysia's fundamentalists have capitalized on the broad desire to maintain calm, imposing a kind of public blackmail to peacefully push the nation toward greater Islamic control.

As in Indonesia, Saudi-funded mosques and religious boarding schools are proliferating in Malaysia. So is the demand for Sharia to take supremacy in a number of areas of law handled by civil courts. One such case was that of Azlina binti Jailani, a Malay Muslim, who in 1998 had herself baptized a Roman Catholic. She changed her name to Lina Joy and made plans to marry her Christian fiancé, a Malaysian Indian. Then the Sharia court stepped in. As defined by Malaysia's constitution, all Malays are born Muslims and remain Muslims for life. They are forbidden to convert and are put at risk of being declared apostate (although non-Malays are welcome to convert to Islam).

Joy and her attorney, Benjamin Dawson, a Christian, took her case through a series of civil courts, arguing that the Sharia court had no jurisdiction over her, since she no longer was a Muslim. Dawson also warned that if Joy was not permitted to marry her fiancé, this would greatly erode Malaysia's vaunted image as a secular state and confirm that it had been overtaken by Islamization. The civil judges supported the Sharia court and ruled against Joy. Extremists threatened her with death, forcing her to go into hiding. Malik Imtiaz

Sarwar, a Muslim attorney who had presented a brief to Malaysia's Appeals Court on Joy's behalf, also was threatened with death. Malik sponsored a series of religious-freedom forums around the country. Reacting to the public firestorm that broke over the Joy case, Prime Minister Abdullah ordered the meetings shut down.

This heightened the already emerging impression that Abdullah was caving in to Islamist pressure. "Malaysia is at a crossroads," Dawson told a reporter. "Do we go down the Islamic road, or do we maintain the secular character of the federal constitution, which has been eroding in the last ten years?" On May 30, 2007, Malaysia's Federal Court rejected Lina Joy's appeal, declaring that "a person cannot, at one's whims and fancies, renounce or embrace a religion." Not surprisingly, Abdullah dismissed any allegations that his country was sliding toward what Americans view as fundamentalism. He likewise brushed aside any suggestion that he was either permitting or encouraging such drift.

We interviewed the prime minister in his office, a spacious, airy room lined with exquisitely carved teak paneling, in the new administrative capital, Putrajaya, an ambitious, planned city south of Kuala Lumpur. He insisted that there was no place under the Islam Hadari canopy for fundamentalists, at least not according to the American definition of the term. "What you describe as fundamentalism, with its references to extremism and terrorism, is associated with the Iranian revolution," he said. "That was the start of political Islam and then it was projected onto the world platform. I don't subscribe to anything like that."

At the same time, Abdullah argued, the Bush administration was wrong, at very least mistaken and possibly outright lying, in insisting that Iran secretly was developing nuclear weapons. He, like other Muslim leaders and intellectuals in Southeast Asia, reminded us that the administration's war-justifying claim that Saddam Hussein held weapons of mass destruction in Iraq's arsenal was false.

The day before our interview, Abdullah had met in the same office with Iranian president Mahmoud Ahmadinejad. The outspoken, often outrageous Iranian, who had said, "Satan inspires Mr. Bush" and vowed repeatedly to "wipe Israel off the map," was on a diplomatic sweep through Southeast Asian Muslim capitals. He assured Abdullah that Iran was developing nuclear power strictly for peaceful purposes. "There is no reason for Iran not to develop peaceful nuclear energy," Abdullah told us. "You don't trust him. But I do. I trust him. I believe him. There is nothing more to say."

The closely related, sensitive question of Israel and Palestine, likewise, was to him an open-and-shut case. "I see the anger here among Malaysians as recognition of reality," Abdullah said. In an apparent desire to have Americans think afresh about its Middle East policies and to identify with the Palestinian cause, he pointed out that not all Palestinians were Muslims; some were Christians. "They're just a group of people who have been deprived of their land and bullied in every sense of the word. The so-called arbiters, the middlemen, have never been fair. These people want their homeland back; they want to be independent and sovereign. This is not a matter just of Islam; it's a matter of human rights, of humanity. United States policy there is simply unjust."

Deputy Prime Minister and Foreign Minister Najib Abdul Razak (whose late father was the dancing prime minister in the old days) further refined Malaysia's position on Israel and Palestine when we called on him in an adjacent office. "We're not asking the United States to turn its back on Israel," Najib said. "Just have a more balanced approach in the Middle East." Such balance would mean Washington insisting on a two-state solution, with Israel giving back the West Bank territory it annexed after the 1967 war. Beyond that, he said, the "tricky part" would be resolving the future of Jerusalem. Recognizing that no American administration could be expected to dramatically shift Middle East policy, Najib said that Israel-Palestine didn't have to be a "zero-sum game" for the United States if it seriously wished to achieve warmer associations with Muslims in Southeast Asia.

"America can improve its relationships by employing soft power instead of always relying on its military might. When the Peace Corps was in Malaysia, America was the most popular country in the world for us. What you need to do in this part of the world is revive programs to help relieve poverty, to improve education, to acquaint people with the better side of American culture. These are things that would go down well with the general population."

Najib paused and, peering over the top of his glasses, added, "Imagine what the United States could do with the $600 billion you've already spent on the war in Iraq if you had used it to help alleviate the world's problems. But, now, history will judge Bush only by his failure in Iraq."

In fact, though, relations between the governments of Malaysia and the United States are better than America's image would indicate. Its law enforcement agencies and its small but well-armed military forces, particularly its navy, deployed in the strategic Strait of Malacca, cooperate closely with their U.S. counterparts. The same week that Iran's Ahmadinejad was making his state visit, Admiral William Fallon was in town, resplendent in summer whites, holding discussions with Najib, who would succeed Abdullah as prime minister in 2009, and senior Malaysian naval commanders. Fallon, chief of the U.S. Pacific Command at the time, was soon to be appointed to replace General John Abizaid as head of the Central Command, in charge of all U.S. forces in the Middle East, with oversight responsibility for the conduct of the war in Iraq. In March 2008, a year after taking charge of Central Command, Fallon was forced to resign from the navy owing to differences with the Bush administration over its policies in Iraq.

Because of public sensitivities, the Malaysian government soft-pedals its cooperation with the United States. "We avoid it because the public keeps bringing up Israel and Palestine and the U.S. rejection of Hamas after free and fair elections," said Najib. Still, under Abdullah, Malaysia had refrained from fueling anti-Americanism. "Mahathir was strident," Najib acknowledged, "but we've never gone around pandering to Islamic objections to the United States. What you see and hear from the public is spontaneous." Conversely, he said, "There are many things Malaysians like about Americans, many things we share in common." He ticked off "rule of law, democracy, and freedom," though many Americans and some Malaysians would argue that Malaysia's adherence to them was debatable. "Also, we're both interested in technology. And we're crazy about McDonald's and Starbucks."

There is no argument about that last part. Just a few steps away from the prime minister's office, in a basement-level food court adjacent to the soaring National Mosque, baristas at the San Francisco Coffee Shop, their hair covered modestly, were serving cups of American Blend and lattes along with bagels and cream cheese to civil servants on midmorning break.

While offering a generally conciliatory overtone, both Abdullah and his deputy, Najib, bitterly complained about the American propensity to lecture, particularly on human rights issues. "The U.S. is always chastising us for our human rights record," said Najib. A special sore point is the draconian Internal Security Act, under which Malaysia (and Singapore, which has a similar law) may arrest without warrant or evidence anyone it suspects of potentially threatening national security and hold these suspects incommunicado, indefinitely, and without trial. Reflecting on the U.S. internment camp at Guantánamo Bay and the Abu Ghraib prison scandal as well as assorted alleged murders in Iraq, Najib said, "Anything we might do here under the ISA is like a walk in the park by comparison. Yet, we don't criticize you. You get away with it and you criticize us."

Despite the Malaysian government's differences with the United States, all centered on foreign policy, Prime Minister Abdullah found in George W. Bush a kindred spirit. The connection, not surprisingly, was faith. Our interview took place on a Friday, and Abdullah was wearing full Malay Sabbath mosquegoing regalia, the *baju Malayu*, a rosy-hued tunic and trousers with knee-length sarong wrapped around his waist and a black velvet *kopiah*, a pillbox-style hat. Abdullah recalled his own Oval Office meeting with Bush in July 2004. In a convincing voice, not unlike Bush's own when he spoke of his first meeting with Russian president Vladimir Putin ("I looked the man in the eye. I was able to get a sense of his soul."), Abdullah told us he could tell that the president was "a very religious man. I could see it in his eyes." He told Bush that Islam Hadari equated with "trustworthy government," and Bush responded, "Amen." Then, continued Abdullah, "I told him that this was Allah's teaching and he said, 'Amen.' He repeated 'Amen' again and again as we spoke."

Abdullah said he was certain that Bush was "sincere about not tolerating *his own perception* [here Abdullah added emphasis] of unjust regimes." But, he said, "his dealing with these regimes, invading Iraq and the hostile reaction to Hamas's victory in the Palestinian election, has gotten him into a hell of a lot of trouble. Now he doesn't know how to get out of Iraq."

The prime minister said he told the president that there were "many shades" of democracy for many countries, "not just Washington and Whitehall," and that his administration was "interfering too much in other people's systems." He questioned Bush intensively on his philosophy of thrusting American-style democracy on Muslim countries. "I asked him, 'Are you telling people that you want them to adopt democracy, but that *you* [again, Abdullah's inflection] have the final veto?' He told me, 'No, I won't do that.' He assured me that he wouldn't interfere. That's why I was so sad when he made his announcement about Hamas and refused to cooperate with a legitimately elected Palestinian government. That's bad. That's why people are angry and why there's so much hatred toward Bush. Unfortunately, you can't divorce Bush from America."

The advent of the Obama administration puts that claim to the test in both countries.

18

The Analysts

Malaysia has an impressive corps of highly sophisticated foreign affairs experts, many of them educated not just at the most prestigious universities at home but also in the United States, Britain, and Australia. To a man, and a few women, they're outspokenly critical of the United States for what they consider biased, heavy-handed policies. During the colonial era, their predecessors used to mock "Britannia" for "waiving the rules." The related vein of ironic disparagement is not coincidental; Malaysia, like much of the rest of the region, still lives with a loathing of colonialism and sees the United States as continuing many of the same tactics.

Although they had their differences with the Clinton White House and its predecessors from both parties, the analysts reserved special disdain for the Bush administration and its Middle East course. They looked forward to the Obama administration with optimism, not only for new direction toward Iraq and Israel-Palestine, but also in providing sorely needed balance for the thousand-pound panda in the room: China.

Much of what these critics had to say grated on both of us (even though one of us adamantly opposed the war in Iraq while the other wholeheartedly supported it). They were unremittingly harsh and unyielding. But to reject their consensus out of hand as so much invective would be mistaken. Rather, we found it instructive to listen more than argue and to recognize points of mutual misunderstanding: They said "Bush" and we heard "America." We said "terrorist" and they heard "Islam."

Many Malaysian analysts personally hold warm feelings toward the United States and Americans and want to see conditions develop that would permit the two governments to improve relations. They believe that by the end of the Bush administration the ball lay idle in the U.S. court. Despite their high hopes for the Obama administration, they worried that more pressing issues would keep it from addressing the underlying causes of Americans' poor relations with Muslims.

The sense of the United States being instinctively anti-Islamic is widespread, and its repercussions are found among some of the most unlikely sources. "I've lectured to a thousand military commanders in Southeast Asia in the last six years," said K.S. Balakrishnan, a political-military specialist at the University of Malaya, "and 80, even 90 percent of them are pleased when bad things happen to the United States." Balakrishnan, an ethnic Indian, said that in addition to the usual suspicions and hostilities, officers criticized the 2006 congressional rejection of a proposal for Dubai Ports World to take over management of several U.S. ports. "That went down very badly," he said. "It was seen as yet another sign of Americans being anti-Muslim." Balakrishnan made it plain that he'd like to see the United States regain the stature it enjoyed when its anti-Communist war in Indochina bought Malaysia and other regional countries the time they desperately required to begin developing their economies. What the United States needs to do to begin offsetting current attitudes is to reach out to "show Muslims that you're not their enemy," he said. But he anticipated that there would not be much of a reversal in public opinion for "at least fifty years" because "that's how deeply emotional things are here."

Mohammed Jawhar Hassan is the chairman of the preeminent foreign policy think tank in Malaysia, the quasi-governmental Institute of Strategic and International Studies (ISIS). An intense man with a whippetlike physique and a piercing stare, Jawhar had served in a number of sensitive intelligence positions and enjoyed unusual access to the national leadership. His assessment of the United States was uniformly hostile: "How can you be so stupid, so naive, so cocksure of yourselves? If you continue trying to force more democracy on the Middle East, you will have far greater problems than you have today in Iraq. You preach and you pontificate; you accuse others of belonging to an 'Axis of Evil' and then you do worse things than they do."

Because the Bush administration established a far-reaching reputation for hypocrisy, said Jawhar, a highly touted tour of the region in 2006 by his public diplomacy chief, Karen Hughes, turned into "a shambles and a failure." Hughes, who had been masterful in honing Bush's persona for American voters, attempted to justify the president's rationale for invading Iraq among Malaysians and Indonesians. But, said Jawhar, "You can't sell rotten fruit."

Like think tanks everywhere, ISIS frequently hosts discussions for diplomats, academics, journalists, and other foreign-affairs specialists at its headquarters in a graceful, colonial-era mansion in a hilly, wooded enclave overlooking Kuala Lumpur. Simons was invited to address a gathering during a visit to Malaysia. The topic was advertised as U.S. policy in Iraq, and more than a hundred guests attended. But the question-and-answer period quickly turned to Israel-Palestine. A retired Malaysian army general with a Sandhurstian mustache rose. "It's a well-known fact that Jews, through their control of the American economy, dictate to your government," the general said in clipped English. How did he know this? He'd read it in *The International Jew*, a four-volume work first published in the 1920s in Dearborn, Michigan, by Ford Motor Company founder and proud anti-Semite Henry Ford Sr., the onetime importer of Malayan rubber. Bookstores in Kuala Lumpur provide generous shelf space for anti-Semitic books and tracts in Malay, English, and Arabic. Prime Minister Mahathir, when he was in office, distributed copies of *Protocols of the Elders of Zion*, a forged turn-of-the-century Russian secret police screed, to all members of the National Assembly.

Privately reviewing the exchange after the forum, Jawhar said that Malaysian bitterness about U.S. policy on the Israel-Palestine issue could not be overestimated. "Look," he said, "Malaysia cooperates very closely with the United States on intelligence, military matters, trade, and a number of other issues. We don't talk about it publicly because, in a democracy, when the people disagree with government policy, you can have real trouble. Our only real issue with the United States is over your policy in Israel, as you heard here today. The fringe of that sentiment translates into violence and even terrorism. The United States is consistently inconsistent when it comes to the behavior of the Israelis and the Palestinians. And more broadly, you always take the hardest line. You don't seem to know how to resolve problems except by terminal threat or actual war."

Lee Poh Ping, a Malaysian of Chinese ancestry, might be expected to have a softer take on the United States and its policies toward Islam. But he did not. Lee holds a doctorate in political science from Cornell University and teaches Southeast Asian studies at the National University of Malaysia. We met in the professor's cluttered office on the university's handsomely groomed campus in suburban Bangi. Shambling and rumpled, Lee said that the United States had yet to reawaken to the importance of Southeast Asia, a region considered so critical during the 1960s and 1970s that fifty-eight thousand Americans died in a failed attempt to save it from communism.

"Except for the terrorism element, the United States has lost interest in Southeast Asia since the Cold War," he said. "Southeast Asia is very much tangential to U.S. foreign policy. Unfortunately, that is typically shortsighted of Americans." Still, he held out a sliver of hope for reengagement once Americans come to realize what the region can mean to U.S. aspirations for long-term world leadership. "You do have considerable manufacturing and marketing involvement here," Lee said. "Well, perhaps one day you'll wake up when you begin to see the value of Southeast Asia in containing China."

A huge influx of visitors from China is immediately evident to anyone strolling through the fabulous new airports, hotels, and shopping malls of Kuala Lumpur, Singapore, Bangkok, and other capitals. Clusters of Chinese tourists have largely replaced

Japanese tour groups, shuffling behind flag-waving guides and spending big. Tourists aren't the only Chinese visitors. Dark-suited delegations of Chinese diplomats, government officials, bankers, businessmen, and investors are everywhere. American counterparts are few and far between. One U.S. embassy official in Kuala Lumpur lamented that the State Department lagged far behind Beijing's Foreign Ministry in funding delegates to attend regional conferences. "If they send ten, we may spring for one," he said. "Or we'll give it a miss altogether. That kind of thing shows disrespect; it shows we don't take the people here seriously; it does tremendous harm."

Professor Lee put it this way: "The Chinese are getting very good at public diplomacy, soft diplomacy, charm offensive, whatever you want to call it. Our perception is that they want to see Southeast Asia succeed. They're using some of their economic advancement to benefit us." By comparison, he pointedly recalled that U.S. secretary of state Condoleezza Rice failed to attend the 2005 Association of Southeast Asian Nations (ASEAN) conference in Kuala Lumpur. Her absence stirred so much resentment that the next year Rice broke away from critical talks on Lebanon being held in Rome to put in a hurried appearance at the ASEAN session. Southeast Asia was the arena in which the United States and China could come together, said Lee. "There's no real conflict between the U.S. and China . . . yet. But I fear that U.S. politicians, Republicans and Democrats, could elevate tensions for domestic political purposes."

When we asked how the United States could improve relations with Malaysia and benefit from its strong links with the Middle East, Lee said, "I'd advise the Obama administration to turn down the rhetoric on Islam. This is calculated to offend." While acknowledging that Muslims can be "too sensitive," he said that some comments ("Islamo-Fascist," for example) were grossly offensive. "The neocons act as if the United States is the world and the world is the United States. The U.S. will have to come to the realization, especially in Southeast Asia, that it is no longer a unipolar world. The point is that the U.S. is the only military superpower, but it can't decide alone what is going to happen in the world." He conceded, though, that "nothing can happen without the U.S."

Of all the strategic analysts we met in K.L., none was better connected to the current government than Abdul Razak Baginda, director of the independent Malaysian Strategic Research Center. He was particularly well plugged in to Najib bin-Abdul Razak, who held the deputy prime minister and foreign minister portfolios. While critical of some U.S. policies, Baginda was more evenhanded and less didactic, skeptical of China as well as the United States. And he was unabashedly candid in expressing his discomfort about the rise of Islamic fundamentalism in Malaysia.

A tweedy type at age forty-six, with droopy, world-weary eyes and an unruly mop of black hair through which he frequently ran his fingers, he was loquacious and at ease using American-style political-science cant. "The United States no longer has a vision for Southeast Asia; just how it fits into the big counterterrorism picture," he said. "I'm beginning to doubt the reliability of the U.S. Invading Iraq was a reckless thing and it did terrible damage to your credibility. It's stunning—the United States of America, with all its brainpower, missed the historically proven need for an exit strategy."

As a self-professed secular Muslim, Baginda said he was proud that Malaysia had become "a shining example" to the rest of the Islamic world by sharply reducing poverty. Other Islamic states were failing to examine themselves from within. Muslims in those countries were fighting against the West because that was the only way for them to express their frustration with themselves and their repressive rulers. But even in Malaysia, "the Puritans" had seized control. "I, like most Muslims, know very little about Islam," he confessed. "So I surrender completely to the Puritans. They dominate the moral high ground. The problem is that this kind of attitude by people like me cedes the upper hand to the extremists. Believe me, 'extremists' is the correct word, because all Muslims are supposed to be 'fundamentalists.'"

He tilted back in his office chair and laced his fingers behind his head. "To tell you the truth, I'm scared shitless, because we're putting religion first, even if it's irrational. If the extremists take over this country, people like me will have no space, no independence. You can't argue when the clincher is, 'It's what the Koran says. It's what God wants.' Hell, what am I telling you, an American? The same thing is happening in your country."After having been subjected to so much unrelenting criticism of the United States, it was refreshing to listen to a Malaysian as he opened up and frankly discussed both of our homelands, warts and all. That's why we were stunned by what happened next.

In October 2006, eight months after we left Malaysia, the gruesome remains of a human body were discovered near a hilltop dam in the Kuala Lumpur suburb of Shah Alam. There was no corpse, really, just bloody hunks of flesh and shattered bone. DNA and chemical testing determined that the victim had been a twenty-eight-year-old woman from Mongolia named Altantuya Shaariibuu. She had been shot twice in the head at close range, then blown to smithereens with C4 plastic explosive.

In Malaysia, only select law-enforcement units may possess this sophisticated material. Investigators soon arrested two members of an elite police unit known as the Special Action Force, which guards VIPs, and charged them with murdering Shaariibuu.

Then police arrested Abdul Razak Baginda. They charged the analyst with abetting the murder. He soon confessed that he'd had an eight-month-long extramarital affair with Shaariibuu, beginning during a trip he made to Mongolia. Malaysian news media, so self-restrained on so many matters, shifted into breathless high gear. Photographs appeared, showing her to be a stunning beauty. Conflicting reports tumbled over each other: the woman was a fashion model; she was fluent in Russian, Chinese, English, and French as well as her native Mongolian; she was secretly married to Baginda; they had a sixteen-month-old love child; she had come to Malaysia to demand money from him.

Then Shaariibuu's mother gave an interview to a newspaper in Ulan Bator, the Mongolian capital: her daughter had never been a fashion model; she was a businesswoman; yes, she was good at languages; yes, she and Baginda knew each other, but her baby had a Mongolian father, as did her two older children; she had flown to

Kuala Lumpur with a sister and another woman, a friend, to meet a business partner. The friend reported her missing. The remains were located three weeks later.

It wasn't long before the Malaysian media moved from Baginda's relationship with Shaariibuu to speculating about his close ties to Deputy Prime Minister and Foreign Minister (and prime minister-in-waiting) Najib: What might this connection signal about the woman's visit to Malaysia and why she was murdered? And what kind of business was she in, anyway? Baginda, it developed, was something of a businessman himself. He and several associates owned a relatively unknown company named Ombak Laut. That company, in turn, owned a company known as Perimekar, and *that* company was a Malaysian defense contractor. In 2002, Perimekar signed an agreement for the Malaysian Navy to purchase two new Scorpene-class submarines from French shipbuilder DCN International and an overhauled Agosta-70 submarine from Spain's Izar for a total of nearly $1 billion.

According to a report at the time in the Hong Kong–based bimonthly *Far Eastern Economic Review*, the three-submarine package included a $100 million commission to Perimekar. Then Ombak Laut sold 40 percent of Perimekar to another outfit, Lembaga Tabung Angkatan Tentera—the Defense Forces Fund Board—a huge social welfare organization operated by the Malaysian Ministry of Defense. Minister Najib denied that the government had paid the $100 million commission—but not that the fee had been paid, possibly by being hidden in the $1 billion purchase price for the submarines. He sounded a bit like former prime minister Mahathir attempting to explain the (relatively puny) $1.2 million payment to Jack Abramoff.

So there was smoke, but what about fire? Enter the maligned onetime deputy prime minister Anwar Ibrahim, who had by then served six years of hard time on charges of sodomy and corruption brought by Mahathir. After his release from prison, some of Anwar's American supporters had obtained for him a sinecure at Georgetown University, where he regrouped for a year. Now he was back in Malaysia, working hard to clear his name and to relaunch a once-skyrocketing political career.

Removing Najib, whom many Malaysians considered the de facto power in the Abdullah government, also would remove a major hurdle in Anwar's way. Anwar, who alleged that he had been railroaded into prison and, once there, beaten by guards, knew a good deal about the dubious independence of the Malaysian justice system. In a public statement on January 27, 2006, he claimed that one of the two police officers charged with Shaariibuu's murder regularly provided bodyguard services for Najib.

Anwar also raised questions over whether Najib, not only Baginda, personally knew Shaariibuu. It seemed that she had gone to Paris with both men and worked as their interpreter in the submarine deal. Anwar wondered if she had had information so damaging that someone in a position of power may have ordered special police agents to murder her and then destroy the evidence in such a singular manner. Perhaps something to do with the $100 million fee? "The facts of the case remain a guarded secret," Anwar offered straight-faced in a news release.

When mainstream media in Malaysia shied away from covering allegations of Najib's involvement in the scandal, the blogosphere erupted. Raja Petra Raja Kamaruddin, the fifty-eight-year-old editor of the popular Malaysia Today site, posted a widely read article alleging government corruption for withholding evidence and influencing the judiciary in the case. He was jailed for sedition. A visitor to Raja Petra's blog, author Syed Akbar Ali, was charged with the same offense for a comment he wrote in response.

On January 5, 2007, Judge K. N. Segara set the trial date for April 10, 2008, more than a year in the future. The reason was a backed-up docket. "Those longest on remand must get the earliest date," the judge told a packed and clamoring courtroom. "That is the system."

That was the first of numerous delays.

On October 31, the High Court acquitted Baginda.

A key witness, one who might have been able to connect the dots among Baginda, Najib, and Shaariibuu, could not be located. He was a private investigator named P. Balasubramaniam. He had been hired by Baginda, who allegedly opened up to him about his friend and mentor Najib. Balasubramaniam filed a declaration stating that the police had deliberately omitted information. The declaration claimed that both Najib and Baginda had a sexual relationship with Shaariibuu and that she was badgering them for $500,000 for her work on the submarine deal. Balasubramaniam quoted a text message Najib sent to Baginda after her body was discovered: "I am seeing IGP [inspector general of police] at eleven A.M. today . . . matter will be solved . . . be cool."

Within twenty-four hours of filing the declaration, Balasubramaniam retracted it, replacing it with one that erased all references to Najib. The detective and his family then disappeared. Their whereabouts remain a mystery.

Shortly afterward, Mongolia's honorary consul in Malaysia, Syed Abdul Rahman Alhabshi, a Malaysian citizen, flew to Ulan Bator and visited Shaariibuu's father, a physician. The doctor later told a French journalist that he handed over his daughter's papers to Syed, who had convinced him that as Mongolia's honorary representative he would work on her behalf. The documents never appeared in court. Syed made public statements absolving Najib of any connection with the dead woman. Then a photograph appeared on the Internet, showing Syed and Najib, posing next to each other in a large, elaborately furnished room. They were smiling.

The allegations of Najib's involvement in the murder were dismissed. In April 2009 Najib became Malaysia's prime minister. The two police officers were found guilty. They were sentenced to hang.

19

The Conservative

As far up the eastern side of the peninsula as it is possible to travel and still be in Malaysia dozes a little rubber-estate settlement with the delightful name of Jeli. On the edge of town, ringed by thick jungle, stands a slightly elevated clearing known as Bukit Bunga. It means Flower Hill. The rise offers a clear view across the shallow Golok River into Thailand and the equally sleepy border town of Tak Bai.

The residents of Tak Bai are subjects of the king of Thailand. But unlike 95 percent of the kingdom's sixty-two million people, they are not Buddhists. They are Malay Muslims, and a few more than a million of them live in Tak Bai and the rest of southern Thailand. Ethnically, linguistically, culturally, and religiously they are the same people as those living a few yards away, on the Malaysian side of the river.

Why this Islamic enclave is encapsulated in Buddhist Thailand is explained in large measure by how the former British Empire handled its real estate holdings, and created unnatural states out of former colonies. Much the same explanation lies behind the partitioning of the South Asian subcontinent into India and Pakistan, with anomalies such as Muslim Kashmir becoming part of Hindu-majority India and the unnatural division known as the Durand Line separating Afghanistan and Pakistan. It is similar, as well, to Britain's bundling of Shia, Sunni, and Kurdish Muslims into modern Iraq. The result in all cases has been open-ended strife. It is this history that feeds the fear and suspicion people in these lands—and throughout the Islamic world—have of the world's great postcolonial power, the United States of America.

While Kashmir and Iraq are well known, the story of the Malays of Thailand is not. Yet more than 3,500 people, Muslims and Buddhists, have been murdered in southen Thailand since 2004, and a full-blown Islamic insurgency is under way. Hardly a day goes by when someone isn't killed.

We will delve more deeply into this conflict when we cross the Golok into Tak Bai. For the moment, it is useful to know that the foundation was laid in 1902, when the Kingdom of Siam, as Thailand was then known, formally annexed the independent Malay Kingdom of Pattani, adjacent to the boundary of British-ruled Malaya. Seven years later, Great Britain and Siam signed the Bangkok Treaty of 1909, in which the British recognized Siamese sovereignty over Pattani. In return, Siam gave up its claim to another Muslim state, Kelantan, which became part of Malaya. The border moved but the people did not.

Today's Malaysian state of Kelantan includes Jeli and Flower Hill. Commuting between Malaysia and Thailand along this stretch of the Golok is a casual affair: either tuck your flip-flops under your arm, hoist your sarong, and wade through the tepid, knee-deep water, or step gingerly into a tippy, outboard-driven, long-tailed boat for a fifty-yard spin. With life on the Thai side frighteningly dangerous nowadays, few Malaysians make the trip. But Tak Bai residents cross all day long, to sell fragrant Thai rice and juicy mangoes in Jeli's amply stocked outdoor markets, to buy cheap batik cloth, or just to gossip with friends and relatives.

According to Thai authorities, some take back ammonium nitrate fertilizer, for making explosives, and unregistered mobile telephones, which they use to trigger bombs. Still, border guards manning wooden observation towers pay no attention to the crossings, although they are technically illegal. The Jeli *Immigresion Pos* was locked and gathering dust when we got there. Elsewhere along the four-hundred-mile border, a twelve-mile wall separates Malaysia from Thailand, and there has been talk of Malaysia adding six miles of fence. But to call the border, which separates two countries with two such distinctly different majority cultures and religions, "porous," in the sense that the U.S.-Mexico border is porous, is an understatement.

Kelantan is Malaysia's Islamic heartland, its Utah, the most conservative state in the country. It is the stronghold of the ultraconservative Parti Islam SeMalaysia, or PAS, which contends nationwide against the dominant and more-moderate United Malay National Organization (UMNO) for the Malay-Muslim vote.

Rohida Mohammed, like many Kelantanese Muslims, has family members on the Thai side of the river, and her sympathy runs deep. Rohida stopped crossing the river to Tak Bai in 2004. That year, on October 25, Thai soldiers and police killed eighty-six Muslims in what became known as the Tak Bai Massacre. "It's too dangerous," she told us. "Some of our family members come here to visit. They come for weddings and funerals. When there is a lot of killing there they all come here for safety. They're in a bad situation."

The Malays of southern Thailand want to reestablish an autonomous Muslim sultanate. The situation causes discomfort for both governments. The Thai government has implied that Malaysia encourages separatist activity, much of it violent. Malaysia heatedly denies this, but has given shelter to Muslims who slip across the border. The refugees can cause awkward problems for the government in Kuala Lumpur—reluctant to offend a neighbor and friend in Bangkok, as well as facing a touchy ethnic and religious issue at home—not wanting to return fellow Muslims to danger.

Rohida was at first uneasy discussing the subject with strangers. She supervises Malay and English instruction in Jeli's schools. We met her one Sunday, when she was working at Darul Falah (House of Success), which prepares girls and boys in public primary schools for exams. One of her colleagues, Eh Wang, a squarely built man with a hearty laugh and a thick thatch of white hair, was more relaxed, probably because of his unique background. As we sat in the shade of an ancient tree on the lush grounds of Darul Falah, snacking on watermelon and small cakes, Eh told us his story:

Ethnic Thai and Buddhist, Eh's family had lived in Malaysia for three generations. Still, he liked to refer to himself as "Siamese," and when traveling in Thailand he went by the Thai name Wang Srisuwan. He was fifty-five, and over the years he had taught

school and worked in the insurance business in Bangkok and Kuala
Lumpur. He felt equally at home in both societies. Now, though,
Malaysia was becoming more fundamentalist, and he worried that
this might soon cause difficulties for him and his family. "Religious
awareness among Malays is growing rapidly," he said. "I believe
it's a result of international influence." Young men from the Kelantan
area had gone to Afghanistan to fight the Soviets, and when they
returned, they were changed. "They brought a new religious para-
digm, a new mind-set. I think that's the same change that's taken
place in the South [of Thailand]."

Listening to his frank assessment, Rohida relaxed and said she
thought he had it right. She was thirty-six and wore a floral scarf
over her head. She said that her mother, who did not cover her hair,
instructed Rohida to do so when she turned thirteen. Now, she said,
lifting her chin toward a long outdoor table lined with little girls in
white head scarves, they start covering as young as seven. "The difference is that people of my parents' generation had very poor education in Islam. They did what the imam told them, and that wasn't
much." Rohida, born in 1970 in the wake of the bloody 1969 K.L.
race riots, received an education suffused with Malay culture and
religion. Now the public school system includes training in Islam
for Malay children—and "morals" for non-Malays. Organized religious discussion groups are part of the workday for all civil servants
as well. "I am a product of those policies," she said.

While she didn't consider herself especially pious, she knew much
more about Islam than her parents did, including how to pronounce
Arabic when she recites from the Koran. Piety, however, did not mean
support for extremists and terrorists. "My religion teaches peace," said
Rohida, "and that's what we teach in school." The government syllabus
did not include Middle Eastern politics or U.S. policy. But "if children
ask about Palestine, for example, we discuss it in terms of the need to
protect our religion." Osama bin Laden and al-Qaeda were off-limits.
"Osama is for violence, and I cannot support that."

A one-hour drive from Jeli is Kota Bharu, the state capital of
Kelantan, the conservative heart of the most conservative part
of Malaysia. About 95 percent of its 287,000 people are Muslim.

In 2005, the local PAS-run government declared that Kota Bharu, which means New City, also would be known as Islamic City. Some regulations the government began adopting are more severe than those of Saudi Arabia: House lights stay on during showings in movie theaters, those few the government hasn't already shut down. Supermarket shoppers must pass through gender-segregated checkout lines. Morals squads can barge into hotel rooms on the hunt for couples, including foreign tourists, who may be breaking *khalwat*, the proximity law. Traditional *wayang kulit* puppet shadow plays, which predate Islam by a millennium and are based on Hindu myths, have been banned.

Five times a day, when the muezzin's call to prayer rings from the city's numerous minarets, and is amplified inside public buildings and shopping malls, all activity must halt for a respectful moment. Alcohol, of course, is banned, as is "revealing" dress. An exposed navel could cost a woman $178, a fine more than twice the cost of the best hotel room in town. Those desperate for relief must flee to Thailand and its relaxed sense of *sanuk* (fun).

By the standards of Kota Bharu, Mohammed Khauri Wan Ali was a moderate. Over glasses of orange juice and a plate of sliced pineapple in a hotel coffee shop looking out on broad, quiet streets, Khauri discussed Islam's discrepancies with Western philosophy. "I ask my friends why they're so het up about the United States," he said. "After all, the Americans bomb everyone, not just Iraq, but Japan, Germany, Serbia, Panama. They're equal-opportunity bombers." Turning more serious, he said he believed that while the United States was treating Muslims harshly, it was doing so to protect its own people. "You can't really blame a country for doing that."

A lecturer at Tunku Ismail International Islamic College, Khauri acknowledged that Islamic piety definitely was on the upswing, and not only in the Malay heartland. Muslims felt themselves under siege and were reaching for the security blanket of religion. But while many Muslims believed that the United States was attacking their civilization, Khauri had his doubts. Americans, by and large, were well-meaning and believed that democracy was a gift they were obliged to pass on to a grateful world. But they failed to understand that democracy, at least the way it was practiced in the United States, had only limited application to Islam, at least in Kelantan. "You Americans are always asking, 'What do most people say? What does the majority think?' But that's not what matters to us. Just because the majority thinks something doesn't mean that it's correct or true."

Muslims in Malaysia and Indonesia rely on a Malay system called *mushawara* (consensus-making) to determine truth. A council of elders discusses the essential elements of a particular issue, and the discussion continues, open-ended, until all sign on. Once the elders reach agreement, the rest of the community must follow. The technique has proven successful enough that ASEAN, seven of whose ten member states do not have substantial Muslim populations, employs it.

Khauri made it sound logical that a select group of men (only), who understand the complexities of a particular issue, iron it out through informed discussion rather than give uneducated people a chance to decide on the basis of inadequate knowledge or emotion.

Malaysians, male and female, have the constitutional right to vote at age twenty-one. In Kelantan, though, more so than in the rest of the country, the power of the ruling Islamic party meant that the extent and effectiveness of democracy were questionable. "People here are parochial," Khauri said. "They consider non-Malays outsiders. They are simple. But at the same time they are trying to be good Muslims. The result is that they vote for PAS because its goal is to promote Islam. This makes it easy for PAS to manipulate them and win their vote." Khauri's evaluation illustrated the pitfalls not only of Islamization within the controlled democratic confines of Malaysia and other predominantly Muslim countries, but also of blurring the line between church and state anywhere.

Back in Kuala Lumpur, we met the deputy president of PAS, Nasharudin Mat Isa. Blending a strong dose of religion with politics still worked in Kelantan, he told us. But, at the national level, it had cost the party badly. In general elections in 2004, PAS lost control of Trengganu, one of the two states it held out of thirteen, and twenty

seats in Parliament. The outcome shook the party because the setback seemed to run counter to the intensification of Islam around
the country. PAS had been well ahead of the curve in agitating for
Islamic statehood and Sharia.

One morning soon after the election defeat, Nasharudin said,
he looked in the mirror and studied the intense face staring back
through wire-rim glasses. He saw a high forehead and long jawline
accented by a substantial black beard. He looked more like an Arab
than a Malay. A light clicked on. He trimmed the beard back to a
goatee. He began meeting people he and the party had long ignored,
Chinese and Indians, Christians, Buddhists, and Muslim moderates.
He appeared on television talk shows, speaking in English. People
were shocked.

> A friend of my wife's called and said that her husband was amazed
> that a PAS leader could speak English. It made me realize we'd
> been making terrible mistakes. For one, we'd written off all non-
> Malays. For another, by trying to merge religion and politics—
> good governance, development, economic advancement, and
> transparency along with Sharia—we frightened a lot of moder-
> ate Muslims. When people thought of PAS they saw images of
> al-Qaeda and Osama bin Laden.

This realization brought awareness that while many Malays
wanted more Islam in their lives, they preferred it in the guise of
moderation. Prime Minister Abdullah's "Civilizational Islam" fit
the bill nicely. "Too many Muslims believed that PAS wanted to
return the nation to the Stone Age," Nasharudin said. "The truth
is that there is no conflict between Islam and modernity. Malaysia is
already a modern nation and what we want to do is get more people
to understand that Islam is a way of life, both for them as individuals
and for the nation; it is not just a way of praying."

In 2005, Nasharudin traveled to the United States on a three-
week tour sponsored by the State Department. He met local politicians, academics, and religious leaders, including three rabbis. "In
Texas, one of the rabbis told me that he was opposed to Israel's

policies with the Palestinians," he said. "That really stunned me." He was also disturbed when he realized that nearly all the Americans he met equated Islam with Arabs. More worrisome, he said, "When you say 'Muslim' to an American, the automatic response is 'terrorist.'" He found that Americans had no sense of his country or the world of difference between religious practice in most of Southeast Asia and the Middle East.

Alarmed both by the 2004 elections and his conversations with Americans, Nasharudin decided that PAS had to rebrand itself. "We have to repackage the party, make it more of a nationally based organization, not just a party of Muslims and Malays. We have to engage with the [Malaysian] Chinese and convince them that Islam won't harm them and their interests."

With this realization as a backdrop, PAS joined a tripartite, moderate alliance headed by Anwar Ibrahim's avowedly multi-ethnic Keadilan (People's Justice) party to contest Malaysia's 2008 general elections. The grouping trampled Prime Minister Abdullah's ruling party, eliminating its two-thirds majority in Parliament for the first time since 1969. Swiftly acknowledging the new reality, the government watered down the Bumiputra system, eliminating the longstanding, politically untouchable requirement that companies reserve 30 percent of their shares for Malays. The election confirmed Nasharudin's enlightenment, for the short term anyway. But while Nasharudin provides an appealing, younger persona to a party long locked into ultraconservatism, he neither wants nor does it make political sense to permanently change direction on the road to full-fledged Islamic statehood.

For the moment, as Malaysia redefines itself as more Islamic, PAS feels the need to move in the opposite direction, temporarily easing off the accelerator. The race it is engaged in with UMNO is more a game of chicken than a flat-out speedfest. For every two steps a competitor takes closer to Sharia and fundamentalism, the other drops back one, wary of losing votes. The direction is set. Only the pace is in question.

PART FOUR

Land of Smiles: Thailand

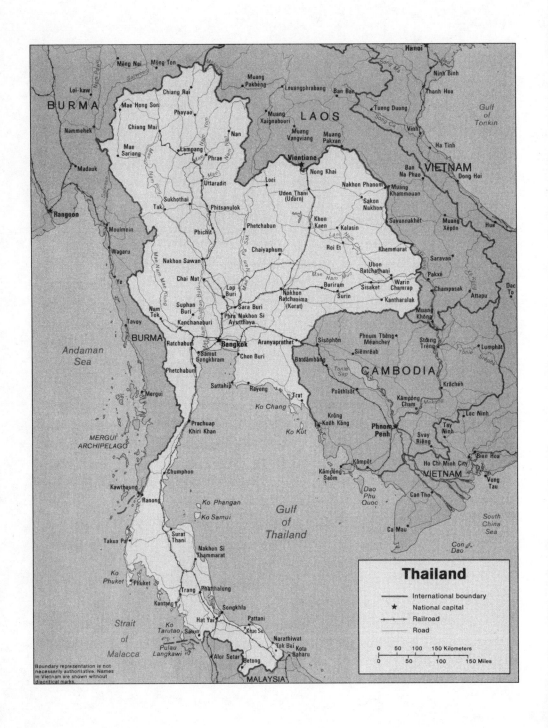

20

The Mother

Safina Garim named her new daughter Najuwa. It means "miracle baby" in Malay. Garim was forty-two when the baby was born. That was six months after Thai soldiers had smothered her twenty-seven-year-old son, Abdul Razak, to death.

Abdul Razak was one of thirteen hundred Muslim men and boys whom the soldiers arrested in Tak Bai, on October 25, 2004, at what was supposed to be a peaceful protest demonstration outside the police station. The heavily armed troops stripped the unarmed men to the waist, bound their hands behind their backs, and piled them face down, like cordwood, five and six deep in open army trucks. Before the trucks left the police station, soldiers shot and killed seven demonstrators.

The soldiers then casually drove the convoy of twenty-eight vehicles around for six hours in the broiling sun while the stacked men died of asphyxiation, one by one, seventy-eight in all, Abdul Razak among them. It was an act of calculated cruelty: the ninety-six-mile trip to the Ingkayuth army base, where eventually they were dumped, normally takes two hours or less. Survivors testified that drivers made long and frequent stops. When the prostrate men cried out for water, soldiers pounded them with rifle butts and stomped them with their boots.

The crackdown at Tak Bai had been ordered by then prime minister Thaksin Shinawatara. He, like most Thais, had little interest in understanding the causes of underlying tensions in the South. Thaksin had been infuriated when, on April 7, 2001, shortly after he had been sworn in, three coordinated bomb attacks struck a railway station, a hotel, and a gas plant. The bombings killed a child, injured at least twenty people, and derailed a train. Thaksin demanded an "immediate" end to the violence. It didn't happen. Then, on January 4, 2004, a group of Islamist insurgents overran a military camp in Narathiwat and seized four hundred weapons, dramatically shifting the equation.

As a former senior Royal Thai Police official and a multibillionaire businessman, Thaksin was accustomed to getting his way with a snap of his fingers. In 2003 he had declared war on Thailand's flourishing narcotics trade, and the swift result was some twenty-two hundred extrajudicial killings. Thaksin now believed he could similarly snuff out unrest in the South with a burst of brute force. That mentality produced the take-no-prisoners tactics at Tak Bai. Thaksin poured gasoline on the fire he had lit by going on the air afterward and claiming that the Muslims in the trucks had died because they were weak from Ramadan fasting.

The Tak Bai Massacre reignited the sputtering fuse on the ethnic time bomb in southern Thailand, a region where restive Muslims of Malay stock have chafed for more than a hundred years under benighted Buddhist rule. Since Tak Bai, revenge killings of Buddhists by Muslims, and counterretaliations by Buddhists on Muslims, school and railway station bombings, arson, drive-by shootings, and beheadings have escalated from occasional to daily events.

In September 2006, Thaksin and his Thai Rak Thai (Thais Love Thais) party were overthrown in a bloodless military coup. The army plotted the coup more in a reflexive response to months of unsettling public demonstrations by middle-class residents of Bangkok against Thaksin's alleged corruption than because of his brutal clumsiness in the South. But the insurgency was a contributing factor. The army chief, General Sonthi Boonyaratglin, the most prominent Thai Muslim, had earlier counseled the prime minister to negotiate with the militants. Thaksin ignored his advice, and Sonthi went on to lead the coup. Sonthi and his junta subsequently tried to quell the uprising through peace talks, and former Malaysian prime minister Mahathir attempted to mediate. Their efforts failed, and the killing grew more brutal. Where, formerly, young men firing rifles from the pillions of motorcycles inflicted most deaths, now killers incinerated schools, temples, and mosques. Roadside bombings grew standard.

Decapitation, with its explicit, face-to-face horror, all but unknown previously in Thailand, became commonplace. The inclusion of these Iraq- and al-Qaeda-style tactics raised fears that Thai Muslims were training with Middle Eastern terrorists or, at least, were studying their skills on the Internet.

In Bangkok, the nation's capital, six hundred miles to the north, the shaky government began caving in upon itself. On August 11, 2008, the ousted Thaksin skipped bail and fled to Britain. From his estate there he played master puppeteer, egging on his vast number of poor, mainly rural supporters. Between August and December, two replacement governments came and went. Opposing hordes of demonstrators, wearing red (pro-Thaksin rural and urban poor) or yellow (anti-Thaksin, middle-class) T-shirts, poured into the streets and forced authorities to close down the glittering new international airport.

The dust settled, tenuously, at the end of 2008 when British-born and Oxford-educated Abhisit Vejjajiva took over the prime minister's office. Although considered personally free of corruption, Abhisit was forced into engaging with a cast of dubious characters in order to form a government. Derided as weak and disdained by the peasant majority, Abhisit quickly visited the troubled south and vowed to raise living standards among Muslims. Few took him seriously.

All this political gamesmanship was unraveling dizzyingly against an epoch-changing backdrop. King Bhumibol Adulyadej, Thailand's beloved, demi-godly monarch for sixty-two years, had turned eighty-one and was showing signs of mortality. When the time came, Crown Prince Vajiralongkorn, whom most Thais consider a short-fused profligate who did not share his father's place in the hearts of the populace, inevitably would succeed the king. Unease ran high.

With the spiritual and political future of the country in turmoil, it was perhaps understandable that few national leaders were paying attention to the bloodbath unfolding in the South and the plight of its victims, such as Safina Garim. Dandling her baby in the shade of an enormous banyan tree outside her home in Tak Bai, Safina reconstructed for us what had happened on that terrible day. Her large almond eyes reddened, but she held her emotions in check. She had been at home when she noticed some teenage village boys walking by her open door. They told her that they were joining a demonstration in front of the police station. The police had been holding six village security volunteers, and protesters were gathering to demand their release. The six, all Muslims, had been charged with giving their government-issued rifles to Islamic militants.

"I asked the boys not to go; it could be dangerous," Safina recalled. "But they said they were only going to look." She didn't know that Abdul Razak, her second-eldest, was already at the demonstration. So was a younger son, Mohammed Nasor. It wouldn't have occurred to her because, as far as she knew, her sons had no involvement in politics. "They were good boys and they minded their own business," Safina said. Like mothers everywhere.

Sometime after six that evening, as she was preparing the celebratory meal to break the day's Ramadan fasting, Safina realized she hadn't seen her two sons all day, and she began to worry. She called friends on her mobile phone. Her husband came home, and they continued telephoning. What they heard was troubling: there had been shooting; people had been killed; others were taken away. But no one could tell them anything about Abdul Razak and Mohammed Nasor.

Early the next morning, after a sleepless night, the phone rang. It was a friend of Abdul Razak's. The friend had seen him outside the police station. He had been loaded onto a military truck (they're called "GMCs" because of America's longtime association with the Thai armed forces, although these days they're manufactured by Mercedes-Benz), but the friend did not know where the truck went. He also reported that Mohammed Nasor had been injured and taken to the regional hospital.

Safina and her husband sped on his motorbike to the riverfront police station, on the main road to the Malaysian border, where they found dozens of photographs posted on a wall. The men and boys in the pictures were dead. Other families swarmed around the photos. Some people were sobbing; others were muted, their hands clasped over their mouths. They did not see Abdul Razak among the pictures, and they went home, presuming the worst, but not knowing.

The couple returned to the police station the following morning. This time they recognized their son's dead body in a photo. He was one of twenty-two with no identification, and the police had sent their fingerprints to Bangkok, where they were checked against driver's licenses. Where was Abdul Razak's body now? Where were the others? The police said they didn't know. More than a month passed. "Thirty-four days after the incident, we received a letter from the police. It said, 'We would like to inform you that your son, Abdul Razak, is dead. His body has been buried in Narathiwat Central Cemetery.' That was all. All that time, we didn't know what had happened, although we assumed that he was dead. All kinds of rumors had been going around: they'd been thrown in the sea; they'd been buried in a mass grave. I tried to trace all the stories. Then, when we got the letter, we went to the cemetery and we found the twenty-two bodies in a single open grave. They were lined up like sardines in a tin. There was no identity for any of them. We had to leave him there."

Abdul Razak had been an important breadwinner for the family. The only one of her children with a steady job, he worked in the Tak Bai municipal office, and he was paying for the education of his three brothers and sisters. He wanted to support them through university. Now, said Safina, "we're trying to keep them in school so that we can make his dream come true."

But the family was having a hard time of it. Not that they were so terribly poor. Safina's husband, Deramae Timasa, earned $89 a month as the leader of their village; in addition, he collected fees for the electricity company, from which he received a small percentage. Their concrete house sported a triangular insert of translucent glass blocks in the front wall, just for show. Mohammed Nasor, his left arm and leg permanently nerve-damaged, was receiving $134 a month working in the district office under a government compensation program for survivors of the massacre. The program would end after ten months.

The family had been given lump sums of $12,000 for Abdul Razak's death and $3,500 for Mohammed Nasor's injuries. In March 2007, the military government distributed a further $1.2 million among the families of the seventy-eight massacre victims. "They said the payments were to 'heal affected families,'" Safina said. She smiled. "Nothing could ever do that." Safina was an elegant woman who paid careful attention to her appearance. Her broad face and hair were closely swathed in a royal blue scarf trimmed in silver brocade, clasped at the throat with a silver brooch; her hands lay still, one over the other, in the lap of a dark batik sarong; her voice was soft, as she spoke in fluent Thai. Few Malay women of her generation speak Thai well. It is the language of the other.

As the overwhelming majority in the South, the Malays have isolated themselves from the surrounding Thai population. They practice their Abrahamic faith and adhere to strict dietary and dress restrictions surrounded by idolaters, who pray not to God but to golden images of a human being, who prostrate themselves at the feet of their king, and whose women wear miniskirts and tank tops: a happy-go-lucky people who consume pork and alcohol. Even in peaceful times it was an uneasy coexistence. Now tensions were sky-high, killing rampant, and Safina foresaw no end to it. "The government doesn't know how to solve the problem," she said, sadly bowing her head. "Muslims and Buddhists don't trust each other. Every day one accuses the other. I see no way out."

Some open-minded Muslims we met in Tak Bai gossiped that separatists wanting to provoke violence had organized the protest rally that resulted in the massacre. Safina acknowledged that the police might have had good reason to open fire on the crowd, although she contended that because they didn't fire any warning shots and barricaded people who attempted to flee they intended to inflict maximum bloodshed.

Shortly after Abdul Razak was killed, an anonymous note arrived at their home. It was addressed to Deramae. In his capacity as the village leader, it alleged, he was acting as a government informant. If he didn't "stay out of our business," he would be killed. The leader of another village had been warned similarly and was gunned down. Writing warnings to potential victims is standard practice, not only in southern Thailand but in Mindanao and other parts of Islamic Southeast Asia as well. Some scholars say the procedure is rationalized in the Koran. Ever since he received the notice, Deramae had become nervous and reclusive and stayed inside the house, away from our discussion. "We don't know whom we can trust anymore," Safina said.

Still, she was doing what she could to help make things better. After grieving bitterly for her son and going through months of uncontrollable hatred, she took it upon herself to speak out for mutual acceptance and understanding. "My husband believes that God is testing our strength and our belief in Islam," she said. A few days before we met, she had traveled to the northern city of Chiang Mai, where she spoke to a meeting of women, both Muslims and Buddhists. Her message was reconciliation. Not everyone received it well. "Most people are very suspicious of the other," she said. "Of course, some Buddhists are suffering, too. But they're not victimized the way we are."

Her bias contained a core truth: Buddhists have taken advantage of Malay Muslims for more than a century. Only in the past few years have the Muslims begun striking back with a vengeance. But it's not the easiest point to make. Thailand is a Buddhist country. Buddhism is widely appealing, particularly among Westerners and, most particularly at this moment, by comparison with Islam. More a philosophy than a religion, it is perceived as forgiving and gentle, its practitioners as calm, even serene. These are admirable qualities, qualities that don't come readily to mind when one considers Islam.

Buddhism, with its glittering gold and red temples, gilded idols, barefoot monks in saffron robes begging silently for their daily rice, kneeling worshippers burning fragrant incense at outdoor shrines—all of these draw eight million foreign tourists each year to Thailand, the Land of Smiles. Buddhism and the gentle Thais, the compliant Thais who, like bamboo, bend with the breeze, the forgiving Thais of *mai pen rai* (never mind). And, of course, the graceful girls and the smooth-skinned boys, the massage parlors, the cheap drugs and cheap sex—all these, too, draw visitors.

So Thailand's message is at once smiling and welcoming with a thick coating of sleaze. But for all of that, it is perceived as neither hostile nor threatening. Unless you are a Muslim. In particular, a young Muslim man, one who is bitter about being unemployed; about not being able to share in the prosperity spreading through much of the country in which you are supposed to be an equal; about the resources of your region being exploited by others; about having to adopt an alien name; about being forced to speak a language not your own and to recite a Buddhist prayer in public school each morning; about being poor. If you are such a young man, you may turn to methamphetamine and other drugs, further dimming your chances in life. Or you may take your bitterness into the street. How many of these young men are actively involved in the southern violence is open to broad speculation. When Prime Minister Thaksin demanded an answer from his generals, he was told that no more than sixty were armed. That gross underestimate had much to do with Thaksin's miscalculation of what it would take to end the uprising.

Police and military officers as well as activist Muslims who claim to have connections among the separatist militants told us the figure might be nearer three hundred. Or three thousand. Perhaps five thousand. One reason for the vagueness is that neither groups nor individuals typically claim responsibility for violent attacks. In a sixteen-month study released in June 2009, the International Crisis Group determined that insurgents have recruited between eighteen hundred and three thousand students from Islamic schools to become armed fighters. A pamphlet found in a raid on one school declared, "Our land is crying and calling and waiting for independence and fraternity. We have been treated as second-class citizens or like children of slaves." According to the study, recruiters invited students who seemed to be "devout Muslims of good character who are moved by a history of oppression, mistreatment and the idea of armed jihad" to undergo guerilla training in mosques and in the guise of football training. There are thought to be five relatively well-organized terror groups operating in the South: Barisan Revolusi Nasional-Coordinate, or National Revolutionary Front-Coordinate, first established in the 1960s to fight for an independent Pattani; Gerakan Mujahidin Islam Pattani, the Pattani Islamic Mujahidin Group, established by Afghanistan veterans in 1995; Pemuda, a separatist youth movement believed responsible for much of the day-to-day sabotage, shootings, and bombings, but not overall planning; the 1960s-era PULO, the Pattani United Liberation Organization; and its offshoot, New PULO, established in 1995.

Some top leaders of these shadowy groups live in political asylum outside the country, principally in Scandinavia, where they are safe from Thai justice. The backgrounds of their groups vary broadly, from those with historical roots in the culture of the Pattani Kingdom to others sparked by the international fundamentalist resurgence of the late twentieth century. Their goals also differ: separatism, autonomy, improved education, reform of the justice system, law and order, economic development, and the spreading of Sharia. By the assessment of Dr. Gotham Arya, a Buddhist and chairman of Thailand's National Economic and Social Advisory Council, any and all of these issues are sufficient grounds for dissent. "The central authorities have not been fair to the Muslims over the course of history," Gotham told us. "They believe, with justification, that the Siamese want to absorb them into Thai culture."

We met with Gotham in his office, a nondescript room furnished in metal and plastic in a nondescript high-rise building in Bangkok. He spends much of his time working in the South. An understated man, he said he believed that poor education more than anything else was to blame for the unrest among young Muslims. A succession of governments had struggled, to no avail, to build a sense of belonging among minority people who consider Thais an exclusionary ethnic group rather than members of an overarching nationality that makes space for them. "The fact is that we have many ethnicities in Thailand and we need to unite them in one nation," Gotham said. "But the approaches have been misguided. We want them to learn the Thai language, but the method is a failure. It's the same as we use to teach English, rote instruction, and the outcome is zero. We impose Thai on them but they speak Malay at home and with each other." The result is that young Muslims coming out of school are unqualified for higher education and better job opportunities are closed to them.

For most of Thailand's population of sixty-five million, the Theravada school of Buddhism is the de facto state religion. So it is no wonder that the three provinces of the Muslim-majority South—Pattani, Narathiwat, and Yala—and their seven million Malays seem remote and inconsequential to their safety. That sense of security suffered something of a setback on New Year's Eve 2006, when nine bombs went off in Bangkok, killing three and injuring thirty-eight, including several foreign tourists. No one claimed responsibility, and authorities were divided as to whether the blasts were set by Muslims or by agents of the toppled Thaksin government. But the event brought awareness of the South closer to home. Both Buddhists and Muslims have learned that it takes very few to wreak havoc.

21

The Widow

Ti Moh was certain that a fellow Muslim had deceived her husband, Maaea Ali. Tempted by a promise of a small amount of money and a large meal in return for assisting in *dawah*—bringing people to pray—Maaea Ali went to the ancient Krue Se Mosque. It was April 27, 2004. The next day, soldiers stormed the sanctuary and shot him and thirty-one other men to death. Since then, Krue Se, like Tak Bai, has festered—an open, ugly wound among the Muslims of southern Thailand.

We found Ti Moh late one afternoon lying curled on the raw concrete floor of a small, square cinder-block house the couple had built after mortgaging their 2.5-acre farm. She lived there, crammed together with her nine children, their spouses, and thirteen grandchildren. Ti Moh was fifty-one, but her shriveled body and yellowed face made her look at least twenty years older. She was so thoroughly exhausted from working all day in the small field behind the house that she could not move or speak to us. She held a pale blue rag to her lips.

The single-story house contained no furniture. A few thin straw mats were spread on the floor. There were no shutters or glass in the window openings, which were punched high into the walls, just beneath the corrugated metal roof. The sole decoration, if one could call it that, was "Allah" roughly spray-painted black in Arabic high on one wall. During the recent rainy season, the house had filled chest-deep with water. Now, broiling in the intolerable heat, the air inside was thick with a strong, dank stench. As we sat on the floor, some of Ti Moh's children told us that they and their mother couldn't decide where their bitterness should be directed: at the soldiers who killed Maaea Ali or at the fellow Muslim who tricked him into being at the mosque. Nor do they know what to believe really happened that day.

According to an official government report, this is what occurred: Eight days before the deadly Krue Se shooting, a group of twenty Muslim "instigators" met to plan an armed assault on a small army post near the mosque. The evening before the planned attack, some of these men and a number of others attended prayers at the mosque and then went to a nearby restaurant for dinner. They returned to the mosque to spend the night. In the postmidnight hours, five of them left to conduct a kind of black magic rite intended to protect them from the bullets of the soldiers they were planning to attack. Drugs may have been involved. More men came to the mosque and changed into black T-shirts, camouflage trousers, and white head-bands—a kind of holy-warrior uniform.

Shortly after five in the morning, about thirty men left for the military post, where they attacked soldiers with machetes and knives, killing one. Voices over the public address system at the mosque, normally used to summon the faithful to prayer, began appealing in Malay for volunteers to join in a "fight to the death." At about the same time, a hundred or so machete-wielding Muslims were attacking military outposts elsewhere in the South. Three police-men and 2 soldiers were killed, as were 106 Muslims. Troops were dispatched to Krue Se, where they surrounded the mosque and exchanged gunfire and grenades with those inside.

By midafternoon, a thousand onlookers had gathered, protesting that the army was unnecessarily damaging the house of worship, which had been erected there in 1578. A modest pink brick-and-mortar structure with Arabesque entrances and rounded pillars, it stood adjacent to a Buddhist shrine. According to local legend, the shrine was built by a woman named Chao Mae Lim Kor Niew, whose brother, a Chinese immigrant, had converted to Islam and built the mosque to honor his adopted faith. When he refused

Chao's demand to renounce Islam, she cursed the mosque. As a result, the dome on its roof was never completed.

At 2:00 P.M., the official report continued, infantrymen and snipers launched an assault, killing thirty-two Muslims inside the mosque. Five automatic rifles, a grenade launcher, eleven knives, and one machete were recovered. All of those killed were men in their thirties, except for two teenagers. (Maaea Ali was sixty-three, a fact not noted in the report. According to his twenty-year-old son, Abdullah Ali, a soldier who had taken part in the raid said his father had been unarmed and was killed while on his knees, presumably in prayer.)

A government-appointed committee was divided in its assessment of the report, the main point of contention being whether the military was wrong not to have attempted to negotiate with those in the mosque. Defense Minister Chavalit Yongchaiyudh, a retired army general, had sent word from Bangkok, ordering the commander on the ground not to storm the mosque and to hash out a resolution. General Pallop Pinmanee ignored the orders, arguing that his soldiers were not trained to negotiate. The killings at Krue Se, certainly, and Tak Bai, perhaps, resulted from violent provocation by Muslim militants. But both incidents were most notable for the use of excessive force.

Despite the Thai reputation for mildness, the army periodically erupts in unspeakable brutality. On October 6, 1976, Simons, then the *Washington Post* correspondent in Bangkok, witnessed soldiers, policemen, and right-wing vigilantes attack some four thousand leftist students at the elite Thammasat University. The students were protesting the return to Thailand of onetime military dictator Thanom Kittikachorn, whom they had successfully forced to flee the country three years earlier. Troops using heavy weapons and automatic rifles assaulted the young people, after first herding them onto a campus soccer field in the heart of Bangkok and trapping them behind tall, locked gates. In a scene that years later would prove eerily reminiscent of Tak Bai, they forced the students, male and female, to strip to the waist and crawl on their bellies to waiting trucks. Anyone who stopped crawling for a moment or who raised his or her head was stomped and beaten. That day, several students were burned alive on pyres of gasoline-drenched tires. Others were hanged by their necks with ropes and belts from tree branches and then battered bloody with steel folding chairs. The official body count was forty-six, a figure that witnesses considered absurdly low.

The events at Tai Bak, Krue Se, and Thammasat share one common outcome: no one was punished. Nor did the revered King Bhumibol step in to demand justice. The paternalistic monarch, whom *Forbes* magazine lists as the world's richest royal, has been on the throne since 1946 and is, quite literally, worshipped by millions of his subjects. He has seen fit to intervene in other political crises, nearly always taking the side of the military. Also mute was the United States, which had begun propping up Bhumibol at the outset of the Vietnam War in return for his strong anti-Communist support. That the king did not come to the aid of left-wing students or Muslims was especially meaningful, and it registered profoundly with both groups. But not expressing their bitterness openly is understandable in one of the few countries in the world where lèse-majesté remains a serious crime. Many of the students who survived the Thammasat massacre fled into the hills, from where their resistance to the rightist government helped prolong a military dictatorship for years and provoked a series of coups. Now Muslim separatists have capitalized on the Krue Se and Tak Bai killings, building support for their cause and extending the daily bloodletting in the South.

Despite the brutality of the southern separatists, the overwhelming majority of Muslims—perhaps 85 percent—do not want to break away from Thailand, do not seek independence, nor do they have any desire to join Malaysia. They certainly do not want the killing to continue. Like most Muslims elsewhere, like most people everywhere, they simply want a fair shake, an opportunity for education, a decent job, a future with some hope.

22

The Counselor

Muslims in southern Thailand live outside the mainstream. Much like the southern Philippines, poverty and underdevelopment assure that they remain embittered, and unwilling and unable to assimilate. While much of the kingdom prospers, in particular Bangkok, with its glittering high-rises and boomtown pace, the South lags sorely behind.

Also moldering in the general economic advance is the northeastern part of the country. There, although the people are Buddhist, most originated in neighboring Laos. To a lesser extent, they share with the Malay Muslims a sense of otherness, of exclusion. Laos, still under Communist rule and slumbering economically, offers little appeal for the people of the Northeast. The same is not true for Southerners, who need only glance across the open border at Malaysia to see how well a Malay Islamic economy can function. They see fellow Muslims in charge of their own destiny. This is particularly irksome to the young men. They feel emasculated in their own homeland by people who, they believe, have no historical right to rule them. In this they are no less irate and frustrated than were their ancestors who struggled for a century without success to restore the Pattani Kingdom, which historically occupied southern Thailand.

What is different now is that they are inspired by the greater Islamic struggle around them. Like their coreligionists in the

Philippines, Indonesia, Malaysia, and Singapore, Muslims from southern Thailand have traveled to Pakistan and Egypt for religious training. Saudis have come to their homeland to teach and have contributed funds to build mosques and religious boarding schools, here called *pondoks*. This cross-fertilization is not entirely a creation of the recent Islamic resurgence. Rather, it is more a revival of exchanges between the Middle East and Southeast Asia that thrived through the nineteenth century, when Pattani, like Aceh, in Indonesia, was an esteemed center of Islamic culture and learning. Once the king of Siam began "Siamizing" the population, the flower of southern Islam was cut from its roots. It is that severed connection that is now being re-grafted.

What distinguishes southern Thailand from the southern Philippines and from Indonesia is that so far neither al-Qaeda nor any regional offshoots, such as Jemaah Islamiya, appear to have gained traction. In 2003, government agents in Thailand seized Riduan Isamuddin, an Indonesian national and the presumed leader of Jemaah Islamiya, who operated as the lead coordinator for Osama bin Laden in Southeast Asia. Known as Hambali, he was a veteran of anti-Soviet combat in Afghanistan. But Hambali was captured not in the South, but in the ancient capital city of Ayutthaya, a popular tourist destination forty-five miles from Bangkok. Three years later, President Bush revealed that he was imprisoned at Guantánamo Bay. The United States paid the government of Thailand a $10 million bounty for capturing Hambali.

In the past few years, Thai police in the South have reported seizing a handful of Indonesians suspected of belonging to Jemaah Islamiya. Still, Thai authorities as well as southern Muslim activists insist that they know of no functioning links between foreign terrorists and southern separatists. In reality, Thailand's separatists, much like the Muslims of Mindanao, would settle for a small measure of autonomy and a crack at economic equality.

"Southern Muslims are influenced by the international Islamic scene, so it's natural to look at what they're involved in as part of something bigger," said Ralph "Skip" Boyce, a former U.S. ambassador to Thailand. "Of course, it's a very big threat to the stability of Thailand, but there is no sign at all of the South being an international playground for Jemaah Islamiya, al-Qaeda, or anyone else." Boyce, whose other assignments have included Indonesia and Iran, is one of the most insightful American diplomats specializing in Southeast Asia. He is an expert on Muslims in the region. "There's a tendency to call what's going on in the South purely a religious conflict, but in reality it's much more an ethnic-Malay-versus-Thai matter," he told us. Like many other foreign and Thai analysts, Boyce placed full blame on former prime minister Thaksin for "making Muslims in the South feel like second-class citizens."

Monsour Salleh, an aging Islamic militant, runs a graphics business in Hat Yai, a southern city of 156,000 about thirty miles from the Malaysian border. Hat Yai is the main railhead on the line between Bangkok and Kuala Lumpur. Sprawling inland from a coastal plain of palm-fringed beaches of the standard tropical-paradise variety, Hat Yai is an unusually cosmopolitan center of ethnic Thai Buddhists, Chinese, and Muslims.

The city also stands astride a major route of the Asian high-way system, which links it with the eastern seaboard of the Malay Peninsula and Singapore. This easy access accounts for a thriving trade in Malaysian and Singaporean tourists, mainly males, who for years flocked to Hat Yai for weekends of low-cost commercial sex. With violence flaring in the area, though, the sex traffic has come to a near standstill. Major streets were all but empty during our visit. Bar girls stood morosely at the doors of empty clubs. The only sound was the sputtering of occasional motorbikes, whipping spirals of red dust across the well-paved roads.

In his youth, Monsour was president of the militant Muslim Youth Association of Thailand. Now, at fifty, he was a counselor to the group. The association has ties to a youth organization in Malaysia run by former deputy prime minister Anwar Ibrahim that provides funding for Thai Muslims to study there. The money is just one of several streams of Malaysian cash that directly and indirectly support the separatists.

A more mundane source of income is a string of Muslim-operated halal soup restaurants near the frontier. Malaysia has denied accusations by Thai authorities that it turns a blind eye to the restaurants' money-trafficking operations. But the claim that these modest eateries are involved in the armed struggle has a ring of truth to anyone familiar with stealthy money operations in Asia. For decades, the government of Japan has chosen to ignore the transfer of funds from expatriate-Korean-owned *pachinko* parlors to North Korea in amounts incalculably greater than anything soup restaurants in Malaysia could generate.

"The way society is organized now, Muslims here don't trust the Thai government leadership," Monsour said during a conversation in his spacious, dimly lit graphics shop in a quiet neighborhood off the main highway. "The young generation of Muslims believes in jihad. They're very spirited and they'll keep on fighting until they achieve their goal. They're very angry about the injustices in their own lives. When you add things like Afghanistan, Iraq, Lebanon, and Palestine to their personal bitterness, you find a will to sacrifice."

Monsour described his charges as "good boys, dignified and committed, who study the Koran. They learn that if they fight to right injustice they will be rewarded in heaven." The Thai leadership in Bangkok failed to recognize any of this, finding it more convenient to dismiss Muslims as common criminals. "The government doesn't understand that this insurgency is about ideology. They have no respect for us." Monsour acknowledged that the government was motivated by the legitimate need to build a sense of Thai nationhood. But he argued that it was doing so at the expense of those who wanted to retain their Malay Muslim identity as well. "We won't stand for that. We're prepared to learn the Thai language, but we also want to be able to speak our own Malay language. People should have the right to choose. I myself, even though I am no longer active in the jihad because of my age and my family responsibilities, worry about my sons and daughters losing their culture. This is not fair; we want the rights a minority should enjoy in any democracy."

The United States, Monsour complained, was not projecting the democratic standards it practiced at home and about which it lectured the Islamic world. "The Americans talk one way, but how they act is another matter," he said with rising heat. "They call people here terrorists. Then they bomb innocent people in Afghanistan and Iraq. The Israelis bomb innocents in Gaza and Lebanon. That's terror, too." The United States was striving to make Muslims in Southeast Asia "moderates," he said. "What that means is Muslims whom the Americans can manipulate and control." He recalled that American representatives of the Asia Society had recently come to Hat Yai to invite members of his youth group to attend a conference in Jakarta on moderate Islam. "We can't accept that. I have many contacts in Indonesia, Malaysia, and Singapore, and I know that the Americans and the Singaporeans are trying to influence things here."

Many Muslims in Southeast Asia look at Singapore with a jaundiced eye, tagging it a U.S. front. Some have similar feelings about the government of Thailand. Over the decades beginning with the war in Vietnam, through extended stretches of military dictatorship and much shorter periods of democracy, the Thais have been faithful allies of the United States. Like the Philippines, Thailand nervously acceded to President Bush's appeal to join the "coalition of the willing" after 9/11. Each sent a small contingent of troops (443 Thais and 51 Filipinos) to Iraq for noncombatant roles. Both withdrew ahead of their scheduled one-year agreements. Three decades earlier, both had deployed armed forces to Vietnam, also to satisfy a U.S. government anxious to project an image of Third World support for an unpopular American war.

Seated quietly until now at the edge of the conversation in Monsour's shop was a client who looked to be in his early thirties. He suddenly joined in, angrily expressing his views of what the United States and its allies were attempting to accomplish in southern Thailand and other parts of the Muslim world. He asked that his name not be used. "If 'moderate' means a Muslim who can be Westernized and manipulated by the United States and Thailand, then I'm against moderation," he said. "We're Muslims and Malays and that's the only thing that's acceptable to us. I'm not in favor of violence, but it's been building for years because of lack of equal rights, lack of justice, and coercion from the Thai state. They want to dominate us. And the only time the government pays attention to us is when we're violent."

23

The Bridge Builder

When American colleges and universities admit students from developing countries, it is with the hope that some will one day become leaders in their homelands, providing high-level contacts and helping improve relations with the United States.

The results are mixed. Some don't return home at all, but remain in the United States and become valued American citizens, though they are sorely missed by their homelands. Some are turned off by their U.S. experience and return home embittered. And some do become key figures in their countries and help build important bridges to the United States.

Surin Pitsuwan is one of those. A Thai Muslim from an observant family that operated a *pondok*, a traditional Islamic boarding school, Surin received the best that American higher education could offer and gave back the best that anyone could hope for. After studying at Thammasat University in Bangkok, he enrolled at Claremont Men's College in California, where he studied political science and graduated in 1972. He did research in human rights and Islamic studies at Harvard and at American University in Cairo. The Rockefeller Foundation funded much of his U.S. academic career. Surin earned a Ph.D. from Harvard in 1982.

Newly minted doctorate in hand, Surin went to Washington, D.C., where he spent the next two years on the staff of New York Democratic congresswoman Geraldine Ferraro. After Ferraro ran unsuccessfully for vice president in 1984, Surin returned to Thailand and joined the faculty at Thammasat. He was elected to Parliament from the Democrat Party in 1985 and was named foreign minister in 1997, holding that portfolio until 2001. In 2008 he became secretary-general of ASEAN.

As a Thai and a Muslim with a first-rate American education and high-level exposure to American politics, Surin is in a unique position to explain a broad range of issues to Westerners, just as he can assess U.S. policies for Thais. He speaks both English and Thai with total fluency, has spent considerable time in the United States, and has influential American friends. His doctoral dissertation, *Islam and Malay Nationalism: A Case Study of the Malay Muslims of Southern Thailand*, became the authoritative source on the issue now racking the country and remains so to this day. Considering that he wrote it in the 1980s, he was extraordinarily prescient in projecting what would trigger the Muslim uprising in southern Thailand and throughout the broader umma two decades later:

> One of the most intractable problems facing developing countries at present is the transfer of loyalty from traditional ties to religious groups, tribal affiliation and other "primordial" bonds, to a more rational allegiance to the state as a new political entity. In many parts of the world today, civil strife, political violence and, indeed, international crises have risen out of these strong but conflicting ties of traditional symbols and modern institutions that are themselves going through a process of transformation. . . . Forming the largest part in terms of population, the Muslims in Southeast Asia will certainly draw attention from the Middle East to the issue of their "unredeemed brethren" in southern Thailand and thus accentuate the level of violence even more.

Surin was blunt in ascribing blame. During an interview with us at Democrat Party headquarters in Bangkok, he charged that political leaders were at fault for having failed to understand even the most basic social, religious, political, and economic motivations of their alleged enemies before they launched armed attacks. In Thailand it was Thaksin, who made the infamous decision to crush the "sixty bandits," and in Iraq it was Vice President Dick Cheney who led the charge, drawing on or influencing false CIA intelligence. "The ill-informed judgment of these two men, neither of whom had any understanding of the complexity of the societies they were considering, led to abuse after abuse and an unending cycle of violence," said Surin. "Both men had been high-powered business executives, accustomed to getting their way without questioning or resistance. Both insisted on overcentralization of power and used know-nothing cronies." Thaksin, he said, took advantage of the Bush administration's war on terror to crack down in the South so he could "deliver the goods" when he met with the president in the Oval Office in September 2005.

Surin rejected out of hand any suggestion that what was unfolding in Thailand and in Iraq was part of a global war by America/democracy-hating Muslims employing terrorism as their chief weapon. Instead, he saw members of Muslim communities in both countries and around the world "standing up in an active and dynamic realization that they have to defend and promote their interests against the fast pace of change that they can neither control nor stop."

Muslims considered the external forces of globalization unfriendly and threatening. Few Americans realized that their cultural exports and their imposition of liberal democracy gave Muslims the clear impression that the United States was invading their space. Muslim concern was nothing more than the understandable fear any smaller, weaker person has for a larger and stronger one. "It's incumbent on the United States most of all to diffuse the boiling situation" in Iraq and the Middle East. "That would help us with our problem [in southern Thailand] because, since 9/11, your problem is our problem; the East's problem is the West's."

But in an environment where lopsided force of arms no longer assures victory, the United States, as the sole superpower, has a particular obligation to go out of its way to understand the motivations of its foes. In his 2001 encyclopedic account of America's long slide into Vietnam, A Grand Delusion, historian Robert Mann illustrated amply that Americans have a long record of not comprehending the people they fight. Mann recounts how, in 1965, President Lyndon B. Johnson, desperate to avoid sinking deeper into the Vietnam quagmire, offered North Vietnamese leader Ho Chi Minh a $1 billion economic assistance package. "Old Ho can't turn me down," Johnson crowed to his aide Bill Moyers.

"But Ho could turn him down—and did," Mann wrote. "Johnson's miscalculation was his failure to see the Viet Cong and their North Vietnamese supporters as committed nationalists. Having fought against foreign domination for more than twenty years, they were unlikely to drop their struggle the minute Johnson promised a billion dollars." Johnson's real failure was that as a politician who thoroughly understood what made Americans tick he so easily misled himself into believing that Vietnamese were no different. "LBJ had no particular grasp of foreign cultures," said National Security Council staff member Robert Komer. "He felt no particular need to delve into what made Vietnamese Vietnamese—as opposed to Americans or Greeks or Chinese. He was a people man and he thought people everywhere were the same."

When Karen Hughes went to the Middle East and Southeast Asia for George Bush in 2005 and attempted to bond with women by telling them that she was "a working mom" who loves kids, though her audiences didn't realize it, they were hearing the ghost of LBJ. Hughes's ear for the Islamic world was made of tin, and the veiled women were not shy about telling her so. "Your policies are creating hostilities among Muslims," Indonesian student Lailatul Qadar shot back after Hughes gave a speech in Jakarta in which she compared Saddam Hussein with Hitler. "It's Bush in Iraq, Afghanistan, Palestine, and maybe it's going to be in Indonesia, I don't know. Who's the terrorist? Bush or us Muslims?"

When Ho rejected Johnson's money, the American president truculently unleashed the Rolling Thunder bombing campaign on North Vietnam and sent the Marines into the South. We know how that worked out. Once again, counter-violence and its unending cycle is a counterproductive response to Muslim violence. The only way to end violence is through helping those who feel oppressed adapt to the world's demand for change. We know that this line of thinking can all too easily be dismissed as pie in the sky, but we also know that the other way does not work.

Said Surin, "If the United States insists that it is fighting a global war on terror, then there is no room for cooperation. What we're looking at is a set of mirror images: each side sees the other as hostile instead of each side seeking mutual respect. Only if both sides work sincerely at trying to heal the rift can there be hope for the future. If both sides feel that they have to kill the other—and the West can't kill a billion and a half Muslims, nor vice versa—there will be no resolution. If the mutual insensitivity now at work continues, what is taking place today could easily lead to a massive clash of civilizations."

A few months after our meeting, Joint Chiefs of Staff chairman Admiral Mike Mullen, testifying before the House Armed Services Committee on the long-term campaign against Islamist terrorism, said in words closely echoing Surin's, "We cannot kill our way to victory."

Recalling his experience as a student, Surin urged Americans to seriously encourage Muslim students from Thailand and other countries to apply to U.S. universities, as well as send more Americans abroad for advanced degrees. While the State Department had begun to recruit young Thais—Surin had recently met with fifteen students who were leaving for the United States—much more had to be done. "Scholarships," he said, "are the greatest way to build bridges."

24

The China Watcher

For better and for worse, whatever the long-term outcome of the turmoil in its Islamic southern provinces, Thailand fully expects China to remain a key player in its national life for as far into the future as anyone can rationally speculate. That much is a given. As for the United States, the Thais are far less certain. They have good reason in both cases.

China has always been closely involved with Thailand. The Thai (or T'ai) people themselves originated in southern China. At least twenty-five hundred years ago, they began migrating down the Mekong River into what would become the states of Indochina and eventually settled in Siam (or Sa'yam), derived from the word for peace in China's Szechwanese dialect. It was only in 1939, when it became a constitutional monarchy, that the country changed its name to Thailand. While travel guides commonly state that the name means "Land of the Free," the literal translation of the name for the country in the Thai language, *Prathes Thai*, is "country of the Thai ethnic group." To the Malay-Muslims of the South, as well as to other minorities, the name implies clearly that Thailand excludes them. Seven hundred years ago, waves of Chinese traders from southern areas of the mainland began making their way to the region in search of business opportunities. They stayed, married local women, and settled down. The two cultures mingled easily, so much so that almost no distinction remains. Few in the Thai ruling class are without Chinese blood. Former prime minister Thaksin's great-grandfather was a poor immigrant who made his fortune by collecting gambling debts.

Early in the twentieth century, great numbers of Chinese families flocked to Siam. This third mass migration helped establish a wealthy, largely urban, overseas Chinese community akin to those throughout Southeast Asia and as far away as the United States and Europe. Ethnic Chinese today comprise 15 percent of Thailand's population and, according to the University of Maryland's Minorities at Risk project, they control as much as 90 percent of the country's business interests. Demarcated Chinatowns are still found in Bangkok and a handful of other large cities, but because of their early assimilation, the Sino Thais have suffered almost none of the animosity and periodic violence to which overseas Chinese have been subjected elsewhere in Southeast Asia.

In the 1960s and 1970s, when China was suffering the chaos and upheaval of the Cultural Revolution under Chairman Mao Zedong and when fear of the Communist menace was at its apogee throughout the world, government-to-government relations between Beijing and the capitalist nations of Southeast Asia—Thailand among them—went into a deep freeze. Overseas Chinese were treated with suspicion, feared as a fifth column for the motherland. With rare exception, such allegations were misplaced, even perverse, since the Chinese had fled in search of economic opportunities and were loath to associate themselves with communism.

Bloody reprisals against Chinese business communities in Indonesia took place against this background. Not coincidentally, this was the time of the great United States–led crusade against what Americans unquestioningly perceived as an international Communist monolith led by a conjoined China and Soviet Union. Southeast Asia became the flash point, the arena in which East and West would battle it out for supremacy. Beginning with the post–World War II Truman administration and ending under Richard M. Nixon, the United States threw its armed might into Indochina. The eventually failed effort to avoid "losing" these three longtime French colonies to communism was a rerun of how a previous generation of Americans had flagellated themselves into believing they had "lost" China and North Korea, as if those countries had ever been theirs to lose. Americans seemed unable to comprehend the desire of others for nationalism and independence.

However, the U.S. misadventure in Indochina did produce one positive effect for Thailand and its anti-Communist neighbors. As leaders throughout the region still gratefully acknowledge, generous U.S. infusions of economic, humanitarian, diplomatic, and security assistance in return for military base facilities during the war years enabled them to develop robust economies. These were the years when brands such as Coca-Cola, Kodak, and McDonald's became household words in Southeast Asia. GIs on R & R leave were treated like heroes on the streets of Bangkok. While the headlines, naturally, went to the war, the quieter story was one of a golden age for Americans off the battlefield.

The central difference between then and now in the United States–Southeast Asia dynamic is that forty years ago, most governments in the region feared communism within their own societies as well as its threat from beyond their borders even more than Americans did. They were, after all, the dominoes. They were small, weak, and vulnerable. They lived well within range of a Chinese invasion. Their populations were peppered with suspect Chinese immigrants.

The admission of defeat in Indochina, declared by President Gerald Ford in 1975, shoved U.S. participation in Southeast Asian affairs into prolonged decline. Three decades later, the invasion and occupation of Iraq provoked the region's Muslims and created an aura of hostility that persists to this day. By contrast, the death of Chairman Mao, one year after the last U.S. helicopter fluttered out of Saigon, followed by the rise of the reformer Deng Xiaopeng and his open-door policies, ushered in a remarkable ascent in China's relationships with the people and governments of Southeast Asia.

The once-frightening prospect of traitors living among them has given way to a broad appreciation for Chinese Thais (as well as Chinese Malaysians, Chinese Indonesians, and Chinese Filipinos) whose personal *guangxi* (connections) on the mainland enable them to conduct mutually beneficial trade and investment activities. In Indonesia, where anti-Chinese bias historically has provoked more bloodshed than elsewhere, the Yudhoyono government expressed its appreciation in 2007 by officially recognizing resident Chinese born in the country as full-fledged citizens. China specialists can't help but compare the rise in influence of what they view as a largely benign China with America's apparent lack of interest, other than the U.S. obsession with terrorism. Few of them share America's all-consuming focus on a global Islamist threat. "China uses diplomacy alone to win concessions," said Thai National Security Council senior expert Surachai Nira. "That's true whether it's in Thailand or elsewhere in Southeast Asia, in Latin America, the Middle East, and Africa. Meanwhile, the United States often combines military force with diplomatic pressure in order to gain what it wants. We accept that the United States is the number-one military power; you don't have to keep on flexing your muscles again and again. It would be much better if the U.S. would use things like economic assistance and education to help us and other smaller powers. You'd get positive results and you'd win hearts and minds."

Surachai and other security analysts with whom we spoke in the region are hardly naive about China. Rather, they consider it natural for the Asian giant to be making its move in their region, and since China has the success story of the decade to tell, they're pleased to listen and learn. At the same time, they are well aware of China's military budget increases (and that it is currently one tenth the size of the U.S. defense budget) and its arms buildup. Much of that buildup is taking place in Southeast Asia, before their very eyes. The Chinese are establishing naval facilities at the Bangladesh port of Chittagong. They are seeking access to the Andaman Sea through the militarist regime in Burma, which China supports and which the United States condemns. China also monitors U.S. and Indian naval activities from Burma's Coco Islands.

Thailand does not support the repressive Burmese leadership. The Thais are saddled with hundreds of thousands of Burmese refugees who have fled across the border in search of safety. But Surachai was quick to point out that while Burma makes a convenient target for U.S. censure, the United States for decades has steadfastly supported the military regime in Pakistan. "They're both dictatorships," he said. "Treat them both the same."

Most experts from small, weak states in the region accept as inevitable the rapid emergence of China as the Asian hegemon. Yet they tend to be more nervous about U.S. military planning than China's. They are keenly aware that while China has far more manpower in its armed forces than does the United States, the Americans enjoy unrivaled technological and nuclear weapons superiority. They consider it ironic that Americans express alarm over China's newfound ability to destroy a satellite, while the United States upgrades its own nuclear warheads. Fearing that they would be the grass trampled by the elephants in the event of a Sino-American war, they grow increasingly nervous each time they hear anti-China drumbeats on Capitol Hill.

"The United States fears that China will be its chief military rival within the next twenty to twenty-five years," Surachai said during an interview at Government House, a tree-shaded, graceful, redbrick building in the old royal quarter of Bangkok. "But to us in Southeast Asia, China shows a different face. When we suffered the financial crisis in the late '90s, China agreed not to change the value of the yuan. That helped establish more positive relations. Where was the United States then?" But even as they nurse resentment, the Thais and others clearly desire the United States to remain active in the region as a balance to China's increasing weight. They worry that as China rises and claims an ever larger portion of the economic sphere and the United States continues to disengage, the outcome will be an increasingly militant America lashing out at Islamic terrorism and at China. And they would be caught in the middle.

The United States' reputation in Southeast Asia today is that of a jealous and hypocritical military giant employing its overdeveloped muscles to beat back any up-and-coming nation at any cost: supplying weapons to Taiwan while damning China for adding to its arms stocks; coddling its chosen dictators while blaming China for nourishing its favorites; outsourcing much of its economy to China and growing slothful on low-cost, made-in-China products while blaming the Chinese for trading unfairly.

Meanwhile, Southeast Asians view China as a vast but still poor nation, one they admire for pulling itself up by its bootstraps and developing an appropriately strong but not overwhelming military to protect its hard-won wealth and growing influence. Any argument that China supports vicious dictatorships, such as those in Burma, Sudan, and Zimbabwe, to milk them of resources, is met with retorts of American double standards: human rights in Burma versus Pakistan is one; nuclear arms in Israel versus those in Iran is another; and, of course, the overriding question of who is a terrorist.

Many Americans may have no difficulty satisfying themselves that they are on the side of justice, but they would find it very difficult convincing skeptics such as Surachai. We see China as future enemy number one, more than likely in a fight to the death over Middle Eastern oil. They see it as a worthy competitor. "This 'global war on terrorism' you're fighting: is it truly a war against terrorists, or is it against Muslims?" Surachai asked. "Or is it a war for Middle East oil—and, ultimately, against China? It's not clear. If you were fighting in Iraq under the UN instead of the U.S. flag alone you'd get much more international support. Instead, you acted on your own. Then you couldn't produce any WMD and you can't explain yourselves to the world."

While Surachai was forgiving of the United States for its assault on Afghanistan, he saw the Iraq war as preemptive, unjust, and potentially threatening to his own country. "We wonder if the United States might not decide one day that southern Thailand is a refuge for Islamic terrorists and launch a preemptive strike there. Of course, we wouldn't expect you to do such a thing without the consent and approval of us, your close ally, but how do we know? You did it in Iraq. Where will you do it next?"

Having unburdened himself of these grievances, Surachai expressed an almost poignant appeal for revived U.S. ethical guidance, a reprise of comments we heard from other Thais. "Look, we believe that the United States is a civilized country and we hope to see it as a moral leader, not just a military power. We want you to set a good example for us to follow."

25

The America Watcher

Surachai's plea indicated the depth and breadth of both opportunity and challenge that China's growing involvement in Thailand creates for Americans. Many Thais are defensive about China's investment in their country. But this is in part because they recognize that both the United States and Japan are ratcheting back, and they have little choice. Meanwhile, Vietnam, with its even cheaper labor, is drawing American investors, leaving Thailand increasingly out of the picture. Thailand claims a low unemployment rate, just 2.4 percent. But underemployment, particularly in the impoverished Northeast and the Muslim South, is vast and crippling. Nearly all decent-paying jobs are centered in Bangkok. This has resulted in economic and social inequality, which the governor of the Bank of Thailand, Pridiyathorn Devakula, has described as among the worst in the world.

If Thailand is to regain the economic vigor it had prior to the 1997 financial crisis it must upgrade its production abilities to more sophisticated, higher-value-added levels, similar to what Malaysia has done. Thailand has only a few years to accomplish the feat to escape a permanent setback. The essential requirements are to drop tariffs and establish preferential trade agreements with its major trading partners, most particularly with the United States. This would enable the Thais to undercut China in some areas and to be competitive with Vietnam when China comes fully on line in a few more years. But suspicions of American intentions continue to worsen. Many Thais in and out of government believe that a free-trade agreement with the United States would benefit only the Americans. Antiglobalization fears like this are hardly unique; we heard them throughout Southeast Asia.

Chaiwat Satha Anand, a distinguished political scientist at Thammasat University and an expert on the United States, was among those who would welcome increased U.S. investment. He also favored further globalization, though he preferred "glocalization," which, he said, "results in happy marriages like pizza tam yam kung and halal KFC buffalo wings." A Muslim, though not a Malay from the South (his mother was Thai; his father, Pakistani), Chaiwat earned a doctorate from the University of Hawaii. He translated the *Federalist Papers* into Thai and is a student and admirer of American constitutional law. "So you know where I'm coming from and what I'm hoping for," he told us. He wanted the United States quickly to reform what he considered its self-destructive foreign policies.

His great fear was that America was on its way to becoming what he called a "weak country," which he defined as "weakness of the soul combined with powerful weapons." Such an out-of-balance America could prove harmful to itself and the rest of the world. "The United States has already made a grave mistake in viewing Islam—and China, for that matter—as your enemy or your potential enemy," he said.

Chaiwat chastised Americans for ignoring the histories of peoples far older than themselves as a means to understanding their motivations and goals. By zeroing in on other cultures only when crises develop, he said, Americans unwittingly create enemies and shut themselves off from positive relations. "With your two hundred years of existence, you ignore the history of China, which is five thousand years old, and of Islam, which is fifteen hundred years old. If you took some time to understand them you would not treat them as simple blocs, but as complex structures filled with a variety of people whose essential interests are not that much different from your own."

Chaiwat's disappointment with U.S. policy turned on what analysts refer to as "enemy deprivation syndrome," which stirred to life with the fall of the Berlin Wall in 1991. The thesis that the United States requires a well-defined foe in order to focus its policies and provide Americans with a clearer sense of purpose has been around a good while. It has its roots in President Dwight D. Eisenhower's landmark "military-industrial complex" speech of 1961. Most assuredly, the need was sharpened by the collapse of the Soviet Union. During the 1990s, under the elder Bush and Clinton administrations, a concerted effort was made to place Japan in the unwelcome position of adversary. Those were the years when Americans learned to fear "Japan as Number One," as Harvard social scientist Ezra Vogel dubbed it, and when autoworkers smashed Japanese cars with sledgehammers on the streets of Detroit.

When Japan's financial bubble burst, Americans tried casting a chorus line of evildoers, among them North Korea, Iran, Iraq, Libya, and Serbia. None quite fit the role. Following 9/11, Vice President Cheney and what Chaiwat described as "some of his more zealous, neoconservative staff members" promoted Islamic terrorism and the "Axis of Evil" as America's worst enemies. That, as well, proved too amorphous for many Americans to sink their teeth into. For some, simply equating terror with Islam sufficed. But for many more, without a clearly defined foreign enemy, internal struggle became the only viable release for pent-up frustration. The bitterness expressed itself in the domestic political arena, with nativists inveighing against immigrants, evangelicals decrying skeptics, and out-of-power liberals cursing ruling conservatives. With the United States now working its way out of Iraq, Chaiwat and other opinion leaders in Southeast Asia worry that China will be next in America's crosshairs. "As with Islam," he cautioned, "you're now reducing China to a caricature."

But while internationally minded Thais such as Chaiwat worried about how their country would be affected if America's anti-China rhetoric turned to action, the more immediate fear was that Thailand was spinning out of control on its own. Domestic political chaos was leading the nation into a downward spiral, and there appeared to be no sign of resolution anywhere on the horizon. A return to military rule in September 2006, a bad habit of long standing that most Thais and their foreign friends believed had been relegated to the trash bin of history, did nothing to resolve the issues that led the army to overthrow Prime Minister Thaksin in the first place. And it ignored the oozing sore in the Muslim South.

Thai attitudes toward U.S. business turned xenophobic, alarming even the normally boosterish American Chamber of Commerce (AmCham). American firms, even those few that may have been considering new investments, were put off in November 2006 when the military regime seized the patent rights of an antiretroviral HIV/AIDS drug from the U.S. pharmaceutical giant Merck & Co. This was followed by a similar seizure from Abbot Laboratories and a move against Sanofi-Aventis's local version of its Plavix heart medication. The junta said it unilaterally broke the agreements with the American companies because too many Thais were unable to afford the cost of the patent-protected medicines.

Little that occurred in Thailand over the three years following the army's overthrow of Thaksin gave cause for optimism. Governments came and went with alarming haste. Riots erupted and were put down, often with armed violence. Only one constant remained: the daily murders in the South. Thailand, which for more than a decade had been stable and inviting, seemed to be crumbling.

PART FIVE

The House That Lee Built: Singapore

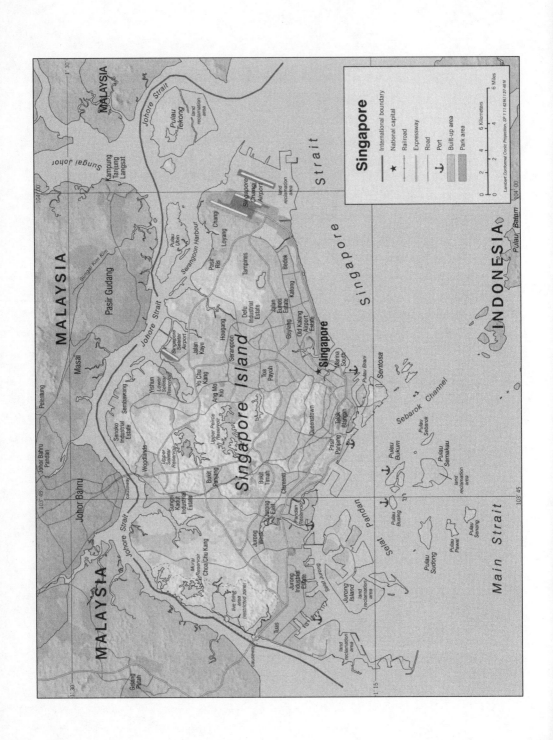

Singapore

- International boundary
- ★ National capital
- Railroad
- Expressway
- Road
- ⚓ Port
- Built-up area
- Park area

0 2 4 6 Kilometers
0 2 4 6 Miles

Lambert Conformal Conic Projection, SP 1°11'42N/1°23'48N

MALAYSIA

INDONESIA

Johore Strait

Singapore Island

Singapore Strait

Main Strait

Selat Pandan

Sebarok Channel

★ Singapore

Pulau Tekong

Pulau Ubin

Singapore Changi Airport

Changi

Loyang

Pasir Ris

Tampines

Bedok

Katong

Jalan Eunos Estate

Old Kalang Airport Estate

Geylang

Marina South

Pulau Brani

Sentosa

Toa Payoh

Serangoon

Hougang

Detu Industrial Estate

Jalan Kayu

Serangoon Harbour

Singapore Seletar Airport

Yio Chu Kang

Ang Mo Kio

Yishun

Sembawang

Lower Seletar Reservoir

Upper Seletar Reservoir

Upper Peirce Reservoir

Seletoko Industrial Estate

Woodlands

Bukit Semang

Bukit Timah

Clementi

Queenstown

Telok Blangah

Pasir Panjang

Pulau Bukum

Pulau Sebarok

Pulau Semakau

Pulau Busing

Pulau Sudong

Pulau Pawai

Pulau Senang

land reclamation area

Jurong West

Jurong East

Peirce Reservoir

Jurong Industrial Estate

Jurong Island

Sungai Kadut Industrial Estate

Choa Chu Kang

Murai Reservoir

fire fight area (restricted zones)

Selat Jurong

Tuas

causeway

MALAYSIA

Johor Bahru

Johor Bahru Pandan

Pelentong

Masai

Pasir Gudang

Sungai Kim Kim

Senoko Industrial Estate

Kampung Tanjung Langsat

Sungai Johor

Johor

Gelang Patah

Johore Strait

1°30'

1°30'

1°15'

103°45'

103°45'

104°00'

104°00'

Pulau Batam

26

The Father

By comparison with Thailand—indeed, with all of the rest of Southeast Asia—Singapore is a rock of stability. That's because the justifiably smug city-state was constructed and is maintained by master builder Lee Kuan Yew.

The project began inauspiciously, in 1959, the year Singapore held its first general elections, still under British oversight. Lee Kuan Yew's People's Action Party won a stunning 54 percent of the vote. Singapore itself was little more than a speck of mudflat and marsh at the tip of the Malay Peninsula. The climate was unerringly hot and muggy. The entire territory measured just a bit larger than Chicago. A million and a half people lived there, three quarters of them ethnic Chinese, the rest mainly Malays and Indians. The island was hemmed in to the north by Malaysia and to the east, west, and south by Indonesia, both with vastly larger populations, mainly of Malay Muslims. It was not an enviable position. Except for a handful of grandiose neo-Romanesque edifices that imperial Great Britain in its hubris had erected to tend this outpost of the Raj in the South China Sea, Singapore was a dirty, dozy, backwater entrepôt.

The wealthy few enjoyed comfortable indolence in shady black and white bungalows, meant to recollect the Tudor style of merrie olde England, which the ruling *tuans* had occupied. The rest lived in decaying, two-story shop-houses in town or thatched huts in outlying *kampongs*. The streets were redolent with the pungent spices of the Indies and the blended stench of open sewers and a polluted harbor. The loudest sounds of activity, residents half joked, were the clicks of chopsticks and the clacks of mah-jongg tiles, punctuated by habitual, lung-clearing hawking. Singapore was poorer than Mexico. Even those who worked hard were not particularly productive.

If only the colonial masters could see Singapore today, with its futuristic, high-rise towers; its manicured public gardens framed in red bougainvillea; its precise, muted subway system; its heavy but orderly traffic of polished, late-model cars; and its street signs banning everything from spitting and smoking to uncompleted toilet-flushing. The few remaining shop-houses have been converted to trendy boutiques and nightspots. The last kampong was about to be razed.

In appearance Singapore has set the tone for Bangkok, Jakarta, and Kuala Lumpur, the other major cities of the region, and it compares more than favorably with the hyper boomtowns of Hong Kong and Shanghai. As a center of technology and finance, Singapore is the goal toward which the others strive. Average income for today's 4.8 million Singaporeans is about $25,000, roughly the same as in Italy. Ninety percent of people own their homes, mostly flats in tidy apartment blocks, financed through mandatory contributions to a superbly managed social security fund. Singaporeans are relentlessly middle-class, well educated, ambitious, and busy-busy-busy. They are, in a word, successful.

And Lee Kuan Yew, whether they love him or hate him, made it all happen. Lee Kuan Yew, brilliant, visionary, driven, and seemingly incorruptible. Lee Kuan Yew, as arrogant as the British ever were, authoritarian, abrasive, repressive, and ruthless. Singaporeans know him as all of that and more. He is the father of their nation.

He is also the father of the current prime minister. But let there be no doubt—and there is none among Singaporeans—Lee Kuan Yew, well into his eighties, still calls the important shots. He *is* Singapore. And in a very real sense, he and his country are the models for much of Asia, where 60 percent of all people on Earth live, and which is positioning itself to lead the world. Lee stepped aside in 1990 after thirty-one years, longer than any other prime minister in the world. But he didn't go very far. With his People's Action Party the only political organization ever to have been elected, he ordained himself "senior minister" to stand over the shoulder of a trusted acolyte he selected to hold the prime ministerial seat while his elder son recovered from cancer. The elder Lee now operates behind a fanciful fig leaf as "minister mentor," still not fully trustful that the nation he created can manage without him. "Even from my sickbed, even if you are going to lower me into the grave, and I feel something is going wrong," he once chastened his fellow citizens in a National Day speech, "I will get up."

There have been times over the years when Singapore seemed too confining to hold Lee and his monumental talent and ego. There were occasional rumors that he would run the United Nations or perhaps the World Bank. But as paterfamilias he could not bring himself to abandon the child he had made in his own image. Instead, he found outlets for his genius as an ad hoc adviser to the leaders of the two countries that matter most to him, China and the United States. There were times, too, when Lee swapped ideologies almost as frequently as he put on fresh white shirts and trousers as a show of political purity. He had entered politics as a self-professed socialist, who at the outset of independence cooperated with the indigenous Communist Party. In the mid-1960s, he was an outspoken critic of all things American. As he achieved success upon success, he touted a Confucian-based, father-knows-best system of "Asian values" and argued that these were superior to Western ideals, such as freedom of expression. Today he is the penultimate conservative, capitalist, and the best friend the United States has in Southeast Asia.

Above all other things, he is a hard-core pragmatist. Lee was reared to be accepted and to get ahead in a world ruled by the British Empire, what the British of the day mockingly called a WOG (westernized oriental gentleman). His grandfather footed the bill for a proper English education and gave him a proper English name, Harry. Harry Lee.

But in 1942, shortly before he was to leave for Cambridge, Japan's Imperial Army stormed Singapore, overrunning the reputedly impregnable British bastion and plowing on across the rest of Southeast Asia. Lee was thunderstruck by the ease with which the Japanese displaced the presumably indomitable British. Yet, although he admires postwar Japan's disciplined approach to productivity, he despised the Japanese occupiers and has never gotten over once being beaten for not standing aside to let a soldier pass him on a bridge. Putting aside sentiment, though, he taught himself Japanese and worked for the occupation force's propaganda arm.

After the war, young Harry Lee went off to England and graduated from Cambridge with some of the highest grades ever achieved at that eight-hundred-year-old university. (His wife, Kwa Geok Choo, received even higher honors.) Soon after the couple returned home and opened a joint law practice, Lee turned whole-heartedly against Britain and became embroiled in the drive to form what would become independent Malaysia—Malaya plus Singapore and parts of Borneo.

But the prickly Lee soon clashed with the easygoing Malay prince, Tunku Abdul Rahman. "Mr. Lee Kuan Yew," the Tunku used to grumble, "is too clever by half." In 1965, after two troublesome years, Singapore was expelled from the new union, to become a freestanding nation. The casting out of the island dashed Lee into deep despair, leaving him sleepless with worry that he and Singapore were doomed to fail. But he soon overcame the black depression and never looked back, forcefully spurring the newly independent ministate onward, from simple entrepôt to towering accomplish-ment as an equatorial Switzerland, a well-ordered center of inter-national finance, investment, light industry, and high technology, as well as a think tank for all of Southeast Asia.

Following the death of Mao Zedong in 1976, Lee was one of the first world leaders to anticipate China's capitalist growth poten-tial under Deng Xiopeng's open-door policy. Having taught himself Mandarin so that he could speak with many of his own constituents, he was able to communicate personally with the Chinese leader-ship. Today, top officials from the mainland flood into Singapore to study at Lee's feet how to apply the lessons of one of Asia's tiniest countries to the world's largest. China's chosen means of opening to the outside—rapid economic development held on a short political rein—is based on Lee's tutelage.

The kernel of his philosophy is that given clean government and enough worldly goods, previously poor people can be kept sufficiently content not to complain about lacking certain freedoms. Creature comforts, the reasoning goes, trump free expression for all but a handful of ivory-tower intelligentsia. And by the time the masses do begin to gripe, their expectations will have been conditioned to a level sufficiently low so as not to seriously upend the system. It has worked brilliantly in Singapore and it is working, so far, in China.

For decades, U.S. presidents have called on Lee as an authentic but comprehensible guide through the mysterious East. Lee was the first foreign visitor President George H. W. Bush received in the Oval Office after launching the first Gulf War. He is the kind of leader American presidents would install in every country in the world if they could: practical, friendly to foreign investors, unemotional, insightful, publicly circumspect, and privately candid to a fault. Throughout Bond's term in the Senate, he has visited Singapore annually and each time been given an hour or more meeting with Lee. These discussions provided Bond with insightful reviews of current conditions in Singapore and throughout the region. American expatriates enjoy living and working in Singapore: it is clean, safe, comfortable (with air-conditioning), and efficient. The subway really does run on time. It is noticeably foreign without being overly exotic. Except for very rare occasions, such as in 1994, when a troubled nineteen-year-old named Michael P. Fay was given six strokes of the cane for vandalizing cars, despite President Clinton's efforts to intervene with Lee, Americans seldom run into serious difficulties. While they would never tolerate Singapore's restrictions back home, they happily enjoy their advantages while posted there.

Most importantly, Lee is that rare creature, the (relatively) benevolent dictator. He rapidly raised living standards by refusing to be stalled by messy, Western-style democracy. The American system, he said some years ago, has no place in Singapore or anywhere in the developing world, "where executive action must be swift to forestall disaster." He is an expeditious, my-way-or-the-highway kind of guy, the kind Americans prefer to deal with because he cuts through red tape and gets things done. Similar appeal lay for decades behind America's shunning of democratic India's squabbling politicians in favor of Pakistan's compliant military rulers. (That hasn't worked out so well, though.)

When Lee has felt himself challenged to any degree at all, whether by foreign news media or domestic political opponents, he has typically retaliated not with arrest or worse, as less subtle strongmen elsewhere do, but with lawsuits. He has bankrupted some of his enemies. He also has drawn on the nation's Internal Security Act, a cherished relic of British colonial rule, to jail others for decades without benefit of trial. When a documentary film was produced in 2007 about seventy-eight-year-old opposition politician Said Zahiri, following his release after seventeen years in prison without trial, the government banned it.

U.S. leaders, far more concerned with results than means, don't seriously complain about human rights abuses in Singapore. Lee in turn does not criticize the United States for holding Muslims at Guantánamo Bay. Every four or five years, the country holds elections and, while the system is fixed in favor of the People's Action Party, seeing news photos of non-Caucasian foreigners stepping up to the ballot box never fails to make Americans misty-eyed.

Keenly aware of Singapore's precarious position as a minuscule ethnic Chinese redoubt in a vast Islamic sea, yet fearful of growing too reliant on big China, Lee has over the past two decades bound the security of his country ever more snugly to the United States. Under an agreement signed with the first Bush administration in 1990 and amended in 1999, Singapore provides docking and logistics facilities to the U.S. Seventh Fleet at its splendid Changi naval base, where it has built a pier large enough to accommodate any American aircraft carrier. Although Changi is nominally a Singaporean base, it functions for all intents and purposes as part of the U.S. Navy. In July 2005 the United States and Singapore signed a strategic framework agreement to expand cooperation in defense and security. Singapore's hospitality to the navy as well as to U.S. Air Force warplanes at the Paya Labar air base has added to its unpopularity, already stoked by its stunning economic achievement, among its Islamic neighbors.

Singaporeans also have learned that close association with the U.S. military comes with another stiff price. In December 2001, Singapore intelligence agents, acting on information extracted from a captive al-Qaeda operative in Afghanistan, narrowly intercepted an advanced terrorist plot. Members of a Jemaah Islamiya sleeper cell were preparing to bomb U.S. vessels at Changi; a bus transporting American sailors; American commercial buildings; and the embassies of the United States, Britain, Australia, and Israel.

The group already had procured four tons of ammonium nitrate to use in explosives and was shopping for thirteen more tons. The ringleader of the plot, which had been taking form since 1997, was identified as Fathur Rahman al-Ghozi, a former student of the virulently anti-American cleric Abu Bakar Ba'asyir at his extremist pesantren in Indonesia. Fathur, who subsequently was arrested in the Philippines, and several others among forty-one alleged Jemaah Islamiya members involved in the scheme had studied bomb-making in Pakistan, Afghanistan, and Mindanao.

Discovery of the plot shook complacent Singaporeans to their eyeteeth. They had long assumed, with paternalistic condescension, that "their" Muslims had no connection to the greater world of Islamic dissent. But when they pried the lid off their very own Pandora's box they discovered a small but furious community of radical Muslims. Most were indigenous Malays, but there were others, of Pakistani, Indian, or Arab origins. They were unified by feelings of marginalization and humiliation in the secular, technologically fueled, consumer-driven, Chinese-dominated welfare state that is today's Singapore. Not to mention that infuriating association with Americans.

In addition, Singapore, like Thailand and the Philippines, but not Indonesia and Malaysia, maintains warm and profitable diplomatic relations with Israel. During the 1960s, Israeli troops lived in Singapore under gossamer cover, training the armed forces. They were referred to jokingly as "Mexicans." Lee had two major reasons for calling on the Israelis for military assistance. First, he has always likened Singapore's circumstances to Israel's: small states with few natural resources; Israel the sole Jewish state in the Arab Middle East (and the world) and Singapore the only Chinese-majority country in Southeast Asia; both peoples surviving nicely by their wits. In his two-volume, 680-page memoir, Lee wrote that his goal was to "leapfrog the region, as the Israelis had done." And second, he admires Jews for what he considers their superior intelligence. Clearly implied in that judgment—and he has come close to saying so publicly—is his belief that Malays lag behind ethnic Chinese in intellect. Needless to say, these attitudes don't go down well in the neighborhood or among Singapore's own Muslims.

The Lees, father and son, were horrified by the discovery of the Jemaah Islamiya plot. Not only did it reveal a shockingly unnoticed flaw in their well-ordered security system, but also they were faced suddenly with the stark realization that their attempt over the years to homogenize Singaporeans of diverse religious, ethnic, linguistic, and cultural backgrounds was in jeopardy. Lee Kuan Yew had worked assiduously to minimize ethnic divisions in the polyglot state ever since 1964, when thirty-six people were killed in race riots between Malays and Chinese and more than five hundred were injured. The outburst was Singapore's equivalent of the 1969 rioting in Kuala Lumpur, and it frightened Lee so much that he vowed that never again would there be disorder in Singapore.

One lasting result was the muzzling of news media, supposedly to avoid unwanted provocations. Public political gatherings of more than five persons were banned, and remain so. Authorities meticulously went about mingling the races, in residential apartment houses, schools, workplaces, and community centers. Even the colorful old Chinatown and Little India neighborhoods, both major tourist attractions for their manicured exoticism, were given infusions of Malay residents. Singaporeans one and all, Lee ordered, would adapt.

Now, despite all his controls and precautions, here was proof of more than incipient unrest on the island. And there were operational links to terrorist organizations just across the short causeway, in Malaysia, and well beyond, to the vast, restive umma. Lee graphically envisioned a recurrence of the 1964 riots, or worse, and he took immediate action. Coordinated by the crack Home Ministry, which incorporates some of Singapore's best bureaucratic minds, police swiftly arrested fifteen suspects. By 2007 they had jailed thirty-nine.

A few have since been released. Another nineteen were allowed to remain out of prison but under close surveillance, what the government refers to as "restrictive orders."

The biggest prize snagged in the dragnet was the leader of the Singapore branch of Jemaah Islamiya, Mas Selamat bin Kastari. He had been arrested in Indonesia in January 2006 and extradited to the city-state. Singaporean authorities believed he was planning to crash a plane into Changi International Airport. Mas was jailed and held without charges under the Internal Security Act. A year later, he fled through a bathroom window. The escape of this high-value prisoner was devastating to the Singapore authorities. They mounted the largest manhunt ever conducted on the little island. To no avail. Mas had slipped away and, either by swimming or on a makeshift raft, made his way to Malaysia. There, in the city of Johor Bharu, just a few miles from Singapore, he remained for more than a year, presumably with the assistance of locals. Malaysian police captured him in April 2009. Needless to say, the escape and subsequent capture by Malaysia were a stinging humiliation to the Lees.

Lee Kuan Yew worries more about Islamic extremists as alien enemies than do his counterparts in Indonesia and Malaysia, so it was not surprising that he supported the U.S. invasion of Iraq. And he believes that U.S. troops must not soon end their occupation. Any outcome that could be construed as a U.S. military humiliation would reverberate throughout the world and, in the Southeast Asian context, be particularly damaging to his little nation.

But never shy about pointing the finger of blame, he charges that the George W. Bush administration committed grave errors in Iraq and that these have blown back to the detriment of the United States and Southeast Asia. "I told [then deputy secretary of defense] Paul Wolfowitz right here, after the invasion, that Singapore supported the United States because removing Saddam was the right thing to do," he told us during an extensive interview in his office. "But I also told him that they were wrong to disband the Iraqi military and police and to hold elections so quickly."

He recalled how, in his wartime youth, the Japanese occupiers, with only a small garrison in Singapore, permitted the British police and civil administration to remain in place while Japanese troops swept on to Java. "It worked," he said. "But Wolfowitz told me that the Americans had to get rid of the Baathists. That was the beginning of your problems . . . ," Lee told us. "After four thousand years of Iraqi history, you think you're going to change society with an invasion? That's a false premise. . . . The result is that you got the clergy mixed up in government. By destroying the old system so precipitously, they committed a grave mistake and they were not prepared for the results."

Two others whom Lee faulted for leading Bush astray were the British-born Princeton Arabist Bernard Lewis and the Zionist intellectual Natan Sharansky, both of whom enjoyed exceptional entrée to the White House.

Lewis's theory of secularizing, modernizing, Westernizing, and democratizing the Arab world was at the center of Bush's vision when he determined to invade Iraq. Under Saddam's Baathist regime, Iraq had been one of the few secular states in the Middle East. Therefore, the administration presumed, it would be low-hanging fruit, ripe for easy plucking and molding into the Lewis-Sharansky-Bush model.

Sharansky, a former Soviet dissident who in 1999 became deputy prime minister of Israel in the right-wing government of Binyamin Netanyahu, idolized President Ronald Reagan for having characterized the Soviet Union as the "Evil Empire." In 2005 President Bush invited Sharansky to the Oval Office and praised his book *The Case for Democracy*, in which he argued that only by the United States forcefully imposing "God's gift" of democracy could the Middle East attain peace. The president told Sharansky that the book had so influenced his thinking that he had included its gist in his inaugural address that January, calling for "the expansion of freedom" around the world.

Having followed the advice of Wolfowitz, Lewis, and Sharansky, Lee told us, the Bush-Cheney team had severely limited its options in Iraq. "Now that they've gotten your country into such a jam you have no choice but to calm the situation and then leave with your tail up," he said. "If you leave with your tail down, the world will be in serious trouble. Quitting is not an option. It would bring disaster to the world."

As we listened, we realized that Lee had mellowed with the years. But not much. He was still highly critical of his neighbors, particularly the Philippines, for their seeming inability to overcome sloth and corruption. He disparaged them as "soft societies." That kind of unsolicited critiquing has won Lee and his country few friends in the region. He was still unapologetic about his views on race and he rationalized his conviction of yellow and white supremacy over browns and blacks with quasi-scientific theories. One of these was based on supposed proof of race-related variations in secretions of the thyroid and other ductless glands. "I started off believing all men were equal," he once stated. "I now know that's the most unlikely thing ever to have been."

He has eased off a bit from tinkering with eugenics, though. For years he had encouraged more "highly educated" (read Chinese) women to marry younger and bear more children to offset higher birthrates among the "less educated" (Malays). His program of official inducements, including tax bonuses and free *Love Boat*–style cruises for courting couples, flopped. He had launched that plan following a too-successful 1970s-era family-planning program, titled "Two Is Enough." It set in motion a still-declining national birthrate. One of his more recent plans was to add another two million people to the island's shrinking population over the next forty to fifty years by inviting educated Asians to immigrate. Also, reminiscent of the *Love Boat* fiasco, the government outsourced to four private companies a kind of *Dating Game*, to draw young couples together.

In addition to a low birthrate, Singapore is plagued by a ceaseless flow of emigration. Each year, six thousand to seven thousand young people leave the island to settle elsewhere. Most are driven away by the island's social and political strictures. For years, Lee dismissed them as weaklings who couldn't make it in Singapore's competitive atmosphere. More recently, the government has conceded the appeal of a more exciting life and challenging jobs in the West and China. The waning population is partially offset by large floating communities of Indonesians, Filipinos, Malaysians, Indians, and Arabs. Most of them work as day laborers or household servants, jobs Singaporeans no longer want to perform.

Lee is intolerably sensitive to the suffocating heat and humidity of Singapore, attributing his sensitivity to his clan's racial origins in the cooler climes of central China, and demands that his home and office be briskly air-conditioned to a precise 71.6 degrees Fahrenheit (66.2 degrees while he sleeps). For years, he wore an old beige zippered golf jacket around the office while guests endured goose bumps in respectful silence. During our latest interview, he was much more elegantly turned out, in a black, Chinese silk tunic with a high mandarin collar. His face, once deeply pockmarked, had smoothed to a babylike texture, and his white hair had crept back, further exaggerating a high, sloping forehead and a heavy, overhanging brow. Having undergone heart surgery and feeling the effects of a "game shoulder," he had given up golf, which he used to play under the baleful eye of machine-gun-toting, mercenary Gurkha bodyguards. He still worked out of the same austere L-shaped office he'd long occupied in the Istana, the former mansion of the British colonial governor-general. A secretary poured tiny cups of green tea. There was no small talk. There rarely is with Lee Kuan Yew. We discussed Islam, China, and the United States, three issues of paramount concern to him. Mainly, he spoke and we listened:

> Oil is at the root of the world's problems with Islam. It gave the Arabs money to influence the moderate Muslims of Southeast Asia. The future of Islam here depends on how things go in the Middle East. The Arabization and fundamentalism we see here come from there.
>
> Southeast Asian Muslims are a different lot; they have neither the emotional nor physical makeup of the Arabs; they don't fly into rages; they're accustomed to living with others. But pockets of them have been converted to the Arab way of Islam by Saudi teachers, by money and travel. This networking and pumping up have been going on for the past thirty years. Now they are linked up worldwide. If we don't contain the extremists in the Middle East we're going to be in deep trouble here.
>
> My pessimistic view is that it's going to take a long time. . . . But after fifteen or twenty years, when the theocrats can't deliver,

modernization will come in. . . . In the end they can't win. They
lack the weapons and the technology. It will be a process of attri-
tion and the Muslims are going to have to decide whether or not
they want to help themselves. Do they want to be taken over by
Hezbollah, the mullahs, and so on, or do they want to have a modern life and a modern religion?

But, he warned, no matter what direction the struggle finally
takes, the rest of the world must dismiss any notion of assimilat-
ing Muslims. "*They* want to assimilate *us*. It's a one-way traffic. In
Malaysia, for example, trying to convert a Muslim is a crime. They
have no confidence in allowing choice."

Until Washington helps "put things right" in the Arab-Israeli
dispute and "pacifies" the Middle East, there was little that
the United States could do to curb the fundamentalist drive in
Southeast Asia. "But you must not let your preoccupation with
the Middle East—Iraq, Iran, the Israelis, and oil—allow others,
especially China, to overtake your interests in Southeast Asia.
The Chinese are not distracted. They're looking for energy everywhere and they're making friends everywhere, including here.
Demonizing China is a mistake. It's purely for [U.S.] domestic
political use. The Defense Department and the State Department
know there is no profit in picking a quarrel with China. You need
them in North Korea and it's in China's interest to keep North
Korean nuclear power under control, or all of North Asia could go
nuclear. On another level, if you put a tax on Chinese goods the
U.S. standard of living will suffer. I also believe that China is wise
enough to adjust."

In his own backyard, Lee said, he was seriously concerned about
the ongoing fighting in Mindanao and the seeming inability or
unwillingness of the Arroyo government to work things out with
the MILF. "I've given up on the Philippines," he said with obvious
disgust, then added, grudgingly, "for the time being, anyway."

As for Indonesia—whose future he believes is central to peace
and development in the entire region—he said provocatively that
overthrowing the Suharto regime, despite its rampant corruption,
had been "a disaster . . . that has set them back fifteen years."

Although Lee has never tolerated corruption in his own ranks, he clearly preferred the certainties of exploitative strongman rule to the unpredictability of freewheeling democracy as practiced today in the Philippines and Indonesia. While acknowledging that "things are looking better" under President Yudhoyono, still, he wondered aloud, "If you press the button, will it ring?"

27

The Son

Despite his elder son being prime minister; his younger son having headed the government-owned telecommunications company (the largest in Southeast Asia); both sons having been promoted to brigadier general in the army by the time they turned thirty; his daughter running the National Institute for Neurology; and his daughter-in-law operating the giant state investment company Temasek Holdings (which bought Thailand's Shin Satellite, leading to a coup against Prime Minister Thaksin, and which recently bought a 15 percent share in the conglomerate the younger son recently took over), Lee Kuan Yew adamantly denies allegations of nepotism.

"We run a meritocracy," he once insisted in an interview with the German newsweekly *Der Spiegel*. "If the Lee family set an example of nepotism, that system would collapse. If I were not the prime minister, my son could have become prime minister several years earlier. It is against my interest to allow any family member who's incompetent to hold an important job because that would be a disaster for Singapore and my legacy. That cannot be allowed."

While these protestations may be exaggerated, few Singaporeans deny that Lee Hsien Loong is exceptionally smart and that he was expertly groomed from childhood to inherit his father's mantle. Even as his son was undergoing cancer treatment in 1992, the elder

Lee declared openly that his elevation to prime minister was "on the cards."

Like his parents, Hsien Loong graduated from Cambridge University with high honors, in his case in mathematics and computer science. He went on to Harvard's Kennedy School of Government and earned a master's degree in public administration. After enlisting in the Singapore army, he attended the U.S. Army Command and General Staff College at Fort Leavenworth, Kansas. He retired from the army in 1984, after thirteen years, as a brigadier general. He was thirty-two years old. Known ever since as B. G. Lee, he immediately launched his career in politics and was elected to Parliament on his first try. The younger Lee rocketed across the political heavens with an unfailing series of reelections and ever-higher cabinet appointments. He was deputy prime minister for fourteen years.

In 2004 he succeeded Goh Chok Tong as prime minister. Goh, a long-standing Lee Kuan Yew understudy, had been regarded initially by some Singaporeans as a seat warmer while the son recovered from his illness and gained experience. That was unfair to Goh, a competent and popular leader, and he stayed in the premier's position for fourteen years. But he also responded to orders with the unquestioning loyalty of a good soldier. In the ensuing job shuffle, Goh slipped into Lee Kuan Yew's former role as senior minister, minus the boss's oversight powers, and Lee created the position of minister mentor for himself.

Although Hsien Loong's meteoric career could be seen as preordained, it wasn't without pain. His wife, a Malaysian-Chinese physician, died in 1982, three weeks after giving birth to an albino son. Rumors spread throughout Singapore that she had committed suicide. Hsien Loong's official biography states that she died of a heart attack. He remarried three years later. In 1992 he was diagnosed with lymphoma and underwent three months of chemotherapy. His doctors announced afterward that he showed "no evidence of any residual disease."

While Hsien Loong certainly could not be accused of being wet behind the ears when he assumed power, he was distinctly rough around the edges. Like his father, who has never suffered fools, gladly or otherwise, he was aloof, seeming to consider himself most people's intellectual superior, and was not shy about letting them know so. He seemed incapable of cracking a smile or a joke. Singaporeans weren't willing to cut him the same slack they'd allowed his intimidating father. Following friendly advice from Goh that he "let his softer side show," Hsien Loong appeared to have enrolled in charm school and graduated with a degree in personality transformation.

In an interview in 1991, when he was finance minister, he had sat rigidly behind his desk, snapping off curt replies and warily projecting defensiveness. This time, slouched comfortably on a cream-colored sofa in his corporate-style office at the Istana, he smiled broadly, naturally, and often. His comments and answers to our questions were calm and confident. He spoke breezily about newly relaxed rules on cultural activities, plans to legalize homosexuality (currently punishable by up to two years' imprisonment), his recent visit to a hip new nightclub, a book on atheism he planned to read, and how he was beginning to wind down the nanny state.

Turning Singaporeans into wild and crazy guys may take some time, though. A franchise of the famed Paris-based Crazy Horse nude dance review packed up and left town in 2007 after just fifteen months, complaining that the government's refusal to allow the show to advertise its most obvious attraction assured poor turnouts. Said Tan Tarn How, a senior researcher on the arts and creativity at Singapore's Institute of Policy Studies, "It raises the whole question of how you maintain the clean, above-board image and, at the same time, want to attract another kind of tourist. [The government] wanted controlled looseness."

Hsien Loong, handsome, youthful at fifty-seven, and self-assured, wore a familiar-looking zippered golf jacket, "a gift from my father," he acknowledged with a grin. What came through was that while he was pacing off his turf as a gradual modernizer, he also was carrying on not only his father's sartorial habits but his views on race and religion as well. For the father, the trigger had been the 1964 riots. The abortive 2001 Jemaah Islamiya bombing plot spurred the son. "In Singapore," he told us, "we're sitting on a global fault line. . . . Ours are communities with direct links overseas—Chinese,

Muslims, and Indians—and Islam in particular is going through a worldwide resurgence. Now it's up to the moderates to lead their fellow Muslims forward and not follow them backward."

He recalled with evident nostalgia how just ten or fifteen years ago it was commonplace for Malay politicians to relax after work with colleagues from other ethnic groups over a steaming plate of fried *mee hoon* and a cold Tiger beer at a Chinese restaurant. "As long as there was no pork, it was okay. Today, those same people cannot be seen in public even entering a restaurant that doesn't have an official halal certificate," he said. "Back then, they were known as Malays; it was an ethnic identity. Now they, and we, call them Muslims. Religious identity is first."

At public ceremonies such as graduations, Malay girls, who are barred by Singapore law from wearing Islamic cover in government schools, either clasp a book or wear gloves to avoid touching the hand of any male handing out diplomas. Such behavior, he said, indicated that Muslims in Singapore, as well as in Indonesia and Malaysia, had "picked up the ritual and form of Middle Eastern Islam, such as dress, no drinking, and fraternizing between the sexes, without any deep understanding. If you want to be well regarded in your community you must adopt these habits."

Disappointed and worried that the government's attempt over the years to integrate Malays into the ethnic Chinese mainstream had come up short, Hsien Loong acknowledged that the discovery of the 2001 bombing plot revealed what Singapore's former UN ambassador Tommy Koh termed the "green tide" of fundamentalism rising on the island. "We have no choice but to ride this tide," said the prime minister. He also acknowledged that a central cause for the new religious fervor was the failure of Malays to match the achievements of the Chinese majority. While 22 percent of Chinese high school graduates went on to university, only 3 percent of Malays did. Some Islamic religious leaders have proposed that Singapore adopt a quota system similar to that in Malaysia, with universities and the government bureaucracy making special allowances to admit Malays.

But the mandarin-style meritocracy Lee Kuan Yew established decades ago would not permit such exceptions. Furthermore, while the Chinese minority in Malaysia has little choice but to grin and bear it, the 80 percent of Singaporeans who are Chinese would balk. "This is not the way we're going to go in Singapore," Hsien Loong said with finality.

Like his opposite numbers throughout the region, the prime minister admonished that there was a central role for the United States to play in cooling Islamic passions, but that under the George W. Bush administration Americans had not lived up to their responsibilities. "Your president doesn't have an academic intellect," he said bluntly. "But he's not dim, either. He does understand issues and he has his views. But, mind you, once he's made up his mind the full complexity doesn't affect him."

According to Hsien Loong, the Obama administration needed to reach out simultaneously in two directions: "You must engage with moderate Muslims in Southeast Asia. Show them that Islam is compatible with modern education, economics, and so forth. Show them that they can be friends of the United States. Stop using exclusionary terms like 'coalition of the willing' and 'with us or against us.' At the same time, you must show more balance in your dealings with Israel, at the very least when they transgress. Palestine is now the number-one topic of discussion in Malay kampongs, and your actions have negatively impacted on your image among them."

By dealing only marginally with Southeast Asian governments, he cautioned, the United States was rapidly losing influence to China. The Chinese were proving adept at exercising "soft power" among the region's governments, while Americans were bogged down with making idealistic demands on issues of transparency and counterterrorism. The United States–dominated World Bank, when Wolfowitz was at its helm, had refused to grant loans to underdeveloped countries whose governments were considered corrupt. Hien Loong counseled greater understanding. "You have to deal with these countries realistically. Most of them are not so bad and they are headed in the right direction." Not that he was advocating the acceptance of corruption, but rational standards would prove more effective than unworkable, puritanical, black-and-white demands. Coming from the son and successor of a man whose hallmarks are incorruptibility and pragmatism, this suggestion warrants serious consideration.

One of Singapore's secrets for keeping its government officials honest is to pay them well, which is completely at odds with
corruption-ridden neighbors such as Indonesia and the Philippines.
As prime minister, Hsien Loong receives an annual salary of
$2.05 million—five times the $400,000 paycheck of the president
of the United States and eight times that of the prime minister of
Japan. Cabinet ministers are paid $1.1 million. To set an example
for his colleagues, Hsien Loong recently promised to donate any
future pay raises to charity.

A well-trained crew aboard a tautly run ship, Singaporean officials
hew to the line cultivated by the Lees. Tommy Koh is one of the
deeper-thinking members of the crew. "It is a big mistake to believe
that you can defeat terrorism with hard power alone," Koh told us
in a separate interview. "You need hard and soft, just as you did
with the Cold War." In Indonesia, with its huge, overwhelmingly
impoverished Muslim population, the most valuable contributions
Americans could make were to help educate children studying in
pesantren and their mothers; to provide sorely needed assistance to
the Indonesian armed forces; and to increase private investment as
a means of creating jobs. "By doing these three things, the United
States would help Indonesia while at the same time help offset the
damage you've done to yourselves through the war in Iraq."
    A serious scholar, Koh also is an effective diplomat. He was
Singapore's chief negotiator in the 2003 free-trade agreement with
the United States, the first FTA Washington established in Southeast
Asia. He described the linkages across international borders among
al-Qaeda, Jemaah Islamiya, Abu Sayyaf, and other terrorist outfits as
"the dark side of globalization." The Iraq war was providing training
grounds for these and other anti-Western extremists who required
front-line experience. "The connections are already there," he said,
"and the longer the war goes on, the worse I fear it will become."
    Koh said that while the vast majority of Southeast Asian Muslims
had little interest in a backward-looking Islam, the "green tide" (a
term he and other Singaporeans used repeatedly) was sweeping
them unwittingly toward stark fundamentalism. In Indonesia and

Malaysia as well as in the tiny, oil-rich sultanate of Brunei, on the northwestern coast of Borneo, "the rising tide is making it extremely difficult for the governments, which are moderate, to crack down." Their difficulties were heightened by explosive levels of corruption, Koh conceded. Corruption also plagued the Middle East, leading Muslims to turn against secularism and toward greater religious fundamentalism. "Arabs, even the intellectuals, have given up," said Koh. "They're no-hopers. They see their only way as through destruction. And in Europe, Muslims are seen as an alien people from an alien culture. It could happen here."

Singapore has developed a two-tiered approach to the terrorists in its midst: the first is to arrest and imprison them; the second is to try to learn from them what led them into radicalism. Imprisonment alone is "not that effective," a top Home Ministry specialist told us, because recruitment manages to stay ahead of arrests. Islamic scholars and clerics dispatched to prisons have reported back to the government that many local terrorists were motivated initially to join Jemaah Islamiya by a sincere desire to learn more about their religion. "They literally signed up for the wrong course," said the official, who asked us not to use his name. "They were shown videos of fighting in Chechnya, Afghanistan, Iraq, and Mindanao. A dozen of them went to fight in Afghanistan and Mindanao. This helped them develop an esprit de corps, similar to gang members in the United States. They have shallow religious knowledge to begin with, and that makes them susceptible to charismatic mullahs. Then they swear oaths, and from that point on they fear the wrath of Allah."

The government's response to these jailhouse informants has been to hire about forty Islamic scholars, formed into the Religious Rehabilitation Group, to "deprogram" them and then instruct them that there are other ways to be a good Muslim. "We're mounting a counterideology program to refute and debunk their distorted views," said the Home Ministry official. "And we're sensitizing local Muslims to the threat at home and from abroad. We have no illusions about effectiveness, but we do see some positive results among the detainees." Nevertheless, the scholars have succeeded to the extent that the authorities have released forty former terrorists, believing them to be fully rehabilitated. None has returned to violence. By comparison, the U.S. Defense Department found that of the 534 prisoners released from the prison at Guantanamo Bay, Cuba, and transferred abroad, 74 had returned to terrorism or other militant activity, a recidivism rate of almost 14 percent. Writing in the *Washington Post*, William J. Dobson, a visiting scholar at the Carnegie Endowment for International Peace, recommended that the Obama administration consider a Singapore-style rehabilitation program as a means of resolving the fate of the 241 prisoners remaining at Guantanamo Bay.

From the Home Ministry source, from Koh, from the Lees, senior and junior, from virtually every government official and intellectual we interviewed, the message was the same: engagement by the United States is vital to heading off Islamic extremism in Southeast Asia. But America is going about it in the wrong way. At the same time, the United States is needed to provide balance for China. But while the United States is entrapped in crises of its own making in Iraq and Afghanistan, an unencumbered China presses ahead. "The perennial problem we face here is that the United States is the chief global power and it's very good at focusing on whatever happens to be the crisis of the moment," said Bilahari Kausikan, a young official in the Ministry of Foreign Affairs. "But it is not geared toward dealing with problems that evolve over time."

With China, as well as India, playing an increasingly high-profile part in the region's economy, the impression has taken hold that the United States "has decided that the game is not worth the candle," said Kausikan. While by beginning to repair its relations with Vietnam and signing an FTA with Singapore the George W. Bush administration had "shown signs of awakening to some degree," the overriding sense among regional governments was that Washington was content to stand "very much on the sideline."

Singapore desperately wants the United States to take center field in regional affairs. But it and the other area powers believed that the Bush administration was determined to rely on its armed might rather than its diplomatic skills. "The U.S. does have power in Southeast Asia," said Kausikan, "but power is not the same as influence." Throughout the Bush years, the United States was seen to be using that power, or threatening to use it, to extract anti-terror cooperation from regional governments, not realizing that from the local perspective, terrorism was just a sliver of the problems they face. More broadly, the region sees Washington as planning for an eventual all-out war if needed to keep itself at the apex of world dominance. Asia, though, was preparing for a galactic shift by China, with India riding the comet's tail.

"As we see it," said Kausikan, "competition doesn't have to mean conflict. But that's not what we hear from Capitol Hill." While conceding that the periodic rise and fall of anti-China rhetoric in Washington was largely meant for domestic audiences, the inherent danger is that over time negativity and hostility can solidify into impermeable walls on both sides of the Pacific. "It's a challenge," he said, "but if you define China as a threat, it will become a threat. And I'm afraid that this kind of finger-pointing is a central part of the U.S. system. It's as basic as the weather."

Kausikan and other bright young technocrats in the Singapore hierarchy sense reverberations of the U.S.-Japan economic tensions of the 1980s in the current strains between Washington and Beijing. The essential difference is that Japan was and remains a staunch ally of the United States, which China, like Russia, all but certainly never will be. Americans' perception of China as the quintessential *other* lurks behind the jittery responses in Congress and the Pentagon each time new information emerges on Beijing's adding weapons to its military arsenal.

Singaporeans judge these American reactions as worn and hypocritical tirades. The United States, after all, owns far more ultramodern weapons of uncontested lethality than any other country has possessed in history, and is developing more all the time. "China is now investing worldwide," said Kausikan, "and as it develops it is natural that it should seek the same type of protection for its wealth as the United States and other advanced nations already have."

The answer, as he sees it, was not for the United States to hold China at an ever-increasing distance, which ensures its remaining an outsider and potentially becoming an enemy. Rather, Washington should help Beijing become what Robert B. Zoellick—a favorite of the Lee team, who succeeded Wolfowitz at the World Bank— termed "a responsible stakeholder" in world affairs. Such a China could be counted on to work cooperatively with the United States and other Western nations, goes Zoellick's argument. This supposition assumes that China is motivated primarily to improve the life of its people rather than to dominate the United States, something that Southeast Asians accept but that many Americans are unwilling to believe.

At the same, time, said Kausikan, Americans needed to learn that their values and beliefs were not necessarily shared by everyone else and that, therefore, they needed to stop interfering, uninvited, in other people's affairs. "If we succeed in drawing China into the world system—and the signs are very encouraging—unlike the U.S., they still will not tell other governments how to run their domestic affairs," he said. Numbers of Southeast Asians express similar confidence, pointing out that China itself is undergoing a massive, albeit controlled, ideological transformation that will carry on for decades.

In Singaporeans' analyses of the variables, Americans speak one way and behave very differently, especially outside their own domain, while China talks and walks to the same beat at home and abroad. "This is the big difference between China and the United States," said Kausikan. "The U.S. has an ideology that requires it to speak in a certain way and that worries some people. The U.S. defines itself by its ideology, and that won't change."

28

The Cheerleader

Singaporeans' insight into how Americans think and function serves their little country well. Much of their understanding is honed at the best colleges and universities in the United States. In 2001, admirers of Lee Kuan Yew formally recognized the value of top-tier U.S. education by establishing a graduate school of public policy for Singaporean scholars in his name at Harvard's Kennedy School of Government.

A glance at the résumés of the ruling elite reveals, in addition to the Lee clan, a long list of Singaporeans with prestigious American degrees. Some are enthusiastic about their experience; others, less so. Some denigrate Americans for a range of supposed shortcomings, hypocrisy in the context of the Iraq occupation being chief among them at the moment. Many would dearly love to have some of Americans' freedoms, particularly free speech, while others fear their society is too fragile to bear the weight responsibly.

Foreign Minister George Yeo Yong Boon (Harvard MBA with high distinction, 1983) stands in a class all his own as a self-professed admirer of the American way. A born-again Christian, he ticked off for us the names of family members who are U.S. citizens, giving special mention to a favorite niece, TV and movie actress Gwendoline Yeo (B.A. from UCLA at age nineteen, summa cum laude, and Phi Beta Kappa.) He proudly waved the red, white, and blue.

"The American Dream has become the Asian Dream," Yeo offered in opening a conversation at his ministry office, in the handsomely renovated British Officers' Mess. "After World War II, the Chinese Revolution, and the wars in Korea and Vietnam, the U.S. showed the way forward for Asians. Many of us went to the States for education and came back to join a great tide involving half the world's people wanting their place in the sun."

Now, having helped create this dynamic force for change in what had been one of the world's great disaster belts, Americans had to face up to the obvious—that Asia will in very short order be bigger, stronger, and richer than the United States and Europe combined. "The big question all of us have to consider is whether we'll have another generation of peace in Asia," said Yeo. "If we don't get the China-U.S. equation wrong, we will have peace. And that doesn't even take into account the emergence of India. So it's very clear: the United States cannot ignore this part of the world, even if it wants to."

But Yeo, like so many other prominent Southeast Asians, warned that the United States was not adapting well to the new multipolar realities. "You can't expect China and India to remain poor. They are growing wealthier by the day, and they will become more powerful. Meanwhile, China in particular takes a broad perspective on its national positions and international strategy. By contrast, the way the U.S. system works—one crisis at a time; your domestic agenda in continuous disarray; elections always coming up—this worries us about you."

Yeo, like the Lees, expressed scant concern about China becoming a military threat, either to the rest of Asia or to the United States directly, for decades at least. Its internal problems are that overwhelming. While he anticipated that the Communist Party would still be in power twenty years hence, he projected that it will have changed enormously, even more so than in the previous two decades. "Like us, they select the best people, based on Confucian methods of testing," he said. "They're in a very creative phase now. In twenty years, maybe less, they'll have democracy, though the United States won't recognize it as such, because it will be democracy with Chinese characteristics. That will make it easier for those of us in the region to work with them, but it will make things more difficult for you unless you enlarge your presence in any and every way you can."

The challenge the United States faces in the region—winning hearts and minds, which it failed to do in the Vietnam War—could turn into a strong and positive force if Americans respond and persist. "So far," said Yeo, "you are losing the battle. But you simply can't afford to withdraw from it. If you can come to terms with Southeast Asia's diversity, you're halfway to managing your Islamic problem around the world."

President Yudhoyono in Indonesia and Prime Minister Najib in Malaysia have the credentials to help clear a path for Americans through hostile territory. But to make the most of these enablers, Washington must appreciate the delicacy of their domestic positions. "They are floating on a tidal force of fundamentalism," said Yeo, "and this requires great sensitivity from the United States."

Another authority on America is Rohan Gunaratna, who also happens to be Singapore's go-to guy for anyone seeking deeper insights into terrorism in Southeast Asia. He holds degrees from Notre Dame and St. Andrew's, in Scotland, and is a citizen of Sri Lanka, which in 2009 finally wrapped up its twenty-five-year civil war with Hindu-separatist terrorists. Gunaratna studies the region from Singapore's Institute of Defense and Strategic Studies, where we spoke with him, and travels often among Islamic terrorist outfits in the region. Although some critics claim that he's overly interested in publicity for himself, nobody denies that he has a superb firsthand knowledge of extremists' motives and tactics.

Gunaratna's take is that while the United States made "a dreadful error" by invading Iraq, it would make an even bigger mistake by leaving prematurely because Iraq had become a lightning rod for Islamic terrorists throughout South and Southeast Asia, the Middle East, and Europe. "Since the United States started the war, many of the old groups, as well as new ones that have spun off from the parent organizations, have grown stronger by exploiting the suffering and anger of fellow Muslims. They now have the will to fight and

to resist; the Americans have only the firepower; they lack the will."
Gunaratna predicted that it would take much longer than Americans
believe to prepare Iraqis to take over enough of their own security so
that the United States safely can withdraw its forces. "Meanwhile,"
he said, "groups in Southeast Asia will continue to grow."

While Southeast Asian governments can legitimately claim that
they have killed or arrested significant numbers of Jemaah Islamiya
and other groups members, "Iraq has mobilized Muslims into coordination and it has increased the threat a hundred times." Much
as in Vietnam, Americans continued to stress the body count, the
number of terrorists killed. But, said Gunaratna, "this is beside
the point. You need long-term plans in strategic counterterrorism
if you're going to change the minds of Muslims. The United States'
and other Western nations' greatest weakness is their failure to
understand and work with Muslims, including the moderate ones in
Southeast Asia. That is why they consider you bullies. They consider
you sinful and depraved and feel that the West has struck them
down and that's why they're so backward. When you published
the [Danish] cartoons, it just twisted the knife. It was proof that the
West just wants to hammer them into the ground and widen the gulf
between 'us' and 'them.' There is a great and widening gulf between
Muslims and the Christian-Jewish West. Things that you laugh at
over dinner are very important to them. Unfortunately, Americans
see the world in black and white. You're very unsophisticated."

According to K. Kesavapany, another prominent analyst and the
director of the Institute of South Asian Studies at the National
University of Singapore, if the United States wanted to do a big
favor for its friends in Singapore, it would invest heavily in people,
by providing funding to alleviate poverty, right social inequities, and
improve education at every level, from kindergarten through graduate school—in Indonesia.

"In short," he said, "you should do everything you possibly can
to make Indonesia a model of a moderate-minded Islamic country.
You need to work on the ground to support Yudhoyono without
making him a lackey, to help him help Indonesia without expecting

him to be a booster for the United States. Indonesia is the linchpin. It has the size, the moderate Islam, and a probusiness administration. It is essential to cooling down the fundamentalist thrust in all of Southeast Asia." Using the instruments under its control, such as the World Bank and the International Monetary Fund, along with public and private sector assistance and investment, the United States needs to "reappraise its policies" and place much more emphasis on Indonesia, he said.

Many economists in the region believe that a free-trade agreement with the ASEAN geopolitical and economic organization should be the central U.S. target, and they have taken some encouragement from the recent U.S. appointment of an ambassador to the group. But a start at a more proactive approach to Indonesia would have a positive impact throughout Islamic Southeast Asia.

Kesavapany, a former Singapore ambassador to Malaysia and an acknowledged expert on Islamic affairs in the region, is far from alone in his view that Indonesia holds the key to locking out radicalism before Southeast Asia, like much of the Middle East already, spins wildly out of control. Even in thriving Singapore, discovery of the 2001 Jemaah Islamiya plot left people feeling unsettled. "We never know when he will strike again. We just know that he will. He has only to hit once; we have to be vigilant 24/7/365."

During a conversation on a palm-shaded campus terrace, Kesavapany predicted, "It's going to become worse and our American friends have done us no good. The U.S. export of democracy in its pure, undiluted form has given us the Shia uprising in Iraq and the election of Hamas in Palestine. The U.S. goes around the world preaching civil rights, individual rights, human rights, and the rule of law. Fine, fine, we all admire you for those. But since the Iraq invasion, resentment among Muslims has grown sharply, and not just toward Americans but toward their friends as well. And in Southeast Asia that means us, in Singapore. The perception that the U.S. invaded for oil and for military bases is widespread and it is undisputed in Southeast Asia, no matter what the Bush administration claimed. We have no choice; we need you here. But we have to hope that there is an exit strategy and that it takes effect soon."

As Kesavapany sees things, the war in Iraq was a classic illustration of good intentions, albeit misguided, gone awry. Had the postinvasion phase of the war gone according to the blueprint drawn up by the neoconservative ideologues in and around the Bush White House, he said, "the neocons would have won the day and we'd all be living in a different world." But they did not understand the geography, the people, their culture, or their enmities. "If they had, they never would have launched the war. Now you don't know how to get out. And 'U.S.' is a hot button with which to stir up the Muslim masses."

The critical importance of the United States helping Indonesia also came up in another interview we conducted with one of Singapore's keener thinkers, Deputy Secretary of Trade Loh Wai Keong. He urged the Obama administration to help Yudhoyono resist fundamentalist pressures by providing training to government bureaucrats, labor leaders, tax assessors, and collectors as well as in agriculture and industry.

While conceding that a "Made in U.S.A. stamp" did no harm in the hugely successful tsunami relief effort, Loh advised, "It would be better if the U.S. were more subtle. Many people in Southeast Asia don't do well with the typical American direct approach. You need much more of a human presence in Indonesia." Put another way, he was advising Americans not to seek short-term credit for their assistance. Better to work quietly at the grassroots level and reap the benefits of gathering friendships over the long term.

Nevertheless, Loh cautioned, with fiery Indonesian clerics crying out against U.S. policies in Iraq and Israel, the reality is that "you're working against the tide. But if you do nothing you definitely will slide back even more. You need to work with the next generation of leaders to develop a more open society. One generous response to one tsunami can't change twenty years of mistakes. The game requires patience, and patience is not Americans' strong suit. You need a long-term plan."

Loh, like others in Singapore, encouraged the United States to pay more serious attention to ASEAN. While Indonesia was not ready for a free-trade agreement of its own, a workable solution would be for Washington to negotiate the agreement with ASEAN. Such an umbrella arrangement would enable Indonesia as well as other member states to gain increased access to the all-important U.S. market. As to China, countries in the region have come to realize that the best way for them to cope with the giant to the north is by further integrating their economies and functioning more as a unified flock of "half a billion sparrows under the ASEAN banner than as ten lone hawks," he said. When and if that happens is subject to legitimate question. Still, said Loh, "the point is that it's widely recognized that integration is ASEAN's only hope for competing with the giants. And there are serious strategic reasons for the United States to improve its relations with ASEAN. We can help each other develop more sophisticated policies in the competition."

Indonesia is key to a unified Southeast Asia. But radical Muslims there oppose both the United States and ASEAN. Their goal is to establish Islamic rule in the Muslim majority states of Southeast Asia, not link arms with the others. Thus, even as Singapore's leaders shout Indonesia's cause from the rooftops, the Yudhoyono administration in Jakarta has reciprocated with unkind and strange gestures. The most recent was cutting off exports of sand. This was by no means petty. Constantly building and adding patches to its tiny landmass, Singapore buys bargeloads of sand to create fill and to mix into concrete. Much of the island's flower-banked coastal highway, leading from its world-class airport to the central city, lies on Indonesian sand. The country hoards sand almost as jealously as the United States stores gold bullion at Fort Knox.

For years, the sand trade seemed like an obvious win-win situation—Singaporean cash for Indonesian dirt. In 2002, though, Indonesia began restricting sales, claiming that entire islands in the archipelago were slipping under the sea to feed Singapore's insatiable appetite for construction. That Indonesia has more than seventeen thousand islands, the great majority remote and uninhabited, didn't seem to matter. The real reason had nothing to do with declining sand levels or rising sea levels. Singapore had refused to sign a long-stalled extradition compact. Indonesian authorities were convinced that Singapore harbored a number of ethnic-Chinese Indonesians, and their money, sought by law enforcement agencies in Jakarta.

It was a reasonable charge. Sino Indonesians have salted an estimated $87 billion in Singaporean banks, wary that Muslim sentiments could again turn against them. Many of them maintain homes on the island, safe havens should the need arise, and where they repair to host lavish parties rather than attract unwanted attention among their Muslim neighbors back in Indonesia. The two governments finally reached agreement on extradition in mid-2007, releasing the stalled flow of sand and money.

Singaporeans believe that the sand wars were based on preternatural envy, the sort that poor people anywhere have for the rich. Given that Singapore's other next-door neighbor, Malaysia, recently began balking over its long-standing agreement to sell the water-poor city-state 350 million gallons of untreated water a day—half of its daily requirement—there does appear to be something to the suggestion that the envious Muslims are using their abundant low-end resources to get even with the rich Chinese across the causeway. In Malaysia's case, the envy is heightened by the vicissitudes of history: when Malaysia expelled Singapore from their union in 1965, the Muslim-majority state had no doubt that it would ascend and the little island would sink. When things turned out otherwise, a more benign variant of the unending antagonism that separates Muslim Pakistan and Hindu-majority India seized hold and continues to bedevil the two countries.

Singapore is seen from Jakarta in two ways, Indonesian legislator Drajad Wibowo told the *New York Times* at the height of the sand fight. It is a role model for development but also an arrogant economic bully, using financial muscle to undermine its poorer neighbors. Many in the region resent about Singapore some of the same overbearing style they detest in the United States. But while Indonesia and Malaysia both accuse the Singaporeans of being selfish and abusive, their own self-interest should lead them in a different direction. Certainly, in their discussions with us, Singapore's leaders argued strongly for the United States to come to the aid of their Islamic neighbor. And from Singapore's own self-interest, a stable and prospering Indonesia, and Malaysia, would better serve Singapore's security and calm its anxieties, in a similar way that a wealthier Mexico would be advantageous to the United States.

PART SIX

Asleep at the Switch: The United States

29

The Digger

During the bleakest period of the U.S. war in Iraq, the State Department's most insightful expert on Islamic radicals was not an American, not a diplomat at all, but a hired hand from the Australian army. In 2004, when the war effort was running up against more stubborn resistance than its planners had predicted, Paul Wolfowitz seconded David Kilcullen, then a thirty-nine-year-old reserve lieutenant colonel who had worked in Australia's Office of National Assessments. Kilcullen assumed his new assignment in Foggy Bottom, analyzing why things were going so badly, and began advising the United States what to do about it. Eventually he and a small team designed the "surge."

Kilcullen was not your run-of-the-mill digger, as Australians call their soldiers. He holds a Ph.D. in anthropology, for which he studied Indonesia's Darul Islam extremists at eyeball-to-eyeball range. As an army officer he trained Indonesian special forces in counterinsurgency tactics, speaking with them in fluent Indonesian. He served in East Timor, Papua New Guinea, Cyprus, and Afghanistan, among other trouble spots.

At the State Department, Kilcullen worked for Coordinator for Counterterrorism Henry A. "Hank" Crumpton, a career CIA agent who had led the agency's campaign in Afghanistan after 9/11. Crumpton, a fellow contrarian, not long afterward quit government service, citing a desire to spend more time with his family. During his three-year stint, Kilcullen wrote a host of authoritative papers in which he pulled no punches against military inflexibility. "We can incinerate any other nation on the face of the globe," he noted in one, "[so] it is no surprise that our enemies have moved out of that quadrant into quadrants where they can survive: irregular, catastrophic, and disruptive." In another major document, titled "Twenty-eight Articles: Fundamentals of Company-Level Counterinsurgency," which he published in March 2006, he declared, "[R]ank is nothing: talent is everything." That Humpty Dumptyish dictum, which flipped a cherished military belief on its head, caught the eye of General David H. Petraeus, who was then about to become the Bush administration's last-best-hope commander in Iraq.

Petraeus, himself a Princeton Ph.D., chose Kilcullen as his chief adviser on counterinsurgency operations. Petraeus saw in the outspoken Australian a source of fresh ideas based not on shopworn, self-destructive U.S. party politics but on expertise hard won in the field and an atypical, nonbureaucratic willingness to tell it as he saw it. In early 2006, Kilcullen joined the general's brain trust of warrior-scholars and went to Baghdad.

Before he left Washington for Iraq, with the Medal for Exceptional Public Service tucked in his pocket, Kilcullen sat down with us in his office on the second floor of the State Department to discuss U.S. policy toward Islam. His easy use of words such as "us," "we," and "our" made plain that he closely identified himself with the American mission. Shaggy brown hair, rosy cheeks, and tan desert boots peeping out beneath dark-blue suit pants contributed to a deceptively boyish mien. But Kilcullen was deadly serious.

The discouraging news, he began, for those who imagined that any kind of victory in Iraq, should it come, would yank the carpet out from under worldwide Islamist terrorism, was that they were off by twenty to thirty years. "This is early days. It's the equivalent of 1953 in the Cold War. What's going on in Islam today is being driven by deep trends in global society and it's causing serious stress. This will continue for at least a full generation." Americans' strategic and tactical approaches to radical Muslims, militarily and diplomatically, were flawed by ignorance and hubris. Thinking was sclerotic, bogged down in a world that no longer existed. That was Kilcullen, the clear-eyed student of national behaviors, unafraid to speak the truth as he saw it to the world's only superpower. But, said Kilcullen, "No one is going to take on the U.S. in a conventional war. So we need to build up the nonconventional side."

To Kilcullen, "conventional" and "nonconventional" apply not only to the armed forces but also to diplomacy and espionage. "If the threat is from nonstate actors," he said, "we need to engage with people rather than governments. If we did, we'd see, for example, that the Iranian people are very friendly to the United States." Indeed, if CIA and other members of the U.S. embassy staff in Tehran had been better plugged into the mullahs around then exiled Ayatollah Ruhollah Khomeini before January 1979, and not just attending upon the shah in his imperial court, the history of Iran and the entire Islamic upheaval might look very different today.

Kilcullen told us that Secretary of State Condoleezza Rice seemed to understand the need to shift U.S. diplomacy from the time-honored practice of elites meeting elites to the more effective sphere of people meeting people. In the early days of her tenure, Rice vowed to move more highly trained Americans out of U.S. embassies, barricaded fortresses in capital cities, and into small-town consulates, where they could mix more naturally with local people. This open style of American representation would require diplomats with advanced language abilities and exceptional commitment. But the payoff could be enormous. However, with the great bulk of overseas spending going to the war in Iraq and the construction in Baghdad of the largest, most heavily fortified U.S. embassy in the world, the trend has been in the opposite direction.

Meanwhile, as the United States had abandoned many far-flung consulates, China has been increasing its diplomatic presence. (To cite two instances, while the U.S. consulate in Cebu, in the central Philippines, was being shuttered, the Chinese were opening one there. In April 2007, China opened another consulate in the Philippines, this one in Laoag, in the north of the country.) American libraries, which used to dot most countries and drew enthusiastic young people to their reading tables to soak up American literature and publications, have been reduced to skimpy "corners." These poorly funded little showcases of what should be America's diverse voices typically stock a handful of magazines and government handouts and are much less appealing to those hungry for an unvarnished picture of our country. On our travels through Southeast Asia, young people groused about this and asked us why the libraries had closed shop. We had to inform them that the U.S. Information Agency, which ran the libraries and conducted much of America's public diplomacy abroad, no longer existed. In 1999 it was absorbed by the State Department, with limited funding.

To find where the money went, look to the Pentagon. The current Department of Defense budget totals $700 billion, while the State Department receives $19 billion. Defense employs 2.1 million personnel, military and civilian; State, 11,000, roughly half of whom are stationed abroad. By comparison, Kilcullen couldn't resist bringing up his own country. The Australian Defense Ministry employs 90,000 men and women. Yet the Foreign Ministry of Australia, a nation of 21 million people, about the same as New York State, fields roughly the same number of foreign-based diplomats as the United States, with its 300 million population. "The U.S. has got it backwards," he said.

America's foreign policy needs to shift far more attention to Southeast Asia. "The extremists are working very hard at getting Southeast Asian governments to turn against the United States. In the Middle East, the genie is out of the bottle. So if we continue to spend a lot there, we may help the situation a little. But if we spend a little in Southeast Asia, we can help a lot. If we lose in Southeast Asia, we'll be well on our way to losing the 'global war on terror.'"

When things go wrong, people tend to identify with the basics in their lives. And nothing is more basic than religion. Southeast Asia is now in the throes of what Kilcullen termed a "piety arms race," one readily obvious example of which is the increasing tendency to wear Arab dress. And extreme fundamentalists are exploiting this rush to faith. "Actually, it's not all that different from what's going on with Christian fundamentalist trends in the United States," he said.

An added complication for any government that is accustomed to dealing with other governments directly is that in Islam, as in Judaism, there is no central authority, no pope, no one running the show. Even in individual mosques there seldom is a single imam

in charge. Thus the frustration for Americans seeking to defeat
something as amorphous as international "Islamofascist terrorism"
is this unanswerable question: who speaks for Islam? All too often
in this vacuum, the United States has chosen to deal with secular strongmen and military dictators such as Hosni Mubarak in
Egypt and Pervez Mushareiff in Pakistan. Often deceptively successful in the short term, these relationships typically backfire and
build up resentment among the masses. From these masses come
tomorrow's middle-class 9/11 hijackers and their armies of illiterate
roadside bombers.

Kilcullen raised a number of related difficulties faced by the
United States: by equating Islam with fascism, Americans were
entirely misguided and off base. If American leaders felt the need
to compare Islam with any "ism," he suggested that communism
came closer to the mark. "Fascism is by nature exclusionary," he
said, "while communism, like Islam, is inclusive. In theory, at least,
all are welcome." A further difficulty is the formlessness of Islamic
terrorist groups. U.S. military strategists tend to consider a battle
won when an organization such as al-Qaeda or Jemaah Islamiya
fragments after some of its key leaders or bomb-makers have been
killed or captured. Kill enough of them, goes this reasoning, and
eventually the fragments are too small to cause us pain.

But what is logical when one nation-state wages war against
another is not when the enemy is a guerrilla band. Just one determined terrorist can kill dozens, even thousands. Patriotic and God-
fearing Americans, some of whose ancestors infuriated Redcoat
commanders by sniping at their precise formations from behind
rocks and trees rather than facing off against superior forces on
open battlefields, need go no further than the family Bible to remind
themselves that Goliath was slain by a boy slinging a stone.

Rising Islamic piety of itself does not necessarily lead to extremism. Extremist organizations in Southeast Asia tend to include
few members who are well versed in their religion. "In fact," said
Kilcullen, "you can argue that those who are better educated in
Islam work *against* terrorism in their homelands." Pious Muslims
are more likely to resort to violence in places such as France
and Britain, where they are in the distinct minority. In a country

such as Indonesia, those who resort to violence are likely to be poor, rural people suffering oppression, real or imagined, from non-Muslims.

Ironically, China—still officially Communist and atheist—is proving far more adept at utilizing the Islamic resurgence in Southeast Asia to its advantage than is the United States, one of the world's most avowedly devout nations. The explanation is that China has its own history of struggle against Japanese and Western imperialists and centuries of intervention by Christian missionaries. Thus it has been able to exploit anticolonial bitterness against the United States, which is considered the inheritor of the colonial mantle. Even though some sympathetic Americans may comprehend this fury intellectually, they don't feel it viscerally. Chinese do.

The United States, with its exported music, movies, video games, and fast food, is a cultural newcomer in Southeast Asia, while China, like India, provides many of the ancient pillars that support social structures in the region. "We can't compete with them on the cultural level," said Kilcullen. "Even the militant Muslims are Buddhist-Hindu at their core." Rather than attempting to dim the Chinese advantage by slapping on more layers of disparagement, the United States ought to decide once and for all how it wants to deal with China. "Americans are schizophrenic on China," said Kilcullen. "Is it a threat or not? Is it a competitor or could it become an ally, or a friend? The neocons are planning to fight China. It's the basic tool we use in our planning. In other words, we are creating a threat."

While China glides gracefully around the terrorism issue, the terrorists are proving expert at elevating the public's widespread resentment toward Americans. Even some pro-American leaders find it difficult to publicly support the U.S. war on terror, more fearful of screaming demonstrators in the streets of their capitals than angry foreigners on the phone.

One major dispute is over how to handle known radicals. The United States and Australia were furious when Yudhoyono released Jemaah Islamiya ideologue Abu Bakar Ba'asyir from prison, ignoring Donald Rumsfeld's demand to keep him locked up and "throw away the key." In fact, Ba'asyir probably did more harm during his twenty-six-month incarceration than he could have done on the outside. "He's an inspirational figure, a mentor," Kilcullen said. "He provides the ideological justification for the crazies. He was a very bad influence while he was among the general prison population. He recruited people who'd already crossed the barrier into violence and crime. In that sense we're better off with him outside, where all he can do is lecture middle-class kids at his pesantren."

It is not uncommon for prison authorities to provide inmates such as Ba'asyir with laptop computers and mobile phones. Kilcullen, who is, remember, a hard-nosed military man, urged the United States to beef up its "soft" spending and help Indonesia build separate prison wings to hold terrorists alongside pedophiles and other criminals especially reviled in Islamic society. "The stigma of being jailed on terrorism charges isn't all that strong in Indonesia," he said. "But put them away with the scum of society, and you really do them harm."

30

The Expat

There's one in every corner of the world: the Bogart character; the American who has lived there as long as anyone can remember; is married to a local; speaks the language like a native; whose understanding of local culture comes from pillow talk and hard-earned personal experience, not just from books; who has deep feelings about the adoptive country but remains an American at heart. They are businesspeople, teachers, journalists, attorneys, travel agents, bartenders, and hoteliers.

In Jakarta, James Castle plays Bogie.

Castle has lived in Indonesia since 1977. He has a doctorate in Indonesian history, is president of the American Chamber of Commerce, and heads CastleAsia, a political risk- and market-forecasting consultancy. A lifelong Republican whose business interests could easily have justified cheerleading for the Bush administration, he managed to hold a balanced keel while negotiating the tricky waters between the two countries. In this, historical perspective served him well.

The judgment of Castle and others like him is an invaluable resource for Americans who appreciate the worth of understanding what others think of us. But the U.S. government makes far too little use of them. "I've spent most of my adult lifetime trying to marry U.S. and Indonesian interests," Castle told us during a conversation in the boardroom of his office in central Jakarta. "Yet when

I ask American and Indonesian leaders to list the ten most important elements in the relationship, never more than two ever overlap." The explanation for that divergence is twofold: first, to Indonesia, the United States is the first or second most important relationship it has in the world, while to the United States, Indonesia may rank fiftieth; second, to the United States, terrorism is the sine qua non, while to Indonesia it is a sideshow.

Castle himself doesn't take Indonesian terrorists very seriously. "There aren't very many of them and they aren't too bright, or they'd be doing something else," he said with a touch of irony. (On the morning of July 17, 2009, Castle was hosting a breakfast meeting of top foreign executives of major companies in Indonesia at Jakarta's Marriott Hotel. He was among more than fifty people injured when a pair of bombs went off, one in the Marriott and another at the nearby Ritz Carlton, killing nine.) But he acknowledged that Jemaah Islamiya and other groups had been able to thrive for so long because most Indonesians were "unwilling to admit that people who kill Muslims in such awful ways could be Muslims. Of course, the terrorists consider themselves Muslims. There's a tendency to support even the worst Muslims over any non-Muslims."

This is behavior that Indonesians cultivated during the Dutch colonial era. "I get nervous in the face of this type of denial," said Castle. "We'll never make progress with that attitude. Look, the terrorists are here. They always have been and they always will be. And so will the struggle over Sharia, because a struggle means that there must be a winner and a loser, and the losers won't tolerate losing. Terror is a means of warfare for people without any other means. The 9/11 hijackers were the epitome. The United States needs much more contemplation about the enemy—who he is and why he is the way he is. For now, we're out of ideas. That's why Guantánamo is still there. Come on! Without a broad plan you can't fine-tune plans for Indonesia and other individual countries. We always have our list of demands. How about asking the other guy for his—and paying attention?"

Castle considers Indonesia's growing fundamentalism more an expression of popular frustration with the pace of democratization, continuing corruption, economic inequity, and injustice within the legal system than part of a worldwide movement. "Unlike in the Middle East, here in Indonesia time is more on our side," he said. "Indonesia is on the cusp of a great democratic revolution. So far, though, no one trusts the institutions, and that includes the courts and every other part of government."

Under the circumstances, many Indonesians have reverted to their intuitive links—family, tribe, local groups, and, ultimately, their religion. If the United States is going to help Indonesia's leaders overcome the public's deep-seated distrust of government, which carries over to the United States and existing and potential American investors, it will first have to better understand what Indonesia requires. "Being seen as pro-U.S. is a danger to the Indonesian government," said Castle. "So yes, we've got to help them relieve poverty, but it must be done with subtlety, not by constantly demanding credit for our good deeds."

While poverty remains a dominant problem in Indonesia, Castle argued that "racism and a feeling of no respect" from the West were more volatile fuels for the fires of radicalism. "The radical leaders, whether they're rich or poor, and there are both here, want the power to make others think the way they do." In comparing Islam and communism, in the sense of them transcending nationalism, as Kilcullen did, Castle said that communism ultimately failed because "it could not deliver the goods." But Islam, he said, would never fail because it alone gives the poor the dignity and respect they can't get anywhere else. "And, besides, the payoff comes later."

Should the United States fail to step into the breach, said Castle, it will soon find it filled by China. "The Chinese are still weak militarily, but people in Southeast Asia want them at the table because they want some balance in the world. Look at it this way: the U.S. is the New York Yankees. Everyone wants us to fail, not because they really hate us but because we make them nervous."

Like many other Republicans living and working in Southeast Asia, Castle bluntly faulted the Bush administration for many of the difficulties people like him face in this part of the world. "The fundamental flaw—from which so many mistakes flowed—was arrogance," he said. One specific change he believed would help stanch this flow would be for the Obama administration to reconstitute the

U.S. Information Agency. "Leave the image-polishing business to those who know how to do it," he said. "We need to be much better at getting American ideas and information out to ordinary Indonesians." As an illustration, he said, "Let's just say that the Iraq war was correct to begin with—and I believed it was, until I saw that Colin Powell had nothing when he went to the UN, and I was appalled—the way it was done was arrogant and it has blown back in our face. It needed a lot more effort for fact-gathering and for coalition-building."

Because this view reflects closely what so many Indonesians and other Southeast Asians say, U.S.-based critics frequently lambaste expatriates like Castle for having gone native. In the State Department, U.S. Foreign Service officers who are perceived as being too close to their host governments are derided as victims of "clientitis." But there is little question that America's low-ebb reputation in the world would be in an entirely different realm if policymakers had followed the advice of those with intimate knowledge of Islam. "We need to reflect on what we're doing in the world," said Castle.

Conclusions

While the world has turned a critical corner, from the threat of mutually assured destruction to the threat of the suicide bomber, the United States remains locked into a foreign policy essentially unchanged from the Cold War era. God-obsessed Islamists have replaced godless Communists as our preeminent enemies, but our guiding strategy has stayed the same: overwhelm the enemy with massive armed force, then bow out as a gratefully liberated nation clicks smoothly into Jeffersonian democracy. It worked more than six decades ago in Germany and Japan (after years of hand-holding and enlightened guidance), but it has not yet worked in Afghanistan or Iraq.

Our efforts in Iraq succeeded in denying al-Qaeda its dream of a base for the caliphate, but at a terrible cost in life and injury, American and Iraqi, treasure, and reputation. Our standing internationally has suffered much more than most Americans realize. We have stirred hostility among Muslims well beyond that already provoked by our friendship and support for Israel. Moreover, whatever success has been achieved came only after the military command under General Petraeus recognized that overreliance on military attacks was counterproductive. Following a visit to Iraq in 2006, Bond called on the Senate to approve more civil assistance. In 2007, the Bush administration adopted new counterinsurgency tactics, based on a "clear, hold, and build" approach. This policy sharply reversed priorities, emphasizing that fully 80 percent of U.S. effort be invested in nonmilitary activities.

President Obama should adjust Petraeus's policy for use in Southeast Asia and begin building before we have to face clearing and holding. We have a genuine and dangerous enemy in radical

Islam. It declared itself so on 9/11. But in dealing with an enemy composed of nonstate actors, we must work quickly and cooperatively with local populations to ensure that these terrorists do not reestablish control. Much as our extensive rebuilding of Japan and Germany turned them from deadly enemies to strong allies, our goal in dealing with radical Islamists should be to support and sustain moderate Islamic governments. We must provide them with assistance to build economic and educational opportunities alongside their security forces to show people a better way forward. To succeed, this assistance must be provided at the ground level—people-to-people, not elite-to-elite.

The authors continue to disagree sharply with each other over the advisability of the United States having gone to war in Iraq. However, we concur that the counterinsurgency's "build" strategy, enabled in large part by the "surge" of thirty thousand additional U.S. troops, allowed Prime Minister al-Malaki to win an election at the end of January 2009 and offer the hope of a relatively secure, relatively democratic, relatively stable country. In Afghanistan the refusal of NATO allies to take on the challenges of the Taliban, especially in the South, will necessitate continued U.S. efforts to build up Afghan military and police forces. In Afghanistan—perhaps even more than in Iraq because it has always been more a collection of tribes than a unified nation—we must focus our attention at the ground level. Key is the development of economically viable farming to obviate the opium industry and to enable a popularly elected government to take over security responsibilities, protect lawful activity, and prevent the country from being retaken by the Taliban and al-Qaeda.

In the Cold War, we achieved the military piece of the puzzle over time in part by terrifying the Soviet leadership into spending its way into bankruptcy. In Iraq, predictably, we crushed Saddam Hussein by rolling over his second-rate, Third World army in weeks. But in both cases, despite the creation of independent political parties and loudly heralded elections, culture has trumped democracy. Russians once again are demonstrating that they're comfortable with strongman rule. In Iraq and Afghanistan, social and political chaos continue, and we still do not know how it will end.

We continue to be in a hot war with Islamists in these two countries. The enemy is agile, integrated into disparate communities on both sides of the Shia-Sunni divide, and motivated to an extent uncommon in modern warfare. After three years of missteps, the Bush administration finally achieved a sensible new strategy with clear, hold, and build. Although Iraq is likely to remain a work in progress, the strategy illustrates that to be successful, it must emphasize economic opportunities and assistance in local development projects that local people believe are high priorities. This effort is to be supported by military operations, not the other way around.

But this is not a strategy that can be used outside a war zone. In the broader world of Islam, the building must be done first, so that clearing and holding do not become necessary. The place to *begin* building the foundation of a lasting relationship with Muslims is not the deserts of the Middle East but the jungles, rice fields, and emerging economic centers of Southeast Asia. The region already is the United States' fifth-largest trading partner and its fourth-largest export market: we sell twice the amount of American products there than we do in China. Americans tend to link Islam with the Middle East and particularly with doctrinaire Arabs, but that is mistaken. Only 20 percent of the world's 1.8 billion Muslims are Arabs. They are outnumbered by the Muslims of the Indo-Pakistani subcontinent and of Southeast Asia. In the complex range of Islamic practitioners, Southeast Asians are among the world's most moderate. Their governments vary in levels of competence, and several are under pressure from fundamentalist forces. But overall they present a brighter picture and a greater promise than those of the Middle East, and they can provide us desperately needed support among their coreligionists there.

Just as critically in a century that is all but certain to be dominated by Asia, they offer a level playing field for peaceful competition with China, the rising power that is fast becoming America's greatest challenge, greater even than radical Islam. While China is gaining trust and influence in Southeast Asia, the United States is sliding backward there. Because its strategy is so narrowly focused on the Middle East, the United States is, wittingly and without apparent concern, losing ground to China in its Southeast Asian backyard. At the same time, free from the costs and stresses of warmaking, the Chinese are concentrating enormous effort on expanding economic and cultural exchanges.

The region's governments and populations have welcomed them with open arms (as is increasingly true in Africa and Latin America). While Southeast Asian Muslims grow ever more suspicious of American attitudes and intentions, few complain about China's rising profile (though many desire greater U.S. trade for balance). This is a stunning about-face from the decades, even centuries, when they viewed China with fear and loathing. The result, unless the United States quickly wakes up and responds in kind, could be a Chinese hegemon in a region that the United States has taken for granted. As Americans should have learned from the blowback of Iraq, we can no longer afford to lose friends anywhere, and certainly not those in such a strategic region.

Southeast Asia itself offers the United States burgeoning markets and abundant natural resources, including significant amounts of oil and natural gas. It also stands astride the vital artery between the China colossus and the volatile Middle East—the Strait of Malacca, the world's foremost oil-transshipment choke point (and one vulnerable to Islamist terrorists). The bulk of the oil transiting the strait originates in Persian Gulf Arab states. Making up some 20 percent of America's energy demand, that single resource constrains U.S. policy in the Middle East and, arguably, worldwide.

Although Americans on both sides of the Iraq war debate have by now largely dismissed oil resources as motivating the 2003 invasion, many Iraqis continue to insist otherwise. They are convinced that if Iraq's oil did not lie closer to the desert floor than Saudi Arabia's, that it was less sulfurous and almost as plentiful, the United States would have been much more hesitant. Countering this belief, however, a blue ribbon commission studying U.S. policy in Muslim nations recommended that a high priority was to lessen our reliance on Middle Eastern oil and thus our need to support repressive governments. It follows that the challenge to the United States to develop more energy resources has significant implications for our relations with the entire Muslim world. Still, no matter how much effort Americans put into greener energy, our requirement for Middle Eastern oil will continue well into the present century. It will, in fact, grow more critical as China and India dramatically step up their competitive demand.

For all these reasons, we are calling on formulators of foreign policy in the Obama administration and in both parties in Congress, as well as business leaders and academicians, to return Southeast Asia to prominence for the first time since U.S. armed forces withdrew from Indochina. Because Americans rarely pay serious attention to other nations until we suddenly perceive them to be a threat, we typically are taken by surprise at the last moment and find ourselves woefully lacking information and understanding. The time for a heads-up notice in advance of a crisis, but none too soon, is now. As long as open-ended struggle with radical Islam remains likely, Southeast Asia will be a critical linchpin. We will make a grave error if we ignore the region any longer. We need to learn and understand not simply the politics and economies of their governments but also the very human feelings and motivations, the passions and hatreds, the hopes and fears of their people. We must get to know their cultures, and we must help them to understand ours better, so that they come to see the United States as a friend, not as a threat.

To know them, we need not boots and bayonets but sneakers and sandals on the ground. Based on the enthusiastic response to calls for national service by senators Obama and John McCain during the 2008 presidential campaign, there should be no shortage of volunteers. Organizations such as Teach for America already have more applicants than places. The Peace Corps must be dramatically expanded. Secretary of State Hillary Clinton, on an attention-grabbing visit to Jakarta as part of her first official visit abroad, in February 2009, announced that the Peace Corps soon would return to Indonesia for the first time since 1965. The United States was also planning to return Fulbright Scholars to the country. The fact that in the recessionary economy many young and not so young Americans are looking for work should raise the numbers of civilians wanting to help abroad. There should be roles for skilled retirees and midcareer specialists, as well. As American mountain climber

Greg Mortenson powerfully related in *Three Cups of Tea*, his best-selling personal account of building schools in Taliban-controlled areas of Pakistan and Afghanistan, almost nothing is impossible given commitment and will.

Many Southeast Asians implored us to respond before the region's Muslims follow their coreligionists in the Arab world and commit to religious warfare. We must focus our vision less on crushing the handful of terrorists and more on transferring American know-how to help meet the needs of the majority via the following:

- education, including exchanges at all levels;
- jobs, through private investment;
- agriculture, industry, finance, and small-business development.

In addition, Americans must do a better job of explaining ourselves through improved public diplomacy: telling the people of the recipient countries what we are doing, why we are doing it, and emphasizing that our goals are long-term and for peaceful, friendly relationships with them.

During the Cold War the Voice of America and other official outlets did an effective job of conveying to people in countries hostile to us the values, aims, and actions of the U.S. government and the American people. More recently, though, we have stopped utilizing these tools well and have fallen into programming popular music and other entertainment seemingly divorced from our diplomatic and economic assistance activities.

Public diplomacy efforts must be coordinated throughout the U.S. government and provided significantly more resources. If we do not toot our own horn, no one else will toot it for us.

At the same time, though, if we are going to recapture the admiration and respect we've lost in recent years, it is critical that we let go of the self-deceiving notion that the rest of the world wants to be American, to live and govern itself as we do. In Southeast Asia, the United States has a rare opportunity to create an entirely new approach to Islam in the twenty-first century, a template that could be adapted for use throughout the world.

This new policy combines *soft power*—diplomatic, economic, educational, and personal outreach—and *hard power*—military force—to create *smart power*.

The concept was well defined by a politically odd couple, neoliberal scholar Joseph Nye and the Bush administration's former deputy secretary of state Richard Armitage, in a 2008 report commissioned by the Washington-based Center for Strategic and International Studies.

"The United States must become a smarter power by once again investing in the global good," Nye and Armitage wrote, "providing things that people and governments in all quarters of the world want but cannot attain in the absence of American leadership." The study recommended that "by complementing U.S. military and economic might with greater investments in soft power," the United States could develop a more intelligent set of policies focused on five critical areas:

- forging new international alliances, partnerships, and institutions;
- contributing much more widely to global development;
- building long-term, people-to-people relationships, particularly among youth;
- expanding free trade to include those left behind in globalization;
- leading the technological drive for energy independence and climate change.

Concurrently, we must improve our use of the new media, including the Internet, to tell our story. Smart power is far less effective without good communication, and we have fallen behind al-Qaeda and others. Smart power could become to Islamist terrorism what containment was to communism: a means to promote the collapse from within of an inhumane doctrine without risking worldwide war. "Smart" also offers the advantage of sounding tougher than "soft." As Bond knows from years of firsthand experience in the Senate, the soft-power component, though prized by experts in the diplomatic and military services, is distrusted by many legislators and, certainly during the previous administration, occupants of the White House. To promote soft policies, they fear, is to be perceived as soft on communism, soft on terrorism.

So they debate missile throw weights instead of rice paddy yields. They avoid encouraging state agricultural extension agents to share their expertise with farmers in, say, Java, ignoring the fact that this would help those farmers produce more. They bypass discussions of sending civil engineers to Sulawesi to help build roads to carry those crops to market; teachers who could help those farmers educate their children; scientists and paramedics who could provide better health care to mothers.

Yet smart power can be the most powerful of weapons. Nothing encourages people to reject radicalism like prosperity, or at least a sense that life is improving. So it was remarkable when, in late 2007, Secretary of Defense Robert M. Gates deplored the "creeping militarization" of U.S. foreign policy and forcefully advocated a budget increase, not just for Defense, but for the rival State Department. "There is a need for a dramatic increase in spending on the civilian instruments of national security—diplomacy, strategic communications, foreign assistance, civic action, and economic reconstruction and development," Gates said in a speech at Kansas State University in Manhattan, Kansas. "We must focus our energies beyond the guns and steel of the military, beyond just our brave soldiers, sailors, marines, and airmen." Though largely unnoticed at the time, this speech and the thinking behind it encouraged Obama to ask Gates to remain at the Pentagon.

A few weeks later, Bill Gates of Microsoft took up the same cudgels when he advised the world's power brokers to transform their basic nature. "We have to find a way to make the aspects of capitalism that serve wealthier people serve poorer people as well," Gates told the World Economic Forum in Davos. Coming from a man who personifies capitalism, this proposal was nothing short of revolutionary. No matter how Bill Gates follows through and whether his fellow billionaires join him, his call to action signals that business and government, whether arm-in-arm or independently, must shift direction.

The government leaders and officials with whom we spoke as well as the broad sweep of Southeast Asians we met universally urged us to encourage more American investment in their countries. This, they emphasized, would not only create new jobs directly but would also allow motivated American companies to help build small and medium-size enterprises through mentoring indigenous entrepreneurs. In turn, the American firms would be ideally positioned to supply the local businesses with economical and intelligently thought-out goods and services. Small- and medium-scale businesses over time expand employment and help build a free market base.

To help this kind of outreach thrive, U.S. tax policy on expatriates must be rationalized. The United States currently is the only major economic power that exacts income tax payment from workers and corporations abroad. These expatriates, who already pay taxes to the countries where they operate, thus are double taxed, although the first $87,000 of their annual salary is exempted by the IRS. As a direct result, many U.S.-based businesses must hire non-Americans to run their overseas operations. In Southeast Asia, many American firms are headed by Britons, Australians, or New Zealanders. This does little to serve the interests of the United States in the region. In 2005, the most recent year for which statistics are available, American firms overseas paid over $111 billion in income taxes to the U.S. government. This is another significant disadvantage for U.S. corporations investing in and creating jobs, fostering small and medium enterprises in foreign countries like Southeast Asia.

Robert Gates, in reversing priorities, had left unasked the obvious: has hard power worked so well for the United States in the past half century that we ought to continue relying solely on it? Part of the answer was provided at about the same time as his speech in Kansas. A poll conducted by the *Wall Street Journal* and NBC News found that 59 percent of Americans said they wanted a new president who would guide the country toward "regaining respect around the world." A majority explicitly acknowledged for the first time what much of the rest of the world had been saying for years: the United States was feared but no longer admired or respected.

Failing to institute a smart power–based foreign policy in Southeast Asia would risk further disintegration of the U.S. relationship with all of Islam. We must begin before religious extremism penetrates deeper and we end up fighting Islamist radicals on a second front. This corner of the world, which the United States has largely ignored for the past three decades, holds the brass ring for defusing our most pressing problems with worldwide Islamic extremism. The Obama administration has the ideal opportunity to grab it.

Having said this—having said everything that has gone before in this book—it may well be that *nothing* the United States undertakes in its efforts to come to terms with Muslims will succeed until and unless we help mediate the unending struggle for survival of Israelis and Palestinians. This is the be-all and the end-all.

It is beyond our competence and the scope of our book to propose yet another peace plan, yet another road map. Ultimately, the road to peace in the Middle East must be plotted and paved and traveled by the people who live there. After sixty years of hostility and bloodshed, that, if nothing else, should be clear. And it very well may be that peace will not come.

In a landmark speech at Cairo University on June 4, 2009, President Obama revealed the tenuousness of his own and America's roles in attempting to diminish the differences separating the warring sides. When he said that "the U.S. does not accept the legitimacy of continued Israeli settlements" in Palestinian territory, his invited audience burst into thunderous applause. But when he referred to America's "unbreakable bond" with Israel, he was met with stony silence. One can only presume that Obama would have received the precisely opposite reaction had he been speaking at Tel Aviv University. Still, for the new U.S. administration, Cairo was the beginning of the beginning.

What we have learned from the people of Southeast Asia on our journey among them is that our people and our government must demonstrate that we are far more even-handed than we have been. We must demonstrate that what we want in the Middle East is for Israelis and Palestinians to live in a country they consider their own. Unless we do that—and do it in a way that rings true with the Muslims of Southeast Asia—we will continue to wield very little influence among them and among the Muslims of the world.

Index